Accession no.
36081971

D0767277

University of
Chester
CHESTER CAMPUS
LIBRARY
01244 392738

...ritain

...magazines

Donation
LIBRARY
ACC No.   DEPT
36081971
CLASS No.
791.4330941 CRO
UNIVERSITY
OF CHESTER

Edited by Emily Crosby and Linda Kaye

British Universities Film & Video Council

British Universities Film & Video Council
77 Wells Street, London W1T 3QJ
Tel: 020 7393 1500   Fax: 020 7393 1555
Email: ask@bufvc.ac.uk   www.bufvc.ac.uk

Copyright © 2008 British Universities Film & Video Council

ISBN 978–0–901299-78-9

All rights reserved. No part of this publication may be reproduced, stored in a retrieval system or transmitted in any form or by any means: electronic, electrostatic, magnetic tape, mechanical, photocopying, recording or otherwise, without prior permission in writing from the copyright holders.

The opinions expressed in this book are those of the individual authors and do not necessarily represent views or policy of the British Universities Film & Video Council.

A catalogue record for this book is available from the British Library.

Cover pictures
Front: Ann Forsyth, presenter of *This Week in Britain* (BFI/COI)
Back: MINI BIKE *Living Tomorrow* issue no. 159, 1975 (BFI/COI)

Cover design by Howard Porter, Frantic Design
Typesetting by Gem Graphics
Printed in the EU through SS Media Limited, 88 Sandy Lane South, Wallington, Surrey SM6 9RQ

CONTENTS

SAFETY PRECAUTIONS IN LONDON'S BUS SERVICE, *This Is Britain* issue no. 9, 1946

BFI/COI

FOREWORD
Murray Weston

I am one of those people who always relished the prospect of the 'full programme' on visits to the cinema. When B movies, short films, cinemagazines, and newsreels were to be had before the main feature, I felt cheated if I missed part of the show. Even the cinema advertisements were exciting to a middle-class boy, like me, who had not experienced moving image advertising before (strange to remember that I was not allowed to watch television advertising in our home until the mid sixties). Later on in life I could never fully understand why many of my cinephile friends would ignore cinemagazines, like *Look at Life,* which were all part of the great British cinema experience. There was clearly a general snobbery about these productions which has been persistent – partly because of their style of production and also, perhaps, because the subjects of many of these films were regarded as rather mundane. But the 'mundane' often becomes the valued record of the future. And so it has been with cinemagazines.

This book, and the accompanying online database, maps out these forgotten, largely undocumented and disregarded British cinemagazines. They have found their fond supporters in Luke McKernan, Linda Kaye and Emily Crosby who worked on this AHRC-funded resource enhancement project at the BUFVC during 2004 - 2007. The project involved pioneering detective work – tracking down ephemera, rare catalogues and documentation from multiple sources – a form of constructive industrial archaeology which will offer a firm starting point for anyone coming again to this field of study; and there is far more left to be done.

The British Universities Film & Video Council has now built a substantial platform of valued online research tools for the scholarly community engaging with moving image content and records from British newsreels, cinemagazines, television and radio. I thank my colleagues for all their hard work in building these research assets and I look forward to the next phase in the work.

Meanwhile I recommend to you this unique and valuable guide to the forgotten world of the cinemagazines in the firm knowledge that it will be bound to inspire more of us to take another look at these intriguing films.

Murray Weston
Chief Executive
British Universities Film & Video Council
May 2008

ACKNOWLEDGEMENTS

This book is one outcome of 'Cinemagazines and the Projection of Britain,' a three-year research project at the BUFVC funded by the Arts and Humanities Research Council. The project was headed by Dr Luke McKernan, then BUFVC Head of Information, with researchers Linda Kaye and Emily Fuller (now Crosby). Maureen Brown, Marilyn Sarmiento and Kevin Fleming also worked on the project, which concluded in March 2007.

The research into the cinemagazines produced by the Central Office of Information would have been far less rewarding if not for the invaluable help and support we received from Film Images (then licensees for COI films but now sadly no longer in business), especially Dave Kent, Tony Dykes, Jenny Hammerton, James Kearney and Angela Saward; and Gavin Houtheusen and Esther Walder at COI Communications. At the BFI National Archive, we would like to thank Ros Cranston, Bryony Dixon, Katy McGahan, Patrick Russell and Sue Woods for their invaluable help and support of our research.

We interviewed a number of veterans of the British cinemagazines for our project. Our thanks go to all those who worked for the Central Office of Information and shared their thoughts and experience, especially Jenny Lucas, John Hall, Adam Leys, Janice Kay, Maureen Irving, Anna Hamlin, Cyril Frankel, Brian Taylor and Peter Steel. From the world of the sponsored cinemagazine, again our thanks for their time and enthusiasm to John and Margaret Chittock, Ken Gay, Deh-ta Hsiung, Robert Kruger, Peter Pickering, Ken Reeves, Roly Stafford, and John Wiles. Recordings of a number of these interviews are now held at the BUFVC.

Many others have helped us along the way. We are grateful to Professor Anthony Aldgate (Open University), Simon Baker (Institute for Historical Research), Dr Tim Boon (Science Museum), Joanne Burman (BP Archive, University of Warwick), Ron Collins, Rhidian Davis (British Film Institute), David Faulkner (COI), Dr Robert Holland (Institute of Commonwealth Studies), Dr Richard Howells (King's College London), Ray Jenkins (Carlton International Media), Simon Murphy (London Transport Museum), James Patterson (Media Archive of Central England), Professor Vincent Porter (University of Portsmouth), Dr Vicky Wegg-Prosser (Bournemouth University), Dr Philip Woods (Thames Valley University) and the late John Turner. Special thanks go to Dr Leo Enticknap and Steve Foxon for the essays they contributed to this publication.

Our thanks go to colleagues past and present at the BUFVC for their support of the research and its expression online, and their help in seeing this book through to publication: Sergio Angelini, Lotfallah Bekhradi, Kevin Fleming, Jeff Hulbert, Luke McKernan, Geoffrey O'Brien, Marianne Open, Nick Townend, Murray Weston and Joanna Yates. Special thanks go to Marilyn Sarmiento for her diligent care in reviewing the final text and compiling the index.

We are grateful to The National Archives for permission to reproduce texts from official documents on *Mining Review* and *Transatlantic Teleview*, to Penguin Books for permission to reprint 'The Magazine Film' by Edgar Anstey; and to Faber and Faber Ltd for permission to reprint the extracts from *The Projection of England* by Stephen Tallents.

Emily Crosby's essay, 'The 'Colour Supplement' of the Cinema: the British Cinemagazine, 1918–1938' was published in *The Journal of British Film and Television*, issue 9, May 2008, and is reproduced with the permission of the publishers, Edinburgh University Press. Linda Kaye's essay, 'Reconciling Policy and Propaganda: The British Overseas Television Service 1954–1964,' was published in *The Historical Journal of Film, Radio and Television*, vol. 27 issue 2, June 2007. Both have been revised for this publication,

Editorial note

Titles of films and television programmes are given in capitals, but title of film or television series are given in italics. For the various cinemagazines produced by the company, the word 'Pathe' is given without an acute accent over the 'e' (in keeping with the usual practice of the company at the time), except for mentions of the French company or its founder, Charles Pathé.

THE OLD VIC THEATRE SCHOOL, *This Is Britain* issue no. 38, 1949

BFI/COI

INTRODUCTION
CINEMAGAZINES: THE LOST GENRE
Luke McKernan

The cinemagazine is both one of the most pervasive yet invisible of motion picture forms. It has a history going back to the 1910s, and a record of usage by a wide variety of producers and sponsors which all bear witness to the vitality and utility of the genre, yet it has been almost entirely written out of history. There is no mention of the cinemagazine in most of the standard film and television reference guides. It has generated almost no critical literature, and certainly no work which has tried to isolate the genre and to provide a single history.[1] This publication is therefore the first of its kind.

The cinemagazine – also known as magazine film, or screen magazine – was a periodically released film series, originally shown in cinemas, which subsequently transferred to television and beyond. Cinemagazines could be issued weekly, monthly or even yearly; they could comprise several items or just the one story. They ranged in length from a few minutes to half an hour or more. In their popular or entertainment form the cinemagazines covered light topics such as travel, sport, hobbies, personalities, animals and fashion, and it is for this kind of seemingly inconsequential material that the cinemagazines are generally known. In this form cinemagazines were a staple of cinemas around the world, flourishing in particular in America and Britain, where they were a common feature of cinema programmes for decades. They were closely allied to newsreels, and several were produced by newsreel companies.

However, the true cinemagazine form ranged more widely than this. Beyond the entertainment cinemagazines, there were those made with a purpose. There were news cinemagazines, industrial cinemagazines, and cinemagazines sponsored by government organisations used for the dissemination of information and national propaganda. However, in each case the didactic or instructional form of the cinemagazine blended with the entertainment function, as the light, insistent mode of regular exhibition combined with soft messages proved popular with sponsors and uncontroversial for audiences which might have rebelled against something more obviously propagandistic.

Britain was the home of the cinemagazine. The first film series that was recognisably in the cinemagazine format was probably the *Kinemacolor Fashion Gazette*, a short-lived series exploiting the world's first natural-colour motion picture system, edited by Abby Meehan and issued by Charles Urban in 1913. However, the first true British cinemagazine was *Pathe Pictorial* (1918–1969), introduced in 1918 as an adjunct to the *Pathe Gazette* newsreel. Pathe became a cinemagazine specialist, introducing a cinemagazine for women, *Eve's Film Review* (1921–1933), and *Pathetone Weekly* (1930–1941), which specialised in showing variety acts. Other newsreel companies followed suit in the 1920s, with *Gaumont Graphic* introducing *Gaumont Mirror* (1927–1932) and *British Screen News* producing *British Screen Tatler* (1928– 1931). The Ideal Film Company issued *Ideal Cinemagazine* (1926–1932, succeeded by *Gaumont-British Magazine* in 1934), the series which introduced the term. *Ideal Cinemagazine* was produced by Andrew Buchanan, who became a leading advocate of the form, seeing it as an educational form ideally suited to bringing light, palatable information to the cinema audience.[2]

Although the cinemagazine was generally dismissed as being among the lightest of cinema fare, there were others who shared Buchanan's belief in it. John Grierson admired the skill of what he called magazines, detecting in them an extension of the popular lecture format, while warning that they 'describe, and even expose, but in any aesthetic sense, only rarely reveal'. Grierson tried to talk down the inherent value of the magazine films but found himself staying to praise them. 'The skill they describe is a purely journalistic skill. They describe novelties novelly ... Within these limits they are often brilliantly done.'[3]

The entertainment cinemagazine, with its frivolous view on life leavened with a touch of sly subversiveness, bowed out by the end of the 1960s, *Pathe Pictorial* closing in 1969 after fifty-one years. But the cinemagazine flourished in other forms. The need for a film series that could show how things were beyond the immediate concerns of the newsreel first emerged in the First World War, with Cherry Kearton's *The Whirlpool of War* (1914–1915). Each of the British newsreels at the start of the First World War issued supplementary newsfilms which gave more space if not necessarily more depth to actuality coverage of the conflict, but only Kearton's *Warwick Bioscope Chronicle* developed a partner series that wove together feature stories from Britain, France and Belgium to create something in *The Whirlpool of War* which reached beyond the headlines.

The most significant news cinemagazine was *The March of Time* (1935–1951), the dynamic series produced by Louis de Rochemont for Time-Life, which revealed the background stories behind the news in a dramatic and multi-faceted fashion. American-produced, it was shown in Britain under a different numbering system with occasional stories shot especially for British audiences (whilst others were excised as unsuitable for those same audiences). *The March of Time* had a startling effect, though perhaps more on commentators than on British audiences, who had some resistance to its insistent, American tone. An admiring Grierson said that 'it gets behind the news, observes the factors of influence, and gives a perspective to events.'[4] It covered politics, international relations, the arts, society and sport, all with equal aplomb and a confident air of having caught the tempo of the times. The Rank Organisation produced its own answer, *This Modern Age* (1946–1951), a polished series that at its best was no less expert in searching for an explanation for current issues. Pathe revealed a more serious tone with its *The Wealth of the World* (1950–1951) on the industrial development of natural resources. The news cinemagazine recognised that the news was not all scoops and headlines, and that it could follow stories through in greater depth, revealing trends and granting the cinema audience greater intelligence than some would have allowed it to have.

The Wealth of the World reflected a presentation of industrial development that had already been demonstrated by industrial concerns themselves. In Britain Shell produced *Shell Cinemagazine* (1938–1952), the gas industry *Mr Therm's Review* (1956) and the steel industry *Ingot Pictorial* (1949–1959), while the mining industry produced the long-running *Mining Review* (1947–1983). Such cinemagazines seldom made it into conventional cinemas (*Mining Review* was shown in public cinemas close to mining communities, and aspired to a wider distribution), but reached targeted audiences through the non-theatrical circuit. These films delivered carefully constructed images of benevolent, forward-thinking industrial concerns for the benefit of investors, schools, societies and clubs, other businesses and their own workers. They borrowed from the entertainment magazine a light touch and a taste for human interest, but combined this with the regular, insistent message of self-promotion.

The cinemagazine form was most effectively employed as a tool of government. In Britain, the Central Office of Information (COI), successor to the wartime Ministry of Information, produced a remarkable number of film series, which were initially targeted at audiences at home and then from the 1950s at an international one. Such cinemagazines were viewed by the COI as a means to project positive images of Britain, to encourage international trade, and simply to provide information to British audiences. They were also a valued tool in a post-Suez climate, when burgeoning television networks around the globe offered new opportunities to get the British message across and to counter the continued 'Americanization' of the world. Hence, after the initial foray of *Britain Can Make It* (1945–1947), which championed innovation in British manufacturing, the COI began to produce a variety of series for distribution to different territories, among them *This Is Britain* (1946–1951), primarily designed to promote Britain's exports overseas; *Transatlantic Teleview* (1954–1958), interviewing British politicians and economists for American consumption; *This Week in Britain* (1959–1979), which disseminated images of British life that stressed both tradition and modernity; *Viewpoint* (1957–1960), *Calendar* (1959–1969), *Carrousel Britanico* (1963–1974), *London Line* (1964–1979), *Living Tomorrow* (1969–1983), and dozens more. These were generally not intended for British audiences, and as a consequence the mistaken idea has grown that the COI lost interest in film production (apart from public information films and the like) in the 1950s, whereas in fact the complete opposite is true. It was simply that the strategic target changed from home to overseas, and the lowly cinemagazine (rather than the revered documentary form) was chosen as the ideal form for conveying these messages.

The cinemagazine was a wide-ranging and various genre, whose precise parameters have yet to be defined. Often it is difficult to determine where newsreels ended and cinemagazines began, especially for British newsreels of the 1960s and 1970s. *Gaumont-British News*, one of Britain's leading newsreels, ended in 1959 when it could not longer compete with television news, but reinvented itself as a cinemagazine, *Look at Life* (1959–1969). Another unclear boundary line is that between the cinemagazine and the documentary film series, such as *Worker and Warfront* (1942–1945). There were also cinemagazines that were produced for children and shown at Saturday matinee cinema clubs. The keenly paternalistic Rank Organisation sponsored *Our Club Magazine* (1945–1950), *Our Magazine* (1952–1956) and *Our World Magazine* (1950), through the Children's Film Foundation.

The cinemagazine was an amalgam of many styles, from the documentary to the newsreel to the travelogue. Its seeming inconsequentiality masked the malleability of the form, which could take on the wishes of a wide range of sponsors, and could adapt itself to many audiences, most crucially making the successful transference from cinema to television. The cinemagazine style eventually became absorbed by the television magazine format but some online and video release examples continue to use the traditional form to this day.[5] What is clear is that the magazine film series of the twentieth century, be they interest-led, information-led, industrial or propagandist, need now to be recognised collectively as a significant and influential part of moving image history, and to be written into those reference works that claim to encompass the motion picture in all its forms.

This publication aims to demonstrate that significance and influence, and to provide researchers with a practical guide to the British cinemagazine. It follows on from the British Universities Film & Video Council's three volumes of *The Researcher's Guide to British Newsreels* (1983, 1988, 1993), which serve as standard reference sources for British newsreels (and also include information on cinemagazines themselves). *Projecting Britain: The Guide to British Cinemagazines* is in four sections. The first, **Articles**, has six pieces on different aspects of the British cinemagazine. Emily Crosby writes on the entertainment cinemagazine in the 1920s and on the sponsored cinemagazines of the National Coal Board, Shell, British Transport and others. Leo Enticknap writes on the Rank Organisation's undervalued news cinemagazine *This Modern Age*. Steven Foxon, film archivist and historian of British Transport Films, gives us the history of the magazine film format as used by the railways in Britain. Linda Kaye's two essays cover the production of cinemagazines by the British government from the 1950s, and the policy of national projection that drove the film and television output of the COI.

The second section, **Documents**, is a selection of original texts on the production and reception of British cinemagazines. There is rare correspondence from 1928 between Pathe and both public and business regarding *Eve's Film Review* and *Pathe Pictorial*; Edgar Anstey, head of British Transport Films, writing on the magazine film for *Penguin Film Review* in 1949;

documents on the production and distribution of *Mining Review*, and the inception of the COI's *Transatlantic Teleview* from the files of The National Archives; and an extract from Sir Stephen Tallents' 1932 publication, *The Projection of England*, whose arguments for the necessity of national projection and its incorporation into British government film policy were decades ahead of their time.

The third section, **Directory**, is an A–Z guide to all of the major and many of the minor British cinemagazines that were produced, primarily between 1913 and 1984. For each series there is a short history of its sponsorship, production and distribution, with further details on where the films can be seen. For many of these series, this is the first time that this material has been made available. The final section, **Resources**, supplies general information for the researcher. There is a guide to archives, libraries and special collections holding moving image, document and sound material related to the British cinemagazine; a guide to the availability of cinemagazines online and for sale; a descriptive bibliography, and a guide to The National Archives as a source of information on British cinemagazines.

Projecting Britain: The Guide to British Cinemagazines is one of the outputs of a three-year (2004–2007) project, 'Cinemagazines and the Projection of Britain', which was funded by the Arts and Humanities Research Council and hosted by the British Universities Film & Video Council through its then association with the Open University. Further information deriving from this project, including 19,000 cinemagazine stories added to the British Universities Newsreel Database, sixty series histories, around 900 biographies of those who worked on British cinemagazines, and a wide range of supporting materials, can be all be found online at http://www.bufvc.ac.uk/cinemagazines. But this is only the start of the research into cinemagazines. The directory is a work in progress and many series, particularly those from the 1980s and 1990s are only now just coming to light. We hope that the database and the underlying investigations from our research team which have led to this guide will encourage others to seek out those areas of this lost history that intrigue them, and help bring the cinemagazines back into general understanding and critical appreciation.

Notes

1   Two exceptions are Raymond Fielding, *The March of Time, 1935–1951* (New York: Oxford University Press, 1978) (though *The March of Time* has often been regarded more as a newsreel than as a magazine film), and Jenny Hammerton, *For Ladies Only? Eve's Film Review: Pathe Cinemagazine 1921–1933* (Hastings: The Projection Box, 2001).

2   Andrew Buchanan, *The Film in Education* (London: Phoenix House, 1951), pp. 64–65. Charles Urban was instrumental in establishing the genre in America, with his *Charles Urban Movie Chats* (1919–1922) and *Kineto Review* (1921–1923) series, both of which were exhibited in Britain (indeed, much of the *Movie Chats* material was subsequently repurposed for Buchanan's *Ideal Cinemagazine*).

3   Forsyth Hardy (ed.), *Grierson on Documentary* (London: Faber and Faber, 1966 [rev. ed.]), p. 145. Grierson was speaking of American series such as the *Fitzpatrick Traveltalks* (1931–1950) produced by James A. Fitzpatrick (a Charles Urban protégé) and Grantland Rice's *Sportlights*. Other American

series in the same vein, which were sometimes shown in British cinemas, included the long-running *Pete Smith's Specialities* (1936–1955), *John Nesbitt's Passing Parade* (1938–1949) and *Screen Snapshots* (1920–1958), all of them popular in their day, though with a flippant humour that has dated badly.

4   Hardy, op cit., p. 201.
5   See Emily Crosby's essay on the sponsored cinemagazine in this volume for some examples.

THE 'COLOUR SUPPLEMENT' OF THE CINEMA: THE BRITISH CINEMAGAZINE, 1918–1938

Emily Crosby

This article looks at the image of interwar society projected by British cinemagazines of the 1920s and 1930s, concentrating on two prevalent themes – working women and fashion. This was the most active period for the cinemagazine as a popular feature in British cinemas, and the essay covers Around the Town, Pathe Pictorial, British Screen Tatler, Ideal Cinemagazine, Gaumont Mirror *and* Vanity Fair, *arguing their value for the study of British social history.*

The interwar cinema programme was a complex and varied delight. A 1922 poll of film exhibitors in the USA revealed that, in addition to the main feature, 22% of exhibitors showed a scenic or travelogue short, 46.22% a one-reel comedy and 21.09% a screen magazine.[1] Contemporary sources suggest that British audiences watched an equally diverse programme of material in cinemas. One exhibitor, for example, cited his idea of a standard programme (in 1921) as containing 'a four-reel feature … a two-reel comedy, a two-reel drama, a single reel comic … a "travel" … a good educational-interest … a cartoon half-reel, and a news film.'[2] This range of viewing material is becoming ever more familiar to film academics and cultural historians alike. In the past, the wider programme was 'largely shrouded in darkness, obscured and overlooked by film historians in favour of what they felt to be more substantial accomplishments of the film industry'; recent studies, however, have placed more emphasis on the wider programme and the experience of cinema-going.[3] Academic discussion about the surrounding trappings of exhibition – the design and architecture of cinemas, the music accompanying silent showings and the social mores attached to audience behaviour – is growing.[4] This better appreciation of the nature of the interwar cinema programme has led to some surprising discoveries, such as the proportion of the 1920s' film industry devoted to serials, or chapter plays. (Pathe financed a good deal of its feature-filmmaking on the back of its highly successful serials sold to second-run houses in the USA).[5] In this article I intend to illuminate further a part of the interwar cinema programme and in doing so, to help fill the gaps in the programme. The cinemagazine, similar to the print magazine in style and content as well as audience, is a vast topic for consideration. As such, I intend, first, briefly to describe the nature of the genre and its history, and then concentrate on the interwar cinemagazine's primary audience and subject – women – through two different representations particularly common to the cinemagazine: work and fashion.

At first glance, the varied and disparate films that have been labelled 'cinemagazines' by their producers, reviewers or film historians seem to have little in common. This form of film was used frequently throughout the world from the early 1910s to the 1980s, and for many different purposes, from entertainment, to education, to propaganda. It might seem that the only unifying characteristic of these films is their form – a ten to twenty-minute film, consisting of one or more light items, produced and distributed on a regular basis. However, at the early stage in the cinemagazine's history, the period 1918–1938, its identity as a genre was at its strongest. The short films market was highly competitive, and the cinemagazine a potentially lucrative film product. During this period of cinema exhibition a segmented, highly varied style of programming was the norm, mainly due to the length of the main 'feature' films. Short features and longer programmes meant that there was a lot of time to fill. Thus the genre was honed to its sharpest, most successful form. The cinemagazine addressed the audience directly, drawing them into the world it portrayed. The flexibility of these films kept people informed and entertained and the frequency of production ensured the popularity of the series with both exhibitors and audiences alike. A typical issue of an early British cinemagazine would try to strike a balance between entertainment and mildly educational stories. A common example might contain an item on a woman's unusual job, shots of celebrities enjoying a party at a London nightclub, a fashion display, a nature item exhibiting the latest advances in cinema technology and a cartoon. Such variety counteracted boredom. An item that did not appeal to one section of the audience would hopefully be followed by a contrasting item which might, and as the entire issue lasted on average around fifteen minutes, it was not unbearable if it simply filled the time until the next feature or serial, or if it provided a little light relief after a miserable newsreel.

The British cinemagazine began in 1918 with the arrival of *Pathe's Weekly Pictorial* on the short films market. Although there is little known about the Pathe company in Britain at this time, and still less known about its production rationale, it is most likely that *Pathe Pictorial* (as it came to be known) was conceived simply to fill time between more substantial films. It was marketed as exciting and educational in equal measure, a mixture of travelogue, fashion, fun and the bizarre, which seems to have been instantly appealing to exhibitors, though there is no information available about

LITERATURE
SCIENCE
ART

AROUND THE TOWN
AND EVERYWHERE

SPORT
FASHIONS
DANCES

BUFVC

Title frame from *Around The Town* issue no. 88, 1921

the audience response to the series. The series was mutually profitable to producer and exhibitor. It was largely made up of library footage and cheaply filmed newsreel-like stories, which made it an easy and inexpensive way for Pathe to advertise its name on cinema screens around the country.[6] The exhibitors in return got a relatively cheap variety reel that could be used to fill the gaps in a programme and to provide a family balance to the otherwise fact-based non-fiction part of the programme (made up as it most often was of a newsreel or two and perhaps a scenic or travelogue feature).

Pathe Pictorial was swiftly followed in December 1919 by *Around the Town*, distributed by Gaumont, Pathe's closest rival on the British market. This cinemagazine had pretensions to be more upmarket than its predecessor, focusing as it did on the arts and science with a very modern-sounding motto, 'Beauty and Celebrity Everywhere'. Either this was a conscious decision on behalf of the series' founder, Aron Hamburger, to carve out a different market from *Pathe Pictorial*, or else he had picked up on a recent trend towards celebrity in other entertainment industries. Whatever its inspiration, *Around the Town* was well-received by the critics, attracting praise for 'visualizing gossip columns ... so popular of late' (*The Times*) and 'introducing to the public all the famous people of the day' (*Fragments*).[7] Exhibitors, too, praised this new approach, the writer of *The Bioscope*'s 'Manchester Notes' claiming that the reel 'has been done very cleverly' so that 'there are few cinemas that will not include them in their programmes every week'.[8]

The success of *Around the Town*, particularly with women audiences, could not fail to attract the attention of Pathe, which retaliated with its own 'feminine' cinemagazine, *Eve's Film Review*, in June 1921. This was a sister series to the *Pictorial*, both advertised with Pathe's news and entertainment products as part of a comprehensive Pathe programme. Although *Eve* shared *Around the Town*'s focus on the more feminine topics of arts, fashion and theatre, it had none of *Around the Town*'s aspirations to high society, and as such fitted more comfortably with the rest of the market. Certainly *Eve* continued to flourish when *Around the Town* foundered in July 1923.[9] Further evidence for this assumption is provided by the example of *Vanity Fair*, an imitator of *Around the Town* which began in January 1922, produced by Walturdaw Co. Ltd. Records only survive for thirty-one issues of this series, which appears to have been short-lived.[10] Again, compared with the success of *Pathe Pictorial* and *Eve* during the same period, it is likely that its aspirational tone proved unattractive to the market. For a couple of years, therefore, *Eve* and *Pictorial* continued as the only British cinemagazines. Indeed, *Pathe Pictorial* was a profoundly successful cinemagazine, the longest-running ever (1918–1969) in its many guises, precisely because the genre was such an adaptable one. This fluid mix of 'fashion, fun and fancy' was malleable in both content and style while still resembling the cinemagazine format. It is therefore no surprise that eventually, in 1927, Gaumont too decided that it needed an home-grown accompaniment to its newsreel *Gaumont Graphic* – the *Gaumont Mirror*.[11] British Screen Pictures' *British Screen Tatler* followed soon after, complementing its *British Screen News* newsreel.[12]

In the meantime, *Ideal Cinemagazine* had begun in January 1926 as a self-described 'happy blend' of 'fact sweetened with frolic, nonsense mingled with news'.[13] With the new *Ideal Cinemagazine* (in some ways, an *avant garde* version of *Pictorial's* original format) its producer Andrew Buchanan was developing a more playful and abstract style of the genre. Buchanan's cinemagazine was made quickly and cheaply to supplement Ideal Films' already lively shorts repertoire. Advertisements to exhibitors in the *Kinematograph Weekly* and *The Bioscope* suggest that it was intended to fit snugly within Ideal's established canon, along with such gems as *Hodge Podge* and the *Sing Song* series, packaged together as the 'Laughter Festival'.[14] The series broke with cinemagazine tradition by having titles for each issue, such as LIMBS ANCIENT AND MODERN and LOOKS AND EYES. Despite this change, the subjects covered in this new cinemagazine were essentially the same as its siblings, still being produced by Pathe and Gaumont in the early thirties. Stories continued to be filmed about bathing beauties and dog shows, with humorous intertitles and later, commentary, and each issue tended to be very loosely grouped around a central theme.

Ideal Sound Cinemagazine's final issue was released in May 1932, but *Ace Cinemagazine*, which ran from 1937–1938, later picked up this same style. This series was among the shortest-running cinemagazines of the interwar period. The logical assumption to make about the failure of *Ace* is that, rather than its subject matter going out of fashion, it was squeezed out by changes in the average programme in the late 1930s. The eventual triumph of sound technology, plus developments in the art of feature-filmmaking meant that by 1938 the cinema programme had changed almost beyond recognition from 1918. Gone were the live acts and orchestras, and now that the feature could last up to three hours, with many houses showing a double feature, there was far less room for the variety reels, comedies, cartoons, and cinemagazines. One newsreel and a single cinemagazine were the most that many cinemas were able to show in a regular programme, and so competition in the shorts market reached a new level. The ever-present *Pathe Pictorial* continued to thrive, but, especially with the rise of news-themed cinemagazines such as the *March of Time*, and therefore, the increased choice available to exhibitors, entertainment cinemagazines were no longer in demand. This is clear from the trade papers: the number of adverts for, and reviews of, shorts dramatically declined during the 1930s (incidentally making their history far harder to trace). With the end of *Ace Cinemagazine*, and with the exception of the unstoppable *Pathe Pictorial*, this type of entertainment-based, commercial cinemagazine would not be seen on Britain's cinema screens again.

Magazines and cinemagazines

Throughout the interwar period the cinemagazine was regularly compared to its print cousin, the magazine, whether in content or style. *Around the Town's* focus on celebrities, for example, drew comparisons with the popular gossip columns. There was similarity in the series' titles – *Eve's Film Review* recalled the print magazine *Eve*, *British Screen Tatler* echoed *Tatler*, while *Vanity Fair* was very probably a direct copy of the magazine of the same name. Those cinemagazines with stable-mates – Gaumont's *Mirror* and *Graphic*, and Pathe's *Gazette*, *Pictorial* and *Eve* – were often advertised together as complementary items in the full supporting programme. As such, the cinemagazines were the 'colour supplement' to the newsreel's animated newspaper. This is particularly apparent with Gaumont's periodicals. The names *Graphic* and *Mirror* are reminiscent of newspapers and Gaumont's advertising describes them as 'Screen Periodical[s]'.[15] When both were run together, they were billed as complementary: 'The News Film and The Pictorial Review for Exhibitors who Think for Themselves,' a slogan reminiscent of today's Sunday newspaper advertisements.[16] There were, in fact, many financial links between the makers of film periodicals and the publishers of newspapers and magazines, mostly forged by the newsreels. Sir Edward Hulton, owner of the *Daily Sketch*, the *Evening Standard*, the *Illustrated Sunday Herald* and a number of Manchester titles, also owned *Topical Budget* between 1919 and 1923.[17] This newsreel, as a consequence, featured several *Daily Sketch* competitions (and incidentally, covered much of 'Lady Hulton's progress through society').[18] In a similar vein, other newspapers collaborated with cinemagazines, including *Around the Town*'s Proverbs competition with the *Kinema Newspaper*, *Eve* featuring the *Daily Mirror* Holiday Beauty competition and the *Gaumont Mirror* covering the *News of the World* fashion competition.[19] Indeed, Hulton was not the only press baron to own a stake in a maker of film shorts. Lord Beaverbrook owned a share in Pathe during the 1920s, at the time when it was producing both *Pathe Pictorial* and *Eve's Film Review*.[20] In 1927, *Gaumont Mirror* even had a direct link with *Good Housekeeping*, running a series of household demonstrations with its endorsement.[21]

When the cinemagazine began, the print magazine was midway through a slow rise in popularity. The market for popular print had been growing throughout the nineteenth century, and increased disposable income, together with quicker and cheaper printing methods, increased the number of titles available to the public. The late 1910s and early 1920s also saw a rise in two particular sectors of the print magazine industry. On the one hand, this was the period in which magazines from America chose to launch British editions for the first time; for example, *Vogue* launched in 1916 and *Good Housekeeping* in 1922. On the other, this period saw increased provision of magazines that catered for readers across class lines, with an emphasis on pictorial journalism, culminating in the launch of *Picture Post* in 1938, when the last of the commercial entertainment cinemagazines (excepting *Pathe Pictorial*) folded. What many of these magazines had in common, like cinemagazines, was their target audience – women. The biggest area of growth in print magazines during the interwar period was the women's periodical, and so too, a number of cinemagazine series either explicitly or implicitly targeted the female audience. The oft-quoted statistic that over 60% of the cinema audience was female along with the general assumption that women were interested in entertainment and men in news, also tends to bear this out.[22] As a regularly repeated part of women's cinema 'diet', the cinemagazine formed a part of the prime influence on women's lives. Films often portrayed a world outside of women's normal experience, and helped them to form views about this world, but cinemagazines also contained a good deal of material that simply presented other women's lives to the viewer. They provided the woman in the cinema with an image of herself and her sex. This process not only entertained, but also influenced the predominantly female audience in their view of the modern woman.

The similarities between cinemagazines and print magazines during this period provide valuable clues as to how audiences viewed them and to how they can be studied now. Most cinemagazines kept to traditional women's topics, with the mainstays of the cinemagazines being travel, beauty, fashion and variety items. While 'the magazine will be friend, advisor and instructor in the difficult task of being a woman,' the cinemagazine too provided help and advice on fashion, beauty and keeping up with the latest trends.[23] It is quite possible therefore that female audience members viewed them in a similar light to their copies of *Peg's Paper* or *Picture Post*. More than this, Jenny Hammerton maintains, that at least *Eve* and *Eve the Lady's Pictorial*, a contemporary print magazine, 'would have been connected in the minds of many of the cinema audience'.[24] This is indeed a possibility. The style of the cinemagazine, its direct relationship with the audience and its knowing humour are indeed reminiscent of the tone of the print *Eve*. Whether this was a conscious effort on behalf of the creators of *Eve* or a happy coincidence is unclear. There are certainly no references to *Eve*'s print cousin in the surviving documents relating to the series. These striking similarities between the print and film magazines lead us to a very useful lens through which to view cinemagazines. Much work has been done on the interwar print magazine, drawing on the vast scholarship of the periodical. It is, therefore, a good starting point from which to address the cinemagazine, focusing on one of the topics that it has in common with its print cousin – women, as both audience and subject.

Surplus women

The period after the First World War saw a marked increase in the visibility of women in the public sphere. Women had played a much larger role in public activities during the war, and as a consequence, had become much more visible in the media. With the realisation that the appalling casualty rates in the trenches would lead to a sharp drop in the male population, the press launched a new phenomenon – 'surplus women'. This hysterical label was used to describe those young women who would not be able to find a husband because of the lower proportion of men in the British population, and thus no longer had a useful role to play in society. The phenomenon was not purely borne out of the fear that there were simply too many women in Britain. Its roots also stem from anxiety over the extension of the franchise to women in 1918. Also, the perceived inadequacy and effeminacy of those men who did return from the war increased anxiety in the press. 'Typically the notion of a deformed, debilitated masculinity was juxtaposed with that of a muscular, healthy "new" womanhood.'[25] Thus, at its heart this problem of the 'surplus woman' had the contrast between the men who wanted to return to their old jobs and their old way of life, and the new, modern woman who had found her place in the world of work. As a result of this anxiety and fear, 'the acquisition of "unfeminine" or "masculine" characteristics of dress, figure and attitudes to sport and work was often depicted as unnatural and freakish'.[26]

At base terms, this was a conflict over the age-old image of woman within the private sphere, a concept that the cinemagazine (and one could argue non-fiction film itself) with its frequent exhibition of the private in public, undermined. In the 1920s women became more public through their adoption of work and the changing patterns of society, and with this, tension within the work/home dichotomy was heightened. The working/public woman was seen as threatening the maternal/private wife. It was this anxiety that was often played out in cinemagazine stories. As Susan Kingsley Kent points out, 'After the partial enfranchisement of women in 1918, public anxiety about women's place in society centred on work.'[27] Where women in cinemagazines are seen doing men's jobs, they are not seen as replacing men, but rather, emulating them. They either become more masculine themselves or else undermine their new roles by showing their feminine character (powdering their noses at the controls of an aircraft, for example). Here, the unease is being both calmed and emphasised through humour, a method that was often commented upon in magazines of the time. As Winifred Holtby noted, '… men find it beneath their dignity to regard a woman as their superior. They find something a little comic about it. The woman boss is a matter for comic pictures and music-hall jokes and sly banter.'[28] The majority of cinemagazine-makers were, of course, men.

Even the types of women's work portrayed served to reinforce the unease with which 1920s' society held the phenomenon. Women were often 'given the chance to see on screen contemporaries very much like themselves – ordinary women doing ordinary jobs and enjoying ordinary hobbies'.[29] Where this occurred, however, these women were rarely singled out as individuals. Instead they were left un-commented upon, the mass of ordinary workers and nothing special. For entertainment value, editors chose to film far more outlandish examples of women at work – women aviators, firefighters and bricklayers, for example.[30] These women who were breaking new social boundaries in doing their jobs were consistently undermined by their portrayal, both visually and in the language of the intertitles. Here I disagree with Jenny Hammerton's discussion of *Eve's Film Review*. She claims that the 'inspirational number of women' featured in *Eve* made out that 'the world is Eve's oyster – she can be anything she desires to be'.[31] I would argue instead that the vast proportion of stories containing working women, portrayed the more traditional occupations – farm work, domestic arts and factory work, and where they did not, the women in more unusual, sometimes masculine, jobs were subtly undermined by both the editing and the intertitles of the cinemagazines.

The most extreme example of this is ODD JOBS FOR EVE, an imported American story for *Eve*, which is a more blatantly negative depiction of women's new occupations than its surviving British counterparts.[32] Its opening section displays a women's volunteer fire department. The action mimics a comic caper as the women hastily load themselves onto a fire truck that is too small to hold them all. As the women struggle to hook up the hose to the water supply, the intertitle reads, 'We could "wisecrack" about women and their hose but that would be a washout,' underlining the humorous tone. This line also cleverly reminds the viewer of the women's more socially acceptable role as female glamour object, thus further undermining their attempts at professional capability. Tellingly, the intertitles for this item also place working women very firmly in the modern world. A young woman 'airplane mechanic and pilot' is singled out as representing 'the modern miss', as though an unusually masculine job was a prerequisite for the modern 'surplus' woman. The woman pilot herself seems nervous at being filmed, and is visibly shy when the camera focuses on her face. The entire scene has a 'staged' quality which highlights the unnatural status of the young aviatrix. The *coup de grace*, however, is dealt at the end, when the working women are contrasted with the 'executive position' of 'bringing up thirteen kids'. A woman is pictured, smiling, amidst all her children, in a tableau much like a traditional family portrait. Here she seems confident and happy, as do her children, in great contrast to the body language and demeanour of the previous subjects. Thus, once again, the efforts of some women are successfully undermined and the audience's assumption, that a woman's role is maternal, is confirmed.

As stated above, this film is somewhat more blatant in its negativity than most of the work stories in cinemagazines of this period, possibly because of its American origin.[33] However, it shares a fundamental characteristic with other stories about 'modern' working girls: it features women singled out as pioneers in their chosen fields, and shows them seemingly embarrassed by the fact. The young blacksmith in THE VILLAGE SMITHY STANDS, for example, writhes and giggles under the camera's gaze.[34] This singling out is in sharp contrast with the mass involvement of girls in more traditional occupations. Hammerton observes, 'There are numerous strangely pleasing films of women doing apparently simple jobs.'[35] In such films as

THE POTATO PICKERS, ANOTHER OCCUPATION FOR EVE – THE KENNEL MAID, and DUNLOP SPORTS SHOES – WATCH THEM MADE AT LIVERPOOL, crowds of anonymous girls are seen going about what is obviously perceived as a normal occupation.[36] What few comments that are made about their sex serve to re-affirm their appropriateness for the job. For example, in ANOTHER CAREER FOR EVE we are reminded that 'The ailments of friend Dobbin afford a ready outlet for feminine patience and sympathy.'[37] Where women in more traditional jobs are seen alone, they are rarely commented on. *Around the Town*'s PHEASANT REARING shows a woman packing eggs into a crate for transportation.[38] Of course, the woman is not the main focus of the film, and as such, she remains an unobtrusive figure. Here sex is not discussed or mentioned. She remains an anonymous domestic worker. This is the case in many cinemagazine stories where women work in more traditional roles; their status as working women is not discussed and certainly not undermined as it is with the more 'modern' or 'masculine' jobs.[39]

Fashion

As one would expect, the more traditional women's interests were very well catered for in the interwar cinemagazine. Fashion parades, for example, are one of the most memorable features of early cinemagazines. A brief look at the types of fashions shown and their mode of exhibition within the cinemagazines reveals a wealth of valuable information to the student of fashion, or indeed, women's history. Pathe started producing short fashion films in the early 1910s, and by the 1920s fashion stories were frequently used by editors of both newsreels and cinemagazines.[40] Paris fashions became a staple of *Eve's Film Review* in particular. The rise in fashion films which cinemagazine fashion stories heralded was in part due to the beginning of the fashion model's popularity. In the late nineteenth century most designers still displayed their designs as sketches, illustrations or as miniatures on dolls. Although pioneers such as Lucile Ltd began to use live mannequins (models) during this period, the profession was still viewed with distaste by society.[41] Even the designers themselves often likened mannequins to prostitutes, and the profession was not considered respectable.[42] Well into the 1910s, to avoid the shame of using mannequins, many fashion houses still relied on sketches or on displaying toiles (rough versions of the garment design) on dress forms when exhibiting designs to customers. The filmmakers' need to shoot moving subjects meant that, until mannequins had become more widespread and more respectable, fashion would remain unfilmable. The change of opinion seems to have occurred by 1920, when the use of fashions in cinemagazines begins its rise. All of the fashions shown in these stories were modelled by real live young women.

The cinemagazine had something of a love affair with the female form. Hammerton has identified and discussed several examples of the fetishisation of the feet and legs in *Eve* stories and also close-up shots that 'break up the body'.[43] It is also worth noting that wherever possible, and often when it was totally unnecessary, cinemagazine editors added a pretty girl. For example, M'LADY'S DRESS WHILE SHE WAITS is essentially a story about dressmaking, which could have been made more realistic through the employment of a dress form.[44] Instead, a dressmaker drapes a live model with fabric (with difficulty); she then admires her own prettiness in a hand-held mirror. 'This is a handy technique for showing both the front and the back of the dress at the same time' but also for the audience to get an apparently unseen glance at the model's shapely form.[45]

What is most striking to a modern viewer of surviving cinemagazines, and most useful to the student of fashion and culture, is the standard of fashions exhibited. From the beginning, *Around the Town*'s fashion subjects were solely haute couture.[46] In keeping with the reel's high-society pretensions, the couturiers featured included Lucile Ltd and Condor Millinery.[47] They were very much 'the latest modes from Paris', reflecting the prevalent view that the French capital was also the capital of haute couture.[48] *Eve's Film Review* seems to have followed suit with this high-fashion bias. *Eve* featured a large number of designers' creations, but the majority of the others were equally prestigious. They too included Lucile Ltd, but also Lucien Lelong, Maison Worth, Maison Redfern, Jeanne Lanvin, Joseph Paquin and Revile Ltd.[49] This focus on prestige and luxury seems quite out of place in the normal *Eve* programme, alongside diving competitions and Felix the Cat cartoons. However, the inclusion of such collections may well have had much to do with the designers themselves. Lucile, Lady Christiana Duff Gordon (1863–1935) was a pioneer in the art of popularising haute couture, particularly through film. Her company, Lucile Ltd, had already supplied Lily Elsie's costumes for the stage production of *The Merry Widow,* when Lady Duff Gordon designed for five films between 1916 and 1921.[50] These films were certainly used to a promotional advantage. The first, THE STRANGE CASE OF MARY PAGE (1916) was advertised 'with reference to its "33 specially designed gowns by Lady Duff Gordon"'.[51] Her designs, paraded by mannequins, appeared in *Around the Town* and frequently in *Eve* throughout the 1920s.[52] Her adoption of the cinemagazine as a legitimate space for collection display may well have inspired her peers to do so, too. Among them were several equally flamboyant characters who easily rose to the challenge. Jean Patou readily embraced popular culture as a way to increase interest in his designs. He dressed tennis star Suzanne Lenglen both on and off the court, and his designs featured in *Eve* issue no. 146.[53] Jeanne Lanvin, on the

BUFVC

Title frame from *Around The Town* issue no. 105, 1921

other hand, had moved into the world of film before her collections were shown in *Eve*. She dressed film actresses such as Mary Pickford off-screen throughout the 1920s.[54]

The adoption of the cinemagazine by the haute couture establishment reflected a widespread move within the fashion industry towards embracing more mainstream culture. Just as prestigious society accepted famous men and women without noble breeding, the haute couture market, too, began to broaden. As interest in high fashion became more widespread, so began the rise in influence of the designers. As more people in more prominent places wore their designs, they became 'authoritative sources of advice about clothes – and by extension – related techniques of femininity'.[55] This relationship was of mutual benefit: 'The role of prestigious imitation … was increasingly accorded to figures in popular culture – first publicity-conscious aristocrats, then film stars and heiresses and because the fashion industry embraced this new trend, couturiers continued to be seen as the pinnacle of taste and beauty.[56] In turn, the couturiers lent some of this aura of respectability and prestige to the cinemagazines. However, haute couture's expansion into the film industry and popular celebrity appears to have little to do with the working-class woman in the cinema. Indeed, 'cinema was always a cheap urban entertainment' and was not yet the middle-class Mecca that Odeon made it in the late 1930s, so there must have been some appeal in the parading of high fashion in the cinemagazines to a working-class audience.[57] The answer to this apparent conundrum is a fascinating insight into the cultural history of the period, brought to life by the cinemagazine.

The cinema, for many members of the audience, represented sheer escapism, the chance to suspend reality and experience a dreamed-of luxury. In this way, 'the cinema, playing on fantasy and desire, enabled women to *imagine* an end to domestic drudgery and chronic want.'[58] High fashion seems to have been the ideal subject for this type of experience. The opulent use of fabrics and the designs, inspired by the Russian ballet or the discovery of Tutankhamen's tomb, were perfectly suited to the tone of exoticism and wonder that the cinemagazines often adopted.[59] Here again is a similarity with the print magazine. As Georgina Howell remarks, 'In violent reaction to hard times and sensible clothes, the longing for escape and glamour brought a wave of fantastic fashion follies into *Vogue*.'[60] The settings of some of *Eve*'s stories even imply 'that the cinemagoer is in the position of purchaser at a design house or boutique.'[61] For many women in the audience, this could have been the ultimate consumer fantasy; a chance to imagine a life of wealth and comfort as remote from their own lives as the far-flung exotic romances screened after the cinemagazine. The exhibition of high fashion in the cinemagazine also gave working-class women the opportunity to emulate those styles in their own clothes. The particular fashions of the 1920s and early 1930s, with emphasis on the simple drop-waisted dress and much freer underclothes, made the fashions easy and cheap to copy, for the first time. By 1925, when fashion coverage in *Eve*, for example, was in almost every other issue, 'everything a woman wore could be cut out of seven yards of fabric and rayon stockings were cheap enough for almost everyone.'[62] This happy accident of style was coupled with the continuing rise in the ready-made clothing industry throughout the early twentieth century. There were 'clothing factories producing cheap frocks and skirts' all over London and the larger towns, and 'the combined effects of the new media, faster distribution, and a retailing emphasis on window display made the idea of constant change in clothing design and detail a widespread aspect of consumer demand.'[63] Thus among many of the more fashion-conscious members of the cinemagazine audience there may well have been a hunger to see the new ideas of the couturiers in order to stay one step ahead of the latest trend.

Some contemporary viewers obviously did see emulation as the draw for fashion stories, as the following comment from *The Film Renter and Moving Picture News* makes clear: 'Close views of sartorial productions … will provide kinema Eves with animated patterns which can be copied. We may yet see … women … descend on kinemas equipped with notebooks in which to record the ideas they glean from these animated fashions.'[64] It is unlikely that all viewers would be such accomplished seamstresses as to be able to copy patterns directly from the screen. However, plenty of anecdotal evidence exists to suggest that cinema audiences did copy their favourite style from films and thus it is credible to suggest that the fashion stories provided at least some inspiration. The editor of *Eve*, Fred Watts, even joked about the audience's adoption of fashion 'on the cheap' in one story. 'Foxy' invites members of the audience to join the '"Get Yourself a Silver Fox" Club'.[65] Women are shown petting and walking fox cubs that will be 'around the neck some day'. The jovial tone suggests that the author was well aware of how tasteless the suggestion is that 'Little Silver Foxes … will grow into furs one day for the Club -!' The entire story was presented with a knowing wink. Even this odd method would not get most of the audience a luxury fur wrap, although the story did provide them with a dubious laugh.

Colour

More regularly than they were played for laughs, fashion stories were an opportunity to display new film techniques or 'camera tricks'. In the case of the cinemagazine, the most frequently used of these innovations was colour process innovation. *Around the Town* tinted its fashion stories, and Fred Watts chose a fashion subject for the first Verrachrome item to be shown in *Eve*.[66] Fashion subjects make up by far the majority of the *Eve* Pathécolor items on record and provide the best examples of those stories that survive. This prevalence was not purely because of an artistic impulse, however. Pathécolor in particular was a stencil colour process that was produced only by the Pathé Cinéma laboratories in France. As most of the fashion stories were filmed in France, either by outside film agencies at the fashion houses themselves or by Pathé in its studios, it was relatively easy for those films to be coloured on the Continent before they came to Pathe Ltd in London for editing and printing. Thus the combination of artistic appeal and practical ease made colour fashions ideal cinemagazine stories. They are also ideal stories for students and researchers now, giving a unique insight into couture exhibition on film in the 1920s and 1930s, but also in some cases, the only surviving record of a design. These colour items also provide yet another parallel with the print magazine. As an infrequent and spectacular occurrence, colour 'carries connotations of novelty'.[67] The inclusion of colour items

14

worked as a lure to audiences in the same way as the innovative photographic spreads in magazines such as *Picture Post*. 'They function as attention-grabbing attractions and incitements to fantasy', heightening the experience of viewing.[68] Both new types of visual attraction provided an hitherto unknown insight into new worlds which appeared 'as special selection', in the cinemagazine's case 'against the background of monochromatic imagery'.[69]

Although one can second-guess responses from audiences to such things as colour in cinemagazines, there is very little factual evidence on which to base this sort of conclusion. Unlike the print magazine, distribution figures are near impossible to find, and even if it were possible to discover how many cinemas took, for instance, *Vanity Fair*, it would be impossible to find out whether the film was screened at each of those venues, let alone how many of the audience present watched the picture. To some extent, this is a common problem for scholars of all types of film. However, the cinemagazine presents its own problems. The nature of the cinema-going experience was such that a shorter item might just as well have been used as an opportunity to use the facilities or catch up on the week's gossip as be watched avidly. Indeed, the cinemagazine was the very sort of item to be left out of a programme if the projectionist thought it too crowded. This casual attitude applied equally in earlier days to the preservation of the issues themselves. Those series made by the smaller companies, such as *Around the Town*, survive more by accident than design, and in scant numbers. What little paperwork that does survive, however, provides precious insight into cinemagazine consumption. Nestled among the accounts and internal correspondence that remain from the Pathe company's 1928 files, are letters from devoted female viewers of *Eve's Film Review*, testament to the existence of many more avid fans of the genre.[70] Much more research needs to be done into this area and also the entire subject of interwar cinema audiences.[71] Along with further study of the cinemagazine itself, this would prove invaluable to film scholarship.

In researching the cinemagazine we are one step closer to filling the gaps in the cinema programme between 1918 and 1938. The cinemagazine, with its richly varied range of subjects and its light, comic, tone is yet another insight into the entertainment enjoyed by the public. However, it is also a valuable source in understanding British social history. The cinemagazines illuminate how women were portrayed and how they saw themselves in the 1920s and 1930s. Alongside print magazines, they reflect the controversies of the time in their portrayal of everyday life and illustrate the fads and trends of the age, through fashion, arts and culture. Further work on these remarkable films, the 'colour supplements' of the cinema, can only increase our knowledge and appreciation.

Notes

1 Richard Koszarski, *An Evening's Entertainment: The age of the silent feature picture, 1915–1928* (Oxford: Maxwell Macmillan International, 1990), p. 48.

2 F. C., 'The Ideal Programme. An Exhibitor's Demands on Renter and Producers,' *Kinematograph Weekly*, 21 July 1921, p. 46.

3 Kalton Lahue, *Bound and Gagged: The story of the silent serials* (London: Thomas Yoseloff, 1968), p. 15.

4 For example, Yuri Tsivian, *Early Cinema in Russia and its Cultural Reception* (London: Routledge, 1994).

5 Lahue, op. cit., p. 35.

6 Just ask an elderly member of the public to name a company that made short cinema films to test the success of this policy – in my experience, almost all of them mention either Pathe's *News* or *Pictorial* series.

7 *Kinematograph Weekly*, 27 November 1919, p. 24.

8 *The Bioscope*, 6 November 1919, p. 130.

9 *Eve* eventually finished in December 1933.

10 Records end on 31 July 1922.

11 The British Universities Newsreel Database records for *Gaumont Mirror* end in May 1932.

12 This series ran from August 1928 until April 1930.

13 *The Bioscope*, 17 February 1927, page unknown.

14 Ibid., p. 7.

15 *Kinematograph Weekly*, 4 November 1926, p. 10.

16 *Kinematograph Weekly*, 26 January 1928, pp. 10–11.

17 Luke McKernan, *Topical Budget: The Great British News Film* (London: British Film Institute, 1992), p. 72.

18 Ibid., p. 74.

19 *Around the Town*, issue no. 88, 4 August 1921; *Eve's Film Review*, issue no. 72, 19 October 1922; *Gaumont Mirror*, issue no. 81, 22 August 1928.

20 McKernan, op. cit., p. 73.

21 Interestingly, this was the same year that *Good Housekeeping* launched a restaurant on Oxford Street in the heart of London. This was a very aggressive marketing strategy, but also, perhaps, a willingness to move into popular entertainments in order to increase market share.

22 Rachael Low, *The History of the British Film 1918–1929* (London: George Allen & Unwin, 1971), p. 32. Arrar Jackson puts the cinema audience at 70% women and girls. Arrar Jackson, 'Writing for the Screen', *The New Survey of London Life and Labour 1934, IX. Life and Leisure* (London: P. S. King and Son, 1935), p. 16.

23 Jenny Hammerton, *For Ladies Only? Eve's Film Review. Pathé cinemagazine 1921–1933* (Hastings: The Projection Box, 2001), p. 39.

24 Ibid., p. 45.

25 Billie Melman, *Women and the Popular Imagination in the Twenties: Flappers and nymphs* (Basingstoke: Macmillan, 1988), p. 20.

26 Hammerton, op. cit., p. 35.

27 Susan Kingsley Kent, *Making Peace: The reconstruction of gender in interwar Britain* (Chichester: Princeton University Press, 1993), p. 100.

28 Winifred Holtby, 'The Man Colleague', *Manchester Guardian*, 21 December 1928, quoted in Berry, Paul and Bishop, Alan (eds.) *Testament of a Generation: The journalism of Vera Brittain and Winifred Holtby* (London: Virago, 1985), p. 62.

29   Hammerton, op. cit., p. 92.
30   *Eve's Film Review,* issue no. unknown, date unknown; *Eve's Film Review*, issue no. 385, 24 October 1928.
31   Hammerton, op. cit., p. 92.
32   *Eve's Film Review,* issue no. unknown, date unknown
33   Hammerton, op. cit., p. 93.
34   *Eve's Film Review*, issue no. 207, 5 March 1931.
35   Hammerton, op. cit., p. 92.
36   *Eve's Film Review,* issue no. 537, 17 September 1931; *Eve's Film Review,* issue no. 601, 8 December 1932; *Eve's Film Review,* issue no. 478, 31 July 1930.
37   *Eve's Film Review,* issue no. 558, 1 February 1932.
38   *Around the Town,* issue no. 88, 4 August 1921.
39   *Eve's Film Review,* issue no. 608, 26 January 1933; *Eve's Film Review,* issue no. 604, 29 December 1932.
40   Hammerton, op. cit., p. 12.
41   http://www.designerhistory.com, accessed 20 September 2005.
42   Jennifer Craik, *The Face of Fashion: Cultural studies in fashion* (London: Routledge, 1993), p. 98.
43   Hammerton, op. cit., pp. 158, 181.
44   Undated *Eve's Film Review* story c.1927.
45   Hammerton, op. cit., p. 77.
46   For example, *Around the Town*, issue no. 43, 23 September 1920 and *Around the Town*, issue no. 54, 9 December 1920.
47   *Around the Town*, issue no. 54, 9 December 1920; *Around the Town*, issue no. 115, 9 February 1922.
48   *Around the Town*, issue no. 114, 2 February 1922.
49   *Eve's Film Review,* issue nos. 77, 79, 131, 136, 187, 395.
50   http://www.designerhistory.com, accessed 20 September 2005.
51   Sarah Berry, *Screen Style: Fashion and femininity in 1930s Hollywood* (London: University of Minnesota Press, 2000), p. 11
52   For example, *Around the Town*, issue no. 54, 9 December 1920 and *Eve's Film Review*, issue no. 142, 21 February 1924.
53   http://www.designerhistory.com, accessed 20 September 2005; *Eve's Film Review;* issue no. 146, 20 March 1924.
54   http://www.designerhistory.com, accessed 20 September 2005.
55   Craik, op. cit., p. 56.
56   Craik, ibid., p. 70.
57   Sarah Alexander, 'Becoming a woman in London in the 1920s and 1930s', in David Feldman and Gareth Stedman Jones (eds.), *Metropolis – London: Histories and representations since 1800*, (London: Routledge, 1989), p. 257.
58   Ibid., p. 247.
59   Georgina Howell, *In Vogue: 75 years of style* (London: Condé Nast, 1991), p. 18.
60   Ibid., pp. 18–19.
61   Hammerton, op. cit., p. 77.
62   Howell, op. cit., p. 43.
63   Alexander, op. cit., p. 257; Berry, op. cit., p. 3.
64   *The Film Renter and Moving Picture News*, 21 May 1921, quoted in Hammerton, op. cit., p. 77.
65   *Eve's Film Review*, issue no. 437, 17 September 1929.

66 For example *Around the Town*, issue no. 88, 4 August 1921; *Eve's Film Review*, issue no. 191, 29 January 1925. Curiously, Verrachrome, a 'natural' colour system, was an invention of Aron Hamburger, the producer of *Around the Town*.

67 Tom Gunning, 'Colourful Metaphors: The Attraction of Colour in Early Silent Cinema,' *The Journal of the Popular and Projected Image before 1914*, vol 2 no. 2 (2003) p. 5.

68 Ibid., p. 11

69 Ibid., p. 5

70 Some of these are reproduced in this volume. See also Jenny Hammerton, 'Letters to the editor of Pathé Pictorial and Eve's Film Review,' *Journal of Popular British Cinema*, vol. 2 (1999), pp. 128–132

71 A few audience studies do exist, such as Nicholas Hiley, '"Let's go to the pictures": the British cinema audience in the 1920s and 1930s,' *Journal of Popular British Cinema*, vol. 2 (1999), pp. 39–54.

THIS MODERN AGE: BRITISH SCREEN JOURNALISM IN TRANSITION, 1945–1951

Leo Enticknap

This Modern Age *was the Rank Organisation's prestigious documentary magazine series, which ran from 1946 to 1951. In this essay, adapted from a chapter in his doctoral thesis,* The Non-fiction Film in Post-war Britain, *Leo Enticknap examines the production history of* This Modern Age, *and considers its political significance and its place within the history of British documentary filmmaking. In particular he argues for its essential difference from the American news cinemagazine,* The March of Time, *with which it is often compared.*

This Modern Age (*TMA*) was one of the most sustained and politically significant cinemagazine series to be produced in Britain. The only other project which approached it in terms of editorial coverage and audience reached was the government's regular monthly release programme of 'information' films, started in 1941 as a propaganda exercise, and which survived in various forms into the 1950s. But it could be argued that these do not stand meaningful comparison with the commercially produced cinemagazine, as they were commissioned from a large number of production units and covered a wide, and essentially unrelated, range of subject matter. Indeed, their only real similarity to their commercial counterparts was the method of their distribution (theatrical and at regular intervals).

TMA is remarkable for a number of reasons. It was made entirely within the private sector, yet draws on many of the cultural and ideological precedents set by the Documentary Movement and associated intellectual film movements before the war, specifically in terms of stimulating discussion, serving an educational function and moving cinema away from the preserve of ideologically neutral entertainment. The highly structured 'debate' format of each film (contrasting arguments for a given position with those against) can in many ways be identified as a precursor to the public service model foregrounded by early television current affairs coverage. It certainly marked a strong contrast to the polemical propaganda which characterised the dying years of the Documentary Movement as demonstrated by, for example, the films of Paul Rotha or Jill Craigie.

Rank and non-fiction cinema

The somewhat prosaic tale of Joseph Arthur Rank's transformation from a Yorkshire flour-milling magnate and staunch Methodist into, arguably, the most successful industrialist in the history of British cinema has been covered extensively elsewhere.[1] It does not need to be repeated here other than to note that the crucial stages of that process took place against the political background of the Second World War. Rank acquired control of Denham and Pinewood studios in 1939, Gaumont-British and the Odeon exhibition chain in the autumn of 1941 and established Independent Producers Ltd, an umbrella organisation controlling the group's production activity, in August 1942.

Rank's interest in non-fiction cinema stemmed firstly from his ownership of the Gaumont-British and Universal newsreels, and secondly from his relationship with the government. The Crown Film Unit operated out of Pinewood Studios, which Rank had leased to the Home Office, and most commercial feature production came under the auspices of the Ministry of Information (MOI) Films Division and its Ideas Committee, which was, according to Porter and Litewski, 'the fount of feature production policy'.[2] This policy was primarily concerned with ensuring that Britain's studios made films with national interest and the war effort in mind, an objective which necessitated close cooperation between Rank and the wartime government.

This public service aspect of Rank's business activities was a significant contributory factor in the monopoly debate. His growing prominence within the film industry had caused left-wing critics and representatives of the Documentary Movement to argue that the extent of his holdings thus ran contrary to the public interest. The result was the Palache Committee, established by the Labour president of the Board of Trade, Hugh Dalton, in 1943. Their report, published in August 1944, and described by an anonymous *New Statesman* journalist as 'really an account of Mr Rank's recent business activities',[3] emphasised that this cultural dimension distinguished the film industry from other comparable economic sectors:

> A cinematograph film represents more than a mere commodity to be bartered against others. Already the screen has great influence both politically and culturally over the minds of the people. Its potentialities are vast, as a vehicle for the expression of national life, ideals and tradition, as a dramatic and artistic medium, and as an instrument for propaganda.[4]

The report implied that Rank's position within the film industry involved certain moral obligations. Although no action was taken on Palache's key recommendations in the short term, the end of the war ten months later brought with it the election of a Labour government and a contraction of the MOI Films Division, including the dissolution of the Ideas Committee. The Crown Film Unit was scaled down, and, with the exception of Humphrey Jennings, its prominent directors dispersed, either to other documentary units, the studios, or, in the case of Pat Jackson, to Holly-wood. Apart from two remaining projects, CHILDREN ON TRIAL (1946 d. Jack Lee) and SCHOOL FOR DANGER (1947 d. Edward Baird), the production of expensive, feature-length 'story documentaries' ceased, and the short-film programme, including the monthly releases, increasingly concentrated on specific informational issues such as road safety and vaccination rather than on the broader political subjects which Grierson and his acolytes had always sought to address. As Rotha complained:

> When the COI replaced the MOI, our Civil Service at the Treasury said, 'No more giving you x-million a year. We'll give you a little here and there. Now you become a service station. If the Ministry of Health wants a film on the immunisation of children from I don't know what, you must make this film for them. So in other words, what happened was they took out all the imagination of the idea from behind the units.[5]

Opposition to Rank, meanwhile, remained constant. The Documentary Movement, having enjoyed its finest hour, was campaigning for state-sector film production to remain at its wartime level (and the numerous cuttings from *Documentary News Letter* which can be found in The National Archives files dealing with films policy during and immediately following the war suggest that it was being listened to), and in 1946–1947 three pamphlets were published suggesting that Rank's religious beliefs and his emphasis on 'quality' production amounted to little more than a front for unbridled mercenary capitalism.[6]

The establishment of a prestigious, high-profile magazine film series, therefore, had the potential to kill two birds with one stone. On the one hand, it would fill the gap left by the MOI's production programme in a way which came under control of the industry rather than the government (a move likely to be approved by exhibitors' representatives) and on the other it would serve to deflect much of the criticism of Rank which centred on moral arguments as opposed to economic ones, of the sort raised by the Palache Committee. Pat Jackson asserts that the original idea for the series stemmed from an approach made by Documentary Movement representatives at the end of the war:

> We wrote a letter to Rank, a lot of us, saying, 'Please don't let this tradition of film-making die because we have really put documentary on the map, the

international map.' […] We knew that our days with the Crown Film Unit were numbered before absolute strangulation took over. […] The answer to what we were asking for was *This Modern Age*, which Rank thought was a fair enough contribution to an analysis of the everyday scene. But, of course, it was not the style we wanted at all. I mean, *March of Time* was doing it far better.[7]

If this account is true, it does much to explain the Movement's dismissal of *TMA*, suggesting that they were attempting to operate to their own agenda but under Rank's patronage. This was not quite the way Rank envisaged things. The obvious similarities with *The March of Time (MOT)*, the American news cinemagazine which had been distributed on a significant scale in Britain in the 1930s, can be explained quite simply: the fixed format and release schedule were necessary, just as *MOT*'s producers had found them necessary, in order to facilitate the widest distribution possible, as exhibitors (the majority of whom operated continuous, double-feature programmes) were able to accommodate a regular series of films of a specific length more easily than an intermittent flow of productions which could last anything between five minutes and an hour. Yet Rank's choice of filmmakers shows that he did not intend *TMA* to be a commercially bankrolled outlet for the Documentary Movement's political and ideological beliefs, as all the key players in the series came either from a feature-film background or from broadcast and print journalism.

The production team

The executive producer was Sergei Nolbandov, a Russian lawyer born in 1895 who had emigrated to Britain shortly after graduating from Moscow University in the mid-1920s. His first job in the British film industry was as an editor and assistant scriptwriter with Ivor Montagu and Adrian Brunel's company, followed by a number of positions in minor studios until he was hired by Michael Balcon and worked at Ealing as a scriptwriter on THERE AIN'T NO JUSTICE (1939). Nolbandov subsequently produced THE PROUD VALLEY (1939) and CONVOY (1940), both directed by Penrose Tennyson. His directorial debut was SHIPS WITH WINGS (1941), which he also scripted, and Nolbandov then directed UNDERCOVER (1943) before leaving Ealing to work for the MOI Films Division in an advisory capacity.[8] He was then taken on by the Rank Organisation to begin preparatory work on *TMA* just before the end of the war. An article written by Nolbandov in 1933 suggests that, having worked in a wide range of production contexts, he believed that established studios with firm financial backing provided a more economic production base than individual filmmakers could:

Producers with a steady working production unit and with powerful financial backing are in this respect much better situated than producers of isolated films, despite the fact that the latter may have more money per individual film. By commanding better studio and technical facilities, by working with a permanent staff, and by careful scheduling of their films in the order of shooting, they can show better results on the screen for much less money invested.[9]

It would seem logical to infer, therefore, that as far as documentary production was concerned, Nolbandov regarded an established unit producing an ongoing series such as *MOT* as a preferable option to individuals working on one-off projects (e.g. Rotha).

Working immediately below Nolbandov was George Ivan Smith, who held the title of 'associate producer and literary editor'. Smith was an Australian journalist who had previously worked in commercial radio, the Australian Broadcasting Corporation and later as head of the BBC Pacific Service. James Lansdale Hodson, the novelist and playwright, was initially a scriptwriter who took over Smith's position in 1947 when the latter left to join the United Nations. In addition to his literary career, Hodson had undertaken a small amount of film work, his only output of any significance being the commentary for DESERT VICTORY (1943). Robert Waithman, a journalist and diplomatic correspondent of *News Chronicle* for the duration of the war, was appointed deputy literary editor in February 1948.

The list of technicians working on *TMA* provides yet another indication that the series was conceived with production values normally associated with substantially budgeted 'A' features. Although not a member of the permanent staff, John Monck directed a number of issues. The commentators were Bruce Belfrage and Leo Genn, both stage actors who specialised mainly in character roles, Robert Harris, a radio journalist, and Bernard Miles, the actor and director, who by the outset of *TMA* had established himself as a prominent filmmaker in his own right.

Eric Cross was the chief cinematographer, and most of his department had worked either in features or newsreels. Among the more prominent cameramen was Clifford Hornby, who had been a locations and second unit director of photography before and during the war, and Ted Moore, whose previous career had been at Elstree Studios and the RAF Film Unit, where he had shot the British sequences for JOURNEY TOGETHER (1945).[10] Sound recordists John Woodiwiss and Don Alton had at their disposal the latest RCA Photophone location sound cameras, capable of mixing up to three channels without the distortion introduced by the previous generation of studio post-production equipment. Music was composed by Muir Mathieson, the acknowledged head of his profession, and conducted by John Hollingsworth, probably the only *TMA* regular to have been mainly associated with documentaries, having joined the RAF Symphony Orchestra when it was formed in 1940. Behind the key creative personnel was an extensive team of researchers, editors and librarians. When the first issue was released, the *TMA* permanent staff numbered over fifty.

HOMES FOR ALL

TMA's inaugural issue, HOMES FOR ALL, was first shown in September 1946 and provides us with a fairly coherent statement both of the filmic style its producers were trying to evolve and of their approach to the subject matter. The topic it dealt with was urban redevelopment, one which had previously been addressed in the Rank Organisation's first feature-length documentary, THE WAY WE LIVE (1946 d. Jill Craigie), released a month earlier.[11]

For a series which would later sell itself on impartiality and even-handedness, HOMES FOR ALL certainly presents a forceful case for the government's planning policy. An intertitle following the opening sequence makes it plain that the film is not restricting itself to a discussion of how Britain should seek to recover from the effects of the Blitz: 'Throughout the world, millions are homeless. Britain's housing problem has the biggest history because Britain led the world into industrial expansion.'

We then see a revisionist account of Britain's social history from the Industrial Revolution to the Great Depression, the commentator concluding that '150 years were spent wrecking a heritage. This is the price we pay for an age of anyhow.' A disequilibrium stage in the narrative is marked by a climactic bombing sequence, and then a hint at its resolution in the last shot from reel one – a Labour campaign poster bearing the slogan 'Let's build the houses – quick!' The second half of the film concentrates on the idea of a planned building programme being the only way to avoid repeating the mistakes of the past, and asserts that massive government intervention is needed to achieve this in the face of economic and infrastructural obstacles, although the message here becomes somewhat contradictory.

Firstly we are told that only state control and standardisation 'can produce the components we need in the numbers we need – in their millions'. This message is reinforced by a montage sequence set to music, recalling THINGS TO COME, (1936 d: William Cameron Menzies) showing pre-fabricated bungalows being produced on an assembly line. Yet the film also warns against 'the old curse of mass-building, the sameness, the monotony, the dreary uniformity … the government must never forget this': cue shots of 1930s slum housing. Thus, while the script of

HOMES FOR ALL endorses the unprecedented extent of the government's involvement in the lives of British citizens, it is a qualified endorsement rather than an uncomplicated celebration of some mythical socialist utopia.

At first glance it might seem surprising that a film financed by big business should be arguing so strongly in favour of public sector expansion. It was well known that Rank was at loggerheads with Labour's policy toward the film industry, and especially the initial architects of that policy, the Chancellor (and instigator of the Palache Report) Hugh Dalton and President of the Board of Trade Stafford Cripps. Indeed, cynical observers regarded *TMA* as essentially a public relations exercise – 'a sop to the socialists' in Jill Craigie's words[12] – one of a number of schemes intended to demonstrate that the Rank Organisation was the responsible face of capitalism, addressing those moral obligations alluded to by Palache and various others. By so doing, they would deflect the criticism of the press and the left-wing intelligentsia, and thus stand a better chance of heading off the more extreme measures, such as state ownership of cinemas, which the latter had proposed. This idea is backed up by much of the critical reaction to *TMA*, as in this review of SHADOW OF THE RUHR (issue no. 21, 1948):

> Mr. Rank's Tory friends were shocked at the most telling tributes the Labour government has had. But what ever you think of monopolies in general and J. Arthur Rank in particular, at least he gives his producers a freedom almost unknown in the cinema world.[13]

Furthermore, credence is given to this view both by a pointed reference to pro-government issues of *TMA* in an 'approved' biography of Rank, written by one of his apologists and published in 1952,[14] and also by the arbitrary nature of Rank's decision to terminate the series in 1949, citing massive financial losses incurred by his production operation, losses he believed were caused by misguided government policy.

But such a theory is not needed to account for the cautious advocacy of government housing policy evident in HOMES FOR ALL. Ever since a feature entitled 'A Plan for Britain' had appeared in the 1941 New Year issue of *Picture Post*, a political lobby dubbed the 'New Jerusalem Movement' by the historian Correlli Barnett had vigorously promoted the idea that an enhanced standard of living at home should be an inevitable consequence of a victory abroad. It was an idea that had gathered steam with the publication of the Beveridge Report a year later, and which culminated in the April 1945 election of a Labour government, one that had been secured largely on the back of a manifesto which had made housing provision arguably the single most important issue.[15] The inaugural production of *TMA* was largely an exposition of these arguments, ones which had already been endorsed by the public at large, and so with hindsight its editorial content was not as controversial as it might seem.

HOMES FOR ALL is far more interesting in terms of its aesthetic content. Carefully framed panning shots, intricate lighting effects and artistic montage sequences contrast sharply with the rough-and-ready cinematography normally associated with virtually every other form of non-fiction cinema being produced at the time. The sound track consists of a literate and tightly constructed commentary, which at times verges on the poetic (the repetition of the 'age of anyhow' motif) and a dense music track. It follows established newsreel practice in that it only incorporates direct synchronised sound, complete with 'dead track,' in one sequence where a person is shown speaking direct to camera (although more use was made of direct sound in the later issues).

Compared with a typical *MOT* approach the film is far more slowly paced, but with a more carefully defined relationship between image and sound. The practice of describing an image in the commentary text, or 'calling the shot', was one that Louis de Rochemont (*MOT*'s founder) had deliberately avoided on the grounds that it retarded the progress of the narrative and thus was less likely to hold the spectator's attention.[16] Instead, *MOT* commentaries were supposed to elaborate on the visual element or instruct the spectator as to how it should be interpreted. For example, the sequence from INSIDE NAZI GERMANY (1938) of a protest meeting against the establishment of a Nazi summer camp near a New England settlement is not introduced (as it might have been in a typical newsreel from the period) with a sentence such as '… these pictures show American citizens protesting against Nazi military activities on the outskirts of their village …'. Instead, it introduces an emotional dimension to the sequence, hence a statement that the principle US Nazi representative '… meets with unexpected opposition in a community long proud of its tolerance'.

The authors of *TMA* commentaries, by contrast, tended to regard calling the shot as a legitimate device for emphasising the intrinsic visual properties of an individual shot or sequence, rather than a narrative defect. Thus, in HOMES FOR ALL, we are told only that 'this was the result [of 1930s slum clearance schemes]', before being shown unaccompanied images of tenement blocks. The overall impression is that the film at this stage is not passing a negative judgement on what was, at the time, regarded as the way forward in housing policy. A more effective example can be found in issue no. 6, PALESTINE (1947). Shots 95–97 of reel two show the devastated remains of the King David Hotel, including the bodies of some of the victims, with the commentator stating simply that '… a wing of the King David Hotel, Jerusalem, British headquarters, was blown up in 1946'. Edgar Anstey's verdict on the slowly paced *TMA* commentaries was that their authors were 'obviously seeking and finding a higher degree of precision in their commentary wording than the genre has yet experienced', and suggested that the result was 'a consequent gain in the freedom and power of the camera'.[17]

Although the first few releases of *TMA* lay down definite markers as to how the aesthetic elements in the series would eventually develop, the techniques which went into them were distinctly experiential, especially as regards sound design. Of issues 1–5, *Documentary News Letter* remarked:

> … it is apparent that the unit still has a great deal to learn about sound-track – what to put on and how to time it with the shots; how to achieve some sort of synthesis so that tracks and visual fuse up into a *film*; and a lot to learn about how the facts, which they photograph so well, can be made intellectually or emotionally exciting.[18]

In many ways this learning curve is evident in all of these films, which show an extensive range of stylistic and narrative approaches.

SCOTLAND YARD

The second *TMA* film, SCOTLAND YARD, opened at the Odeon, Marble Arch, London on 10 October 1946. Again concentrating on domestic affairs, it examines the problem of black marketeering using the case study of a woman arrested for causing a disturbance. A police officer identifies the stockings she is wearing as having been stolen from a warehouse in which a security guard had been murdered. The Scotland Yard machine then goes into action in an attempt to identify and apprehend the criminal responsible.

The entire film is built around this structuring narrative, an approach similar to the one taken by the story documentaries made during the war. The crucial difference is that none of the characters have speaking parts, apart from two moralising monologues delivered by the Metropolitan Police Commissioner, Sir Harold Scott. The film depends to a large extent on effective editing and a virtuoso commentary spoken by Bernard Miles. Immediately after the opening scene in which the woman is arrested we see a montage sequence of filing cabinets and card indexes as Miles' voice drops to a monotone and warns:

> If you have ever been convicted, you are indexed here, under your name and every one of your aliases. The sort of crime you commit and how you go about it

ITV PLC (Granada International)

Frame still from SCOTLAND YARD *This Modern Age* issue no. 2, 1946

– picking a lock, breaking a window, using a jemmy – all are noted in this room. Even knowledge of the offence and how you did it, without a name, may be enough to track you down.

The understated yet unsettling way in which direct address to the spectator is used here contrasts sharply with the bombastic approach which had become the trademark of *MOT*, heightened by the fact that the track is, at this point, completely silent apart from the commentary. In a later scene showing the interrogation of a suspect, Miles imitates the voices of both protagonists interspersed with that of the third-person commentator, the reflection of one on the other eliciting an almost Brechtian sense of identification followed by detachment. The film does, at times, verge on the melodramatic ('… the mysterious world which police and criminals live in is very much a world of their own, with a hint of strangeness, even by day …'). In the concluding scene we see the Commissioner warn against the purchase of black-market goods on the grounds that trivial crimes can lead to more serious ones. There then follows a shot of the suspect's cell door, upon which is a black-board stating that he has been charged with murder. Given that this offence carried a mandatory death penalty in 1946, the sequence leaves little to the imagination. However, the overall impression of the film is of the immense possibilities offered by what is essentially a very simple technical and structural formula.

The ideological message being put forward in SCOTLAND YARD is contained primarily in the two book-end scenes of the Commissioner. It follows the lead established in HOMES FOR ALL (which justifies a centralised planning policy as something which the public voted for and therefore deserved to get) in that crime is expressed as something of concern to society as a whole rather than as a problem which only the police can deal with. Thus we are told that 'science works hand in hand, but the policeman on the beat is as necessary as ever', as the visuals take us from the Scotland Yard map room and powerful new police cars to images of a policeman checking that front doors are locked and talking to someone on a street corner.

The Commissioner specifically emphasises the nature of the current crime wave as a consequence of the war, noting that shop-breaking and tax evasion have doubled since 1938, but that personal violence, murder and the use of firearms by criminals had not increased (statistics which tend to undermine the narrative which follows). In the closing speech he augments the direct address in the commentary by again stressing that the prevention of crime is up to the spectator as much as it is the duty of the police:

> … when we buy goods under the counter we forget that we are pandering to the black marketeer who gets his stuff from the thieves in our midst. These thieves flourish because of the demand …

The moral of the story was not lost on the critics, nor on the Metropolitan Police, who persuaded Rank's General Film Distributors (GFD) to re-release the film a year later in conjunction with a publicity campaign against the black market.[19] Jympson Harman in the *Evening News* noted that:

> The film has a 'black market' message for the public. It shows how a simple thing like accepting a pair of stockings 'under the counter' encourages the present crime wave and in this case leads to murder.[20]

The first two issues of *TMA*, therefore, are notable more for style than for content, an important conclusion in view of the repeated comparisons between *TMA* and *MOT*. The political standpoint advanced in them is not quite that of the strict neutrality which would later be promoted as the hallmark of the series, but the debates they address are opened up to a greater extent than had been the case in most newsreels and government films from the period. Housing provision and the crime wave are shown to be a direct consequence of the war and dealing with them is said to be the responsibility both of official agencies and the public at large.

The next three films, TOMORROW BY AIR (issue no. 3, 1946), FABRICS FOR THE FUTURE (issue no. 4, 1947) and THOROUGHBREDS FOR THE WORLD (issue no. 5, 1947) are concerned with industrial and technological issues rather than overtly political ones. They did not have such a favourable reception as the earlier releases, largely because they were deemed to be stylistically weaker. *Documentary News Letter*, in its review of TOMORROW BY AIR, hinted at the way in which there seemed to be a formulaic narrative applied to each subject *TMA* dealt with in turn, by sarcastically remarking that 'there ought to be a legal way of banning the line "Then came war! (boom-boom)" from commentaries for the next ten years.'[21] As for THOROUGHBREDS FOR THE WORLD, the only positive comments 'M.E.C.' in the *Monthly Film Bulletin* could come up with were that 'the shots of horses and foals of all ages are lovely, and, since the breeding of bloodstock is such an essentially British practice, the film should be of interest to cinema audiences overseas.'[22]

PALESTINE and SUDAN DISPUTE

Issue no. 6, PALESTINE (1947), is significant for two reasons: it was the first film in the series to address foreign affairs, and it was also the first *TMA* issue to be advertised and marketed in a way that stressed editorial impartiality, and these two precedents are very much connected. Whereas the topics that had previously been dealt with by *TMA* were essentially matters of social consensus, the Empire in general and Palestine in particular were the subject of intense controversy and volatile public opinion. A wave of terrorism perpetrated by Jewish extremists had been taking place in the province as a result of Britain's refusal to admit large numbers of refugees from the Nazis (a policy dating from the Versailles negotiations, at which Britain, in the Balfour Declaration, had given an undertaking not to allow Jewish settlers to outnumber the indigenous Arab population). When President Truman applied pressure on Churchill at the Potsdam Conference to increase the number of immigrants, the Palestine question went instantly to the top of the British foreign policy agenda, a question which the Jews regarded as a struggle against British oppression and British public opinion regarded as American imperialism.

Shortly after Labour was elected, Attlee agreed to a joint Anglo-American inquiry, but the government refused to issue any more immigration permits. In the meantime, Aneurin Bevan tersely commented that as the Jews had already waited 1,900 years for a national home, then another twelve months would not make much difference.[23] But it was the explosion of a terrorist bomb on 22 July 1946 at a Jerusalem hotel which hardened government policy and turned public opinion decisively away from the Jewish cause. The incident claimed ninety-one lives and caused a wave of jingoist rhetoric in the press. On 24 July the *Daily Express* even published a recruiting advertisement for the Palestine Police depicting heavily armed militia and captioned 'How to Join a Crack Force'. During the whole of 1946, seventy-three troops and over 300 civilians had been killed or wounded.[24]

By sheer coincidence, a *TMA* unit was in Jerusalem at the time of the hotel bomb and shot footage of the acting high commissioner, Sir John Shaw, directing rescue operations. Researchers in London had also pulled off a journalistic coup by uncovering a Nazi newsreel in which the Grand Mufti of Jerusalem (a senior Arab official) appeared to give a Nazi salute to what were supposedly Muslim troops of the SS. It was these two items which formed the basis of PALESTINE, around which a commentary was written stressing British impartiality in the face of terrorism and subversion. A prologue shows footage of General Allenby entering Jerusalem which, according to the commentary, 'marked the liberation of Palestine'. GFD's press release for the film assures us that 'the Arab and Jewish stories are shown separately,' but they are shown to a very specific end, as the text makes clear:

> Britain had led the way in freeing Palestine: her Balfour Declaration lead to the League of Nations mandate which made it possible for Jews to go back to Palestine. The film emphasises that Britain was charged with ADMINISTERING PALESTINE FOR ARAB AND JEW.

Of the Arab–Nazi connection:

> German newspaper photographs are shown of the Mufti in Germany with Moslem troops of the Wehrmacht. Arabs claimed that these were faked by Nazi propagandists. 'THIS MODERN AGE' presents a sensational answer – a captured Nazi newsreel, which is shown for the first time in the free world. In it the Mufti of Jerusalem is seen, in the presence of Nazi officers, giving the Nazi salute to Moslem troops of the SS during the war.

Of the Jewish terrorists:

> With equal force the film condemns Jewish extremists who resort to terrorism. Wanted members of the Stern Gang, and the Irgun, are shown. Graphic shots of the 1946 bomb outrage at the King David Hotel were taken by the Unit's cameramen shortly after the explosion. [...] Britain was forced to hunt out the terrorists.

31

The camera covers searching in streets and in settlements. Among the results are discovered dumps of illegal weapons which Jews all over Palestine had been storing for the final showdown.[25]

Slightly less evident than the scrupulous even-handedness toward Arab and Jew is the distinctly anti-American tone of the film. The King David Hotel scene is introduced by shots of British security police sealing off an area of Jerusalem, while the commentary tells us that the Anglo-American Inquiry's recommendation that Britain should admit a further 100,000 Holocaust victims had not been matched by any offers of financial support. After the Nazi newsreel sequence there appears an animated map of the Middle East as the commentator asserts that '… the US has conflicting interests, which lead to support for anti-British Jews at home, and appeasement of Arabs for new American oil concessions in Saudi Arabia.' The closing scenes bring together these three tropes which form the bulk of the narrative – the Arab involvement in Palestine, the Jewish involvement in Palestine (with both the structure of the film itself and the publicity surrounding it emphasising impartiality where each is concerned) and the American interference in Britain's administration of Palestine – to argue that Britain had been left in an 'honest broker' situation in which she was obliged to contain a civil war within the province itself and what her government believed to be an unsatisfactory response from the international community.

GFD's extensive publicity appears to have paid off. When PALESTINE was released in February 1947, the critical response to the film concentrated more on the impartiality angle and on comparisons with what was perceived to be the level-headed, rational and therefore British attitude of *TMA* with the crude propagandising of its American counterpart, than on the more subtle political ideas it contained. *Documentary News Letter* concluded that '… the balance struck leaves each side equally deserving, each equally blameworthy.'[26]

Over half of *TMA*'s output dealt with international affairs (twenty-two out of forty-one films), and Rank's publicists would seek to associate this discourse of even-handedness with each and every one, especially those dealing with the transition of Empire countries to independence. Taken together, the distinct narrative blueprint evident in PALESTINE can be identified, in some shape or form, in all these films. It consists of four key elements:

Firstly, there is a historical overview designed to justify Britain's involvement in these countries in the first place. A typical example is SUDAN DISPUTE (issue no. 8, 1947), in which the opening sequence briefly explains the immediacy of the debate, namely the upcoming renewal of the 1936 Anglo-Egypt Treaty. This is abruptly followed by an intertitle which reads simply, 'What are the facts? What is the Sudan?' This also evolved into a recurring *TMA* device, dividing the film into a sort of three-movement structure consisting of *introduction – intertitle – exposition, development – intertitle – conclusion* (another example being WHERE BRITAIN STANDS, from 1950). We are told that General Gordon entered Khartoum to put down slavery and that Kitchener 'was the first man to speak of Sudan for the Sudanese', followed by a brief description of events leading to the establishment of the Anglo-Egyptian administration of the country in 1899.

The second phase of the film describes what had been achieved as a result of that administration, designed in narrative terms to lead into a discussion of the opposing viewpoints in the debate at hand, and in aesthetic terms to show off the extensive production values on which *TMA* also marketed itself. This consists of a sequence running over 300 feet of tribal dancing in a Sudanese village. The images appear to be professionally lit and shot on quite slow panchromatic stock, and so look remarkably sharp and contrasty. They are accompanied by a Muir Mathieson score and synchronised location sound of almost studio quality. This in itself sets it apart from the low-budget travelogues which audiences would have been familiar with, but the object of the exercise was not simply aesthetic quality. In a sparse but shrewdly interjected commentary we are told that the tribes-people were 'slaves in the past, free men today', and that the revival of these indigenous cultural practices was made possible by the introduction of modern agricultural techniques which broke up a nomadic culture and encouraged the establishment of permanent settlements.

The third sequence leads into the debate itself. Britain's favoured option, an independent Sudan, is rejected by Egypt because Sudan contains the source of the Nile, and the presence of a modern sovereign state in control of Egypt's main natural resource is seen as a threat to her economy and national security. Britain favours complete independence as she feels that half a century spent developing the institutions of a democratic state have adequately prepared Sudan, and that continued Egyptian administration could lead to civil unrest. This leads to the second intertitle: 'This is the result of fifty years' administration by the Sudan government.'

The concluding phase of the film suggests that the debate will be settled by the emergence of political parties established by the Sudanese, ending with images of a public meeting and the summing up:

Are the Sudanese to determine their own future? Egypt says no, Britain says yes. A vital principle is at stake. The people must have the right to decide their own destiny in this modern age.

This narrative model is most clearly evident in the *TMA* issues addressing international affairs. It turned out to be extremely successful in deflecting any suggestions of bias and concentrating critical reaction towards the notion of impartiality. As with PALESTINE and SUDAN DISPUTE, the idea was rammed home by GFD publicists throughout the existence of *TMA*. A catalogue issued in 1950 defined the difference between *TMA* and Rank's newsreel operations as follows:

> *This Modern Age* is not biased in any way. It has handled many controversial and important topics since the series was started four years ago and the latest four issues are of equal significance. They tackle the problems of nations and peoples who are playing important parts in the political and economic structure of the post-war world. Their difficulties are boldly explained and all possible solutions given a hearing. [...] It is this quality which has lifted its reputation above that of any other feature and given it first place in the minds of cinema-goers.[27]

A brief review of SUDAN DISPUTE in *The Times* agreed, noting simply that the film was 'admirably photographed' and that 'the opposing points of view are fairly stated.'[28] But although this view was widespread, it was not universal. 'G.F.' in the *Manchester Guardian* hinted at some of the possible drawbacks to the rigidly formulaic structure used in PALESTINE and SUDAN DISPUTE when, in respect of the latter, he suggested that *TMA* was oversimplifying the subject matter:

> Although there is a clear definition of Egypt's claim to control of the Nile, the conflict of British and Egyptian opinion on the future of the Sudan is presented purely as a question of whether or not the Sudanese are entitled to govern themselves as an independent nation.[29]

But dissenting voices such as his were the exception which proved the rule: that the *TMA* approach was generally welcomed by critics, whose two key criteria for appraising the series were the documentary-realism discourse and comparisons with *MOT*. Reflecting on the legacy of *TMA* shortly before its demise, Roger Manvell asserted that 'at no time since before the war was the pattern of world affairs portrayed so consistently on the British screen.'[30]

British affairs

When it came to domestic politics, *TMA* did not feel the need to be quite so circumspect. Between PALESTINE and SUDAN DISPUTE came COAL CRISIS (issue no. 7, 1947) and DEVELOPMENT AREAS (issue no. 9, 1947). The former, directed by the Documentary Movement veteran Edgar Anstey, was a vehement indictment of what he perceived to be the lack of investment in coal by the Labour government since nationalisation. The film argues that under private ownership, the coal industry had updated obsolete equipment and maintained safety standards, and that by not doing so, the government was failing in its duty. Miners, we are told, are 'the Royal Engineers of this underground battle for coal', and a dramatic narrative is built up around the idea of coal being an essential source of energy needed for the country to function properly. This point was reinforced by the timing of the film's release in April 1947: the fuel crisis resulting from the severe winter of 1946–1947 had caused colossal power cuts, widespread cold-related illness and direct losses to industry put at over £200 million.[31]

The polemical statements in those *TMA* films dealing with domestic politics as opposed to the formulaic way in which the series addressed international affairs had become apparent as it approached the end of its first year. DEVELOPMENT AREAS applied the HOMES FOR ALL blueprint to industrial deprivation ('Industrial Britain … a proud history shot through with the tragedy of unemployment'): the post-1918 boom was deflated by a worldwide depression and punitive import tariffs, cue stock footage of the Jarrow marches, followed by the intertitle, 'What peace could not do, war accomplished.' Centralised planning of industrial distribution, we are then told, is the only way to prevent the boom-and-bust cycle from being re-established. DEVELOPMENT AREAS, however, is a lot less subtle in terms of its political message. We are shown chiaroscuro-laden images of Welsh mining villages while Hodson's commentary reels off their names, reminiscent of Thomas Chalmers in THE RIVER. Emotive similes and metaphors are used throughout the film ('… men rust and rot in idleness as do iron and steel …'), more often and more prominently than in HOMES FOR ALL, SCOTLAND YARD or COAL CRISIS. *Documentary News Letter* thought this a positive step, and preferred it to the methodical detachment of PALESTINE or SUDAN DISPUTE:

> The treatment is forceful and, compared with the mouselike timidity of many films on similar subjects, as bold as a lion – a circus lion, anyway. It is on issues such as this, rather than 'SUDAN DISPUTE', that *This Modern Age* should build a reputation as an adult, entertaining, informative, reliable screen periodical.[32]

Three further releases completed *TMA*'s first full year of operations: RAPE OF THE EARTH (issue no. 10, 1947) on soil erosion, HOME AND BEAUTY (issue no. 11, 1947), a social interest piece in the vein of TOMORROW BY AIR and FABRICS OF THE FUTURE, and ANTARCTIC WHALE HUNT (issue no. 12, 1947), which built, to a certain extent, on the aesthetic experimentation in SCOTLAND YARD.

ANTARCTIC WHALE HUNT also introduced another foil to the *TMA* armoury, as it drew on the travelogue-documentary genre, one which had hitherto occupied a sort of cultural limbo between the 'interest' film, a low-budget form of production which relied essentially on an attractionist aesthetic, and the ideological values and narrative structures evolved by documentarists. This combination of authentic images, removed from the everyday experience of most British film audiences, together with a political dimension, offered the ideal outlet for *TMA*, given that the series was marketed on the basis of feature-quality production values and the ability to present controversial ideas fairly and effectively.

These developments set a pattern which would be reflected in the bulk of the *TMA* releases for 1948 and 1949. The films which dealt with foreign affairs did so either through the formulaic narrative by which the early examples such as PALESTINE and SUDAN DISPUTE were seen as a relevant but non-partisan contribution to those debates, or by foregrounding the extraordinary production values which the series had come to represent. But the issues concerning domestic political and cultural issues tended to make far more polemical statements, and it was these films which tended to attract a greater amount of critical interest.

In WILL BRITAIN GO HUNGRY? (issue no. 13, 1947), *TMA* appropriated images of the dust bowl to condemn the government for failing to introduce intensive farming techniques. THE BRITISH – ARE THEY ARTISTIC? (issue no. 16, 1948) attracted a large amount of press coverage. This is hardly surprising, as the film tackled head on the ideas of 'high' and 'low' culture which had emerged during the war, and, specifically had underpinned the agenda of the film education movement and the magazine *Penguin Film Review*. As Richard Winnington noted in the *News Chronicle*, the film could not be accused of subtlety.[33] It opens by describing the growing popularity of 'serious' art forms, including a lengthy sequence from Arthur Bliss's latest ballet, a Benjamin Britten opera and the obligatory footage of Dame Myra Hess playing in the National Gallery. A concerted effort is made to emphasise that this phenomenon is not restricted by conventional class barriers, citing examples including the Army Bureau of Current Affairs and the London County Council Art Class. The commentator then warns that 'all the same, we'd better keep our feet on the ground … Thrills, crooning and Jazz appear to be our chief delights.' In this way, an arbitrary comparison is established between 'high' and 'popular' culture, an idea which reaches its climax in an interview with Robert Donat, whom we see posed on a Pinewood set, opining that '… since the war, we've made some very fine films – but we've also made some very bad ones.' Interestingly, Donat concludes with the idea that quality is directly related to public preference ('… if you insist on the best, you'll get it. After all, you pay for it.'), reflecting Roger Manvell's view that the war had democratised the notion of a film culture based on indigenous artistic traits rather than purely economic parameters. However, if the audience accepted this point, then the overall message of THE BRITISH – ARE THEY ARTISTIC? hardly complimented its audience. The closing sequence intersperses books about art with titles such as *Bed for Beginners: Being a Gentleman's Guide to Scientific Seduction in Eight Easy Lessons*, a pianist in a pub and the Bliss ballet.

Much of the press coverage pointed out that this dichotomy was an extremely crude one. A reporter for the *Daily Telegraph* even questioned the validity of the premise embodied in the film's title, 'A good many Britons would probably reply, cheerfully, "No, thank you – we leave that sort of thing to foreigners." Most foreigners would think the question silly.'[34]

A more typical reaction was to accept the premise but to argue that it had been grossly oversimplified. According to Richard Winnington in the *News Chronicle*:

> The conflicting choices at the end – the broad and narrow roads which face the stunted Briton – are not subtly posed. It is not a choice between music and pin tables, ballet and roller skating, but between the quartet and the theatre organ, Dostoyevsky and Dorothy Whipple.[35]

And a correspondent for the *Daily Graphic* was not entirely convinced by Donat's evangelising, complaining that 'I keep on insisting on the best, but I don't get it.'[36] Nevertheless, with THE BRITISH – ARE THEY ARTISTIC?' *TMA* began to look at the cultural issues facing British society in the immediate postwar period, and, in doing so, probably achieved a greater impact on audiences and critics than had been the case with their issues on foreign affairs or the strictly political approach they had hitherto taken to domestic matters.

The next of these films was WOMEN IN OUR TIME (issue no. 22, 1948), a vaguely structured survey of 'the position of women in Britain today', as it was advertised. Taking the suffragette movement as a starting point (complete with exhaustive repetitions of Ethel Smyth's 'March of the Women'), the film examines the growing number of women in professional occupations and argues that the war acted as a catalyst in this respect. The narrative does, however, oscillate abruptly between describing a utopia in which both sexes enjoy complete social equality and a clichéd affirmation of what is an implicit status quo. In one staged scene we see a woman attend to her crying baby while her husband buries his head in a pillow in an attempt to ignore the situation; meanwhile, the commentator informs us that 'it is women's beauty and graciousness which does so much to enrich our lives.' Even so, the weight of critical opinion pronounced WOMEN IN OUR TIME to be an incisive contribution to an important social issue.

A more challenging treatment can be found in EDUCATION FOR LIVING (issue no. 27, 1949). In this film (directed by Nolbandov), *TMA* put forward a strident defence of the recent legislation that had raised the school leaving age from fourteen to sixteen. 'A schooling in the democratic way of life is not an easy one' is the position from which the film argues for the massive expenditure required by the new system. Full-scale secondary education, we are told, is necessary to maintain Britain's industrial competitiveness, for the cultural benefits it offers the population and for its ability to produce individually minded citizens. Although many of the traditional *TMA* hallmarks are still apparent (the sound quality in the opening sequence showing a primary school assembly is so clear that the acoustics of the hall are easily audible), in this case they serve to enhance the message of the film rather than to substitute for it. Taken as a whole, EDUCATION FOR LIVING makes an impressive counterpoint to Warren Chetham Strode's play *The Guinea Pig* (and the subsequent film directed by Roy Boulting in 1948), an account of an East End boy who wins a scholarship to a prominent public school, which had aroused a great deal of controversy at the time the Education Act was in preparation. *TMA* followed up the film with FIGHT FOR A FULLER LIFE (issue no. 30, 1949), which made similar arguments for further and higher education.

The two remaining *TMA* issues on British affairs were WHEN YOU WENT AWAY (issue no. 33, 1949), a lightweight survey of the tourism industry, and WHERE BRITAIN STANDS (issue no. 36, 1950), a summing-up of what Britain had achieved between the end of the war and the 1950 general election. The film can also be seen as summing up *TMA*'s contribution to the film industry and film culture of that time, bringing together the industrial advances which had been necessary to safeguard the country's economic position, the wide-ranging social reform at home and the retrenchment of the Empire and Britain's changing role in world affairs.

The *TMA* issues on British affairs, therefore, gradually became more self-assured as the series progressed, and they experimented with a number of filmic styles and techniques. From the minimal story documentary narrative in SCOTLAND YARD to the different strands of argument followed through in EDUCATION FOR LIVING, *TMA*'s filmmakers actively sought ways of making non-fiction cinema into a medium which could bridge the paradox between entertainment and discursivity, rather than rely on the sensationalism upon which *MOT* depended. An anonymous writer in the *Times Educational Supplement* observed that in 1949 *TMA* won the Cinema Exhibitors' Association poll for best money-making shorts, and 'now public affairs are beating Donald Duck':

This Modern Age deserves success, for it has never bought victory as entertainment at the price of integrity. As it gradually develops an extremely difficult technique, bounding complex problems in a twenty-minute nutshell, some will inevitably turn out more satisfactorily than others.[37]

The Dalton Duty

The Rank Organisation incurred substantial losses in the closing years of the decade, ones which Rank believed were due to failures in the government's response to the balance of payments crisis as it affected the film industry. Reducing dollar expenditure on American films had been a stated intention of the Attlee government ever since it took office, but the discussions which had taken place during 1946 and the spring of 1947 had been geared towards developing a compromise solution: this would have allowed the import of American films to continue, but limits would have been placed on the export of their earnings. Unfortunately, the loan by the US to the UK of $3,750 million agreed in December 1946 had been approved only on condition that sterling be made convertible with the dollar by 15 July 1947. Dickinson and Street conclude that this, in conjunction with the severe winter of 1946–1947, had forced the government's hand, and emergency measures to restrict the purchase of American films by British distributors (which were paid for in dollars) became inevitable within a very short space of time.[38]

Thus, on 6 August 1947, a Board of Trade order was made under the 1932 Import Duties Act which placed a 75% *ad valorem* tax on the revenue earned by all imported cinema films (this subsequently became known as the 'Dalton Duty,' after Hugh Dalton, then President of the Board of Trade). What the government had not bargained for was Hollywood's response: less than two days later the Motion Picture Producers' Association of America (MPPAA) announced that it was completely boycotting the British market until such time as the order was rescinded.

The effect of this for the production sector of the British film industry was both profound and immediate. At the time the order was introduced, fewer than one in five features shown in British cinemas were British films. Thus without a massive domestic production drive, exhibitors faced the real possibility of a film shortage that would result in cinema closures. In an attempt to overcome the shortfall, it seems that the government approached J. Arthur Rank personally and tried to persuade him to throw his massive production resources into low-budget, high-quantity filmmaking in order to counteract the Hollywood embargo.[39]

The effect of the 1947–1948 production drive can be seen from the figures: of all feature films registered for quota purposes in 1947 and 1948, registrations of films over seventy-two minutes in length increased from forty-eight to sixty-eight, and those between thirty-three and seventy-two minutes (that is, cheaply made 'B' films, descendants of the notorious 'quota quickies') almost doubled, from fifty-eight to 101 registrations.[40] Virtually all of this increase can be accounted for either by Rank-produced features, or by independent films for which GFD had guaranteed distribution in advance. Needless to say, the Rank Organisation had stretched itself financially by this production drive, and guaranteed exhibition was essential. Unfortunately, when Harold Wilson became President of the Board of Trade following a cabinet reshuffle in October 1947, he promptly negotiated a settlement with the MPPAA, signed on 11 March 1948. Almost a year's backlog of Hollywood films flooded into Britain just as the early results of Rank's production drive were ready for release.

The Dalton Duty, and the timing of its revocation, has largely been blamed for the massive losses sustained by the Rank Organisation and the production slump of 1949. Rank certainly blamed the government for reneging on its promise to protect his post-1947 output from American competition. If Wilson's recollection that the imposition of the duty was 'really to establish a negotiating position', and not a long-term measure, is correct, then there are certainly grounds for believing Rank was misled.[41] In any case, the debacle resulted in Rank sustaining net losses of £16,286,521 between the imposition of the duty and the annual shareholders' meeting in September 1949. At that meeting, Rank stated clearly that he blamed the government's U-turn, suggesting that 'even if all our films had been of the quality that we hoped, the unusually strong competition would have made it difficult to achieve satisfactory results.'[42]

Inevitably, the first stage of the retrenchment programme needed to offset these losses involved cutting back on those uncommercial activities which had hitherto been subsidised by the more profitable elements of the business, of which *TMA* was by far the most expensive. On 15 December 1949, a Rank spokesman announced at a press conference that a further twelve issues were in production, concluding, 'after that we cannot say.'[43]

The decision to terminate *TMA* elicited a strong response from the quality press, which generally took the line that the series had maintained the prestigious reputation of the British film industry for non-fiction in an industrial climate which had finished off a large proportion of the Documentary Movement's production base. The political columnist Norman McKenzie wrote:

It has done a worthwhile job; it has been free of any suspicion of Government propaganda, and it has held the breach for British documentary production at a time when less fortunately placed units have had to go out of business.[44]

As 1950 wore on, support for *TMA* grew more intense, although it was by and large restricted to the sector of British film culture which had a track record of emphasising the quality–realist discourse (i.e. broadsheet newspapers and the Documentary Movement). Joan Lester, writing in *Reynolds News*, asserted that:

If anything deserves to be rescued from the wreckage of the producing side of the Rank empire, it is this monthly film review. For four years I have watched it grow from a slightly uncertain and stodgy beginning to a sturdy, distinctive feature, owing nothing to imitation, combining information with cinematic entertainment, often good, and sometimes brilliant.[45]

Interestingly, Paul Rotha made an economic case for retaining the series. He suggested that *TMA* could find an important niche market as television assumed a wider role in news coverage:

This Modern Age is a long-term venture which is being cut short before it has scarcely had time to grow. It is being allowed to vanish, moreover, at a time when television is making the news-reel of less importance and when the need for balanced, editorialised news on the cinema screen has never been more needed.[46]

A number of proposals emerged as to how *TMA* might be saved. McKenzie argued for 'a philanthropic foundation to underwrite the losses', likening the problem to that faced by the Army Bureau of Current Affairs after the war when the Carnegie Foundation took it over. A more realistic idea seemed to be public subsidy: the government had established the National Film Finance Corporation (NFFC) a year earlier, but this was designed to loan money to producers unable to cover short-term production costs, not a system for subsidising unprofitable films. The NFFC's director, speaking at the 1950 BFI summer school, said that he had given 'a great deal of thought' to *TMA*, but that the provisions of the NFFC Act precluded any direct subsidy.[47]

It is likely that there was very little political inclination to keep the series in business. The attraction of *TMA* to the government, if any, lay in the fact that it was a purely commercial operation (unlike other areas of documentary production) and thus was not associated in any way with the public sector – or, as McKenzie put it with rather less subtlety, 'free of any suspicion of government propaganda'. Thus if *TMA* were to be funded by the taxpayer, it would no longer be seen to have that political autonomy. In the event, TURKEY – KEY TO THE MIDDLE EAST (issue no. 41), released in January 1951, marked the end of *This Modern Age*.

Conclusion

The arrival of *MOT* in Britain in the 1930s marked a turning point in the development of an indigenous non-fiction cinema, despite, and because, of its American provenance. For the first time, a regular series of factual films (other than newsreels) had proven their commercial viability. Although its 'news as entertainment' formula drew a certain amount of fire from the then nascent intellectual film culture in Britain, no one could deny that, in one crucial respect, *MOT* had succeeded where its only comparable alternative – the Documentary Movement – had demonstrably failed: in reaching a mass audience.

What were these crucial differences between the production strategies of *TMA* and *MOT*? In aesthetic terms, expenditure and production values were important, and emphasised aspects of the series. J. Arthur Rank believed that 'quality' in a film could be assessed in proportion to how much money it made, and *TMA* was no exception to this credo. Unlike Louis de Rochemont's dictum that the medium should be made to fit the message, the visual and sonic properties of the medium itself were very important to Nolbandov and his technicians. Thus, every single shot in every single issue (with the exception of footage included for historical reasons, notably Allenby's entry into Jerusalem and the Nazi newsreel in PALESTINE) was originated on slow 35mm negative stock by studio-trained cinematographers. As one newsreel cameraman observed, '*TMA* looked beautiful, but was like cracking a nut with a sledgehammer.'[48]

Combined with this emphasis on aesthetic quality was a more open-ended editorial policy. A typical instalment of *MOT* depended on a polemical (and preferably controversial) *locus standi*, and every other aspect of the production was subordinate to that, hence its use of deceptively obtained or quite simply faked footage. The producers of *TMA* consciously sought to avoid sensationalising their subject matter in that way, possibly because the *MOT* idea was increasingly being seen as irrelevant, or, to quote the *Times* review of ANSWER TO STALIN, '[it] would not pretend to objectivity.'

Perhaps because of the emphasis on even-handedness which informed many of *TMA*'s documentary precursors, or perhaps because of the preconception that objective journalism was, in the words of another *Times* editorial, 'a virtue, or a vice, the world has agreed to regard as exclusively English', this idea was at the forefront of the *TMA* project. Evidence of this can be seen both from the films themselves and the publicity material and critical reaction to them. Many of the *TMA* issues, most

42

importantly those dealing with foreign affairs, evolved a narrative structure analogous with the format of a formal debate, consisting of an introduction, arguments for and against, a summing up and a conclusion. The press releases, posters and distributors' catalogues which accompanied the films stressed their impartial stance time and time again. While the films dealing with foreign issues emphasised this discourse to a far greater extent than the domestic ones did, the notion that *TMA* represented a consensus view rather than a partisan one was never far away from Nolbandov's choice and treatment of subject matter.

There was an important connection between the aesthetic and the editorial strands of the *TMA* idea. The often crude production values apparent in *MOT* (underexposed shots, duped or pirated footage and the almost total absence of location sound) tended to be mitigated by the cogency of its arguments. *TMA*, however, frequently had to turn to other devices to offset the sometimes complex and unglamorous points being expressed by its commentaries. For example, the cinematography in ANTARCTIC WHALE HUNT and the high-quality synchronised recording of tribal rituals in THE FUTURE OF ONE MILLION AFRICANS (issue no. 39, 1950) more than compensate for the slow progression of their narratives. In critical terms, they rescued these films from being dismissed as little more than glorified travelogues.

So, what of the political cinemagazine post-*TMA*? A number of other series had emerged during the late 1940s, most of them produced by the government. The documentary arm of the Pathe newsreel company launched *The Wealth of the World* in 1948, but this only lasted six months longer than *TMA*. The emergence of television was, however, a crucial factor. The BBC *Television Newsreel*, which started in 1948, was given an expanded format in 1950 when the BBC also started to undertake a wider range of current affairs production, and it could well be argued that the work of *TMA* in developing aesthetic and editorial approaches to the documentary idea can be seen most clearly in early television. Ironically, television was also the indirect cause of one of the last major magazine film series to be produced in Britain: when the Rank Organisation pulled out of newsreels altogether in 1958, it replaced Gaumont-British and Universal with a one-reel weekly series, *Look at Life*, which continued for over a decade.

It is certainly significant to note that *TMA*'s dates coincide almost exactly with those of the Attlee governments. While Geoffrey Macnab has noted suggestions that this points to a direct institutional link between the two, I think it is more useful to see the series as having been a component in the wider industrial and cultural developments which make those years a key period in the history of British non-fiction cinema.[49] That is not to deny the existence of a continuing, but changing, relationship between cinema and state, but it must be stressed that *TMA* was conceived and executed as a purely commercial enterprise. Furthermore, it was one which depended on that commercial status for the viability of its often prominent claims to impartiality. The termination of *TMA* was also a commercial decision, albeit one which Rank blamed the government for having to make. Although it had evolved against the background of the 1930s, *MOT* and various other influences, *TMA* was most definitely, to borrow Richard Harkness's conclusion, 'a film series which had arisen to meet the challenges of its time'.[50]

Notes

1   The most commonly quoted accounts are Geoffrey Macnab, *J. Arthur Rank and the British Film Industry* (London: Routledge, 1993) and Alan Wood, *Mr Rank* (London: Hodder & Stoughton, 1952). See especially pp. 105–110.
2   Vincent Porter and Chaim Litewski, 'The Way Ahead', *Sight and Sound*, vol. 50, no. 2 (1981), p. 110.
3   *New Statesman and Nation*, 12 August 1944.
4   Board of Trade, *Tendencies to Monopoly in the Cinematograph Film Industry* (London: HMSO, 1944), para. 7.
5   Interviewed in Eva Orbanz (ed.), *Journey to a Legend and Back: The British Realistic Film* (Berlin: Volker Speiss, 1977), p. 36.
6   Ralph Bond, *Monopoly: The Future of British Film* (London: ACT, 1946); R. J. Minney, *Talking of Films* (London: Home & Van Thal, 1947); Frederic Mullally, *Films: An Alternative to Rank* (London: Socialist Book Centre, 1946).
7   Elizabeth Sussex, *The Rise and Fall of British Documentary* (Berkeley: University of California Press, 1975), p. 166.
8   Accounts of Nolbandov's work at the MOI vary: several newspaper reports from the period describe him as an 'associate producer', while Sidney Bernstein recalls that he was a film editor. See Caroline Moorehead, *Sidney Bernstein: A Biography* (London: Jonathan Cape, 1984), p. 164.
9   Sergei Nolbandov, 'Costing Productions' in Adrian Brunel, *Filmcraft* (London: George Newnes, 1933), pp. 179–180.
10 For an account of his pre-war career, see Clifford Hornby, *Shooting without Stars* (London: Hutchinson, 1941).
11 These two films are so similar in construction and argument that it would seem reasonable to speculate that their production was in some way connected.
12 Quoted in Macnab, op. cit., p. 137.
13 *Reynolds News*, 19 September 1948. The author is Joan Lester.
14 Wood, op. cit., p. 205.
15 Correlli Barnett, *The Lost Victory: British Dreams, British Realities, 1945–50* (London: Macmillan, 1995), p. 152.
16 See Raymond Fielding, *The March of Time, 1935–1951* (New York: Oxford University Press, 1978), p. 81.
17 Anstey, 'The Magazine Film', *Penguin Film Review*, no. 9 (May 1949), p. 20 [reproduced in this volume].
18 *Documentary News Letter*, vol. 6, no. 56 (1947), p. 89.
19 See the *London Evening Standard*, 16 September 1947.

20   *Evening News*, 27 September 1946.
21   *Documentary News Letter*, vol. 6, no. 56 (1947), p. 89.
22   *Monthly Film Bulletin*, vol. 14 (1947), p. 16.
23   David Leith, 'Explosion at the King David Hotel' in Michael Sissons and Philip French (eds.), *Age of Austerity, 1945–1952* (2nd edition, Oxford: Oxford University Press, 1986), p. 55.
24   Ibid., p. 57.
25   Press release for PALESTINE released by GFD/This Modern Age Ltd (from microfiche in BFI National Library). Author's emphasis.
26   *Documentary News Letter*, vol. 6, no. 56 (1947), p. 89.
27   GFD distribution catalogue, 1950, back cover. Copy in GFD subject file, BFI National Library.
28   *The Times*, 24 April 1947, p. 6.
29   *Manchester Guardian*, 23 April 1947.
30   Roger Manvell (ed.), *The Year's Work in the Film, 1950* (London: Longmans Green, 1951), p. 27.
31   K.O. Morgan, *Labour in Power, 1945–51* (Oxford: Clarendon Press, 1984), p. 340.
32   *Documentary News Letter*, vol. 6, no. 58 (1947), p. 119.
33   *News Chronicle*, 14 February 1948.
34   *Daily Telegraph*, 6 February 1948.
35   *News Chronicle*, 14 February 1948.
36   *Daily Graphic*, 13 February 1948.
37   *Times Educational Supplement*, 6 January 1950.
38   Margaret Dickinson and Sarah Street, *Cinema and State: The Film Industry and the Government, 1927–84* (London: British Film Institute, 1985), pp. 184–187.
39   Macnab, op. cit., pp. 181–182.
40   Board of Trade figures, reproduced in Dickinson and Street, op. cit., p. 192.
41   'Margaret Dickinson and Simon Hartog Interview Sir Harold Wilson', *Screen*, vol. 22 no. 3 (1981), p. 13.
42   Rank's statement to shareholders, September 1949 (copy in BFI National Library).
43   *Daily Mail*, 16 December 1949.
44   *New Statesman and Nation*, 29 April 1950.
45   *Reynolds News*, 6 August 1950.
46   Rotha, 'Time Stands Still – But Why?' *Public Opinion*, 8 December 1950, p. 3.
47   *The Times*, 21 August 1950, p. 6.
48   Norman Fisher, quoted in James Ballantyne (ed.), *Researcher's Guide to British Newsreels*, vol. 2 (London: BUFVC, 1988), p. 33.
49   Macnab, op. cit., p. 137.
50   Richard Harkness, *This Modern Age* (research paper, Department of Radio–Television–Film, Temple University, Philadelphia 1974), p. 25 (copy in BFI National Library).

LIBRARY, UNIVERSITY OF CHESTER

THE RISE AND FALL OF THE SPONSORED CINEMAGAZINE

Emily Crosby

The 1950s and 1960s saw a rapid rise in the use of the cinemagazine by commercial companies. Here Emily Crosby describes the origins of the sponsored cinemagazine and examines how it was utilised within this sector for public relations, internal relations and advertising. She concludes by arguing that the decline of the cinemagazine in the 1970s did not lead its demise, merely its reincarnation within a different medium.

The commercially sponsored cinemagazine was one of the cinemagazine's most successful and popular incarnations.[1] In addition to the vast number of cinemagazines made for the British government under the auspices of the Central Office of Information, huge numbers of cinemagazine series were funded by industrial and commercial companies, and even charities, in Britain. Most of these films were made by non-fiction film units under contract from sponsor companies, but a few public relations departments went so far as to create their own film units, the mainstay of which was the cinemagazine. Large and small organisations found these series to be an effective way to put across information to both employees and the public and their use continues to this day.

The first industrially sponsored cinemagazine series was *Shell Cinemagazine* (Shell, 1938). It coincided with the end of the entertainment cinemagazine boom which had brought such titles as *Pathe Pictorial*, *Gaumont Mirror* and *Ace Cinemagazine* to the public's attention. It appears that this early sponsored series was an attempt to copy these popular cinemagazine styles, combining light-hearted features about 'raising water through the ages' with more educational content such as 'oil tankers'.[2] The similarity of its name to the contemporary *Ace Cinemagazine* confirms this attempt at popularity. Other companies did not copy the idea of sponsored cinemagazine series until the late 1940s. But, in the meantime, the cinemagazine had gained credibility for commercial use through two very different occurrences.

Firstly, series such as *The March of Time* showed the versatility of the cinemagazine format by adapting the issue structure to create documentary-style illustrations

46

and discussions of contemporary events. This made the cinemagazine an attractive prospect to bodies with a message to get across, an alternative to the more circumscribed newsreel format or the light-hearted *Pathe Pictorial* model. Secondly, it was this new style of cinemagazine that prompted the government to use newsreels and cinemagazines as part of its wartime information policy. At a time when vast groups of people needed to be kept informed of national developments, it was necessary to be able to distribute the same message to all, in a format that they could easily relate to and understand. The cinemagazine was a familiar form to both producers and consumers, and as such, seemed the perfect choice for government-sponsored film. Thus series like *Britain Can Make It* came into existence.

Given this government-led development, it is not surprising that the longer-running industrially sponsored cinemagazines, the forerunners of the sponsored cinemagazine boom in the late 1940s and the early 1950s, were sponsored by nationalised companies. The National Coal Board (NCB) in particular was heavily influenced by the government's film programme and the proposed (though apparently not produced) *Factory Newsreel*. The NCB faced a similar task to the wartime government in informing and inspiring a large number of disparate communities in order to present a united front to win the peace, and they addressed this task with a product very similar to the government's – *Mining Review* (NCB, 1947). London Transport's *Cinegazette* (London Transport Executive, 1947) likewise was of this breed, as was the cinemagazine of Richard Thomas & Baldwin's (RTB, later British Steel) *Ingot Pictorial* (RTB, 1949). These films consciously projected the various different parts of large companies in order to emphasise their unity in the face of competition, anti-nationalisation campaigns, and the poor industrial conditions following the war.

Why sponsor a cinemagazine?

When discussing sponsored films one must never forget economics. As Arthur Calder-Marshall reminds us, 'the financiers are out to get results, either in sales or in state of mind.'[3] All of these series needed to be considered economically viable to the company sponsoring them – there were, after all, other products available to industry for promotion and public relations. The case for film had to be proved. For the NCB, the case for *Mining Review* seems to have been made by the perceived success of government models and the apparent gap in the government's Monthly Release programme. *Mining Review* could be shown for free to what appeared to be a willing audience at cinemas across the country. Effectively, the NCB was taking advantage of a vast, established distribution network, in to which all it needed to drop was a relatively inexpensive product – a regular film. Here was a ready-made exhibition of NCB achievements without all the hassle of venue hire, exhibition stands and on-site staff.

A similar incentive was provided to most sponsors by the increasing 16mm market from the late 1940s onwards. By providing free, regular 16mm films through their own libraries or the government's Central Film Library, companies such as Shell-Mex and BP Ltd, Butlins and Unilever, were able to take advantage of the richly diverse audiences available through schools, social clubs, churches and unions. The potential audience was indeed vast. In 1954 Sir Harry Pilkington, president of the Federation of British Industries, reported that 'in this country there are some 23,000 16mm projectors in schools, institutions, industrial centres and so on. The number of viewers which it is possible to reach in this way must be colossal.'[4] For less than the cost of television or periodical advertising, companies could be guaranteed willing, captive audiences for their message in addition to a product that they could present at other times to employees, customers, and investors.

Sponsored cinemagazines were not just financially attractive to the sponsor. Most of the sponsored cinemagazines of the 1940s and 1950s were contracted out by commercial companies to non-fiction film units such as the Documentary and Technicians Alliance (DATA). To them, in the precarious documentary industry, following the demise of the Empire Marketing Board and Crown Film Unit, the opportunity for regular work on a monthly series must have been welcome indeed. DATA was keen to maintain its annual contract with the National Coal Board for *Mining Review*, which provided it with financial security, and the Film Producers Guild was very proud of its work on *Oil Review* (Anglo-Iranian Oil Company, 1950) and *Ingot Pictorial* because of the regular publicity that these titles brought them.[5] Cinemagazines represented a guaranteed monthly income, which after set-up time and costs could be run on a few days' work a month.

The range of style and content of sponsored cinemagazines was almost as diverse as the companies sponsoring them. Organisations from Anglo-Iranian Oil to Burroughs Wellcome to Butlins sponsored cinemagazine series in the twentieth century, and each had a character reflecting that of the sponsor and the message it wished to promote. However, for the boom period of the mid-century these styles fell in to three broad categories: public relations, internal relations and advertising. Considered in turn, these types give us an insight into the world of commercial film promotions during the 1940s, 1950s and 1960s.

Sponsored cinemagazines for public relations
The middle of the twentieth century saw many industrial concerns turning to film as 'an important means of communicating ideas to 'carry an up-to-date message'.[6]

Many went in for prestige projects – well-shot, lavish documentaries on oblique topics intended to raise the public profile of the firm, rather than directly advertise the company's products. Among some of the earliest sponsored cinemagazines, the public relations cinemagazines seem to have been an extension of this prestige filmmaking, inspired by the documentary film movement. Oil and petroleum companies were particularly keen to maintain a favourable profile through film. This may in part have been due to continued petrol rationing until 1952 and the need for companies to maintain brand awareness in the minds of the public. Thus *Shell Cinemagazine*, which continued until 1952, and *Oil Review* came into being as regular expressions of the breadth and impact of their sponsors' interests. The emphasis in these cinemagazines was on the worldwide expansion of the sponsor, through stories such as PROVENÇAL OIL REFINERY or THE GULF RUN, and their modern and capable developments overseas.[7] Ronald Tritton, writing at the launch of *Oil Review*, hoped that 'its public relations job will be done solely by the credit titles and by the association of ideas in its content – that the oil industry is a fascinating, worldwide activity carried on to the increasing convenience of mankind, and that the Anglo-Iranian Oil Company takes a leading part in the Industry.'[8] This regular public relations cinemagazine, borrowed by various social groups from the Petroleum Film Bureau, but also shown to shareholders and interested parties at company headquarters, could present the best face of the company whenever and wherever it was needed. It was even shown around the oil fields themselves: 'Up to the early summer of 1951 the company's films, with excellent Persian soundtracks were widely shown on commercial circuits in Teheran and other cities of Persia.'[9] It would be a mistake to conclude that public relations-sponsored cinemagazines were only made by massive multinational companies. It is an indication of the broad popularity of this format that even Slough County Council had its own series, *Borough Gazette* (Slough County Council, 1948).

Shell-Mex and BP Ltd produced a range of these public relations series during the 1940s and 1950s. They were aimed at the agricultural community, one of the largest petroleum markets at the time. *Scrapbook* (Shell-Mex and BP Ltd, 1949) was a general cinemagazine series with stories about new tractor inventions and farming innovations, but all the time portraying the modernity and suitability of Shell-Mex and BP fuels by association. Often these films were shown as part of an extensive presentation to farming communities, extolling the virtues of the mechanised life. The company believed that these shows created 'an atmosphere of goodwill which is hard to measure, but which cannot fail to provide a background favourable to sales'.[10] They were not alone in presenting such a programme. Esso sent out a mobile film unit showing, among technical and instructional films, *Farm Review*

(Esso, 1950), a cinemagazine along similar lines. Farming, in particular, seems to have attracted this sort of cinemagazine, as several other companies circulated similar titles. For example, *David Brown Newsreel* (David Brown Tractors, 1963) featured 'DB equipment at work under varying conditions in different parts of the world' purely as a promotional tool.[11]

The internal workings of the sponsor company were often the focus of these public relations cinemagazines. *Unilever Magazine* (Unilever, 1950) and *Laing News Review* (John Laing & Co. Ltd., 1954), to name but two, featured the work and culture of diverse parts of a large organisation. They aimed to dispose the public more favourably towards the company by persuading them of the friendly and inclusive nature of the organisation. These films were not only shown at public showings by social groups and organisations, but also through exhibition stands and displays at the company headquarters. *Unilever Magazine* was 'available free to all responsible organisations'.[12] Despite the obvious public relations nature of this story, they were also in demand as educational resources, so much so that a 'demand has grown for stories from the magazines to be made available separately, for users with a special interest in one particular subject.'[13]

Sponsored cinemagazines for internal relations

For many other sponsors during the 1940s and 1950s, the cinemagazine was 'a house magazine in film form' – a regular insight into the workings of the company, the social lives of the staff and new developments from management.[14] It was a product whose 'purpose was to integrate', 'presenting, to paraphrase the newsreel slogan, the Company to the Company'.[15] The promotion work of these series was far more internal in focus.

These sponsored cinemagazines of the 1950s must be seen as a symptom of the culture of paternalism which prevailed in many industries during this period. In the cases of *Ingot Pictorial*, *Mining Review* (to some extent) and *Cinegazette*, they functioned as extensions and visual representations of the company's interest in and care for the workforce, and indeed, the wider society surrounding its works. They were celluloid attempts at 'fostering a sense of community'.[16] *Panorama* (ICI, 1951) was an internal relations cinemagazine, very much aimed at uniting the divisions through education. This was explicitly illustrated in its 'Other People's Jobs' feature, profiling an employee of a different division in each issue. The cinemagazine was part of a complete programme of 'films for internal relations – films to increase the individual's knowledge of ICI's activities, to be of assistance to employees and to explain or amplify anything about the company which is not perhaps fully understood.'[17] From 1948 onwards, they were seen by workers as part of a travelling film show. Three units were sent out to all ICI divisions twice during the autumn and winter. After hours, shows of 'cartoons, shorts and on occasions, full-length feature films,' as well as *Panorama*, were put on in works' canteens, theatres or local halls, to an average of 40,000 viewers a year.[18] The company was happy to report that this policy 'has given to ICI workers a sense of unity'.[19]

Through *Ingot Pictorial*, Richard Thomas & Baldwin (RTB, later British Steel) also made a conscious effort to make 'every employee understand and accept his individual responsibility' as part of 'the company of which we are team members'.[20] This was reflected in the visual style of the series. The camera crew made sure to 'purposely linger where the normal cinema would show only a flash – for example, in scenes showing groups of employees, crowds at a football match, and so on – in order that employees will have a chance to identify themselves on the screen'.[21] Emphasis was placed throughout on workers' ownership of the series. Verity Films used 'quite a number of Works personalities completely unused to the microphone' as commentators, to ensure that local voices were heard and identified with by the audience.[22] *Ingot Pictorial* also regularly featured 'Sports Flashes' detailing recent successes from RTB's various teams as well as features on the Cookley Operatives Training Scheme and a new steel works at Velindre, for example.[23] The repeated emphasis on team sports was hoped to be a reflection of the working relationship with which the viewers identified themselves. RTB claimed that *Ingot Pictorial* 'records achievement and induces a sense of pride and loyalty … By covering such other aspects of the company's activities as education, medical and canteen services, sporting and social events, it illustrates the company's concern for the human factor in its relations with employees.'[24] It was produced in conjunction with a house newspaper and a 'magazine of the *Picture Post* type', again, as part of a company wide programme of internal relations.[25] 'Here for the first time people "in the works" were being given a picture of, as it might be, a finished jigsaw puzzle of which previously they had only known one or two pieces.'[26] Mobile van projection was key to the distribution of this series. In 1952, a tour of thirty works reached an audience of 7,000.[27] But RTB also allowed the issues to be shown in a handful of public cinemas in the area of works in order to reach steel-working households and the wider community.

Where *Ingot Pictorial* attempted to capture the character of its audience, other internal relations cinemagazines took on a more centralised, paternalistic character. Perhaps the epitome of these paternalistic sponsored cinemagazines was *Cinegazette* issue no. 5's story, FOOD FOR THOUGHT. This profile of London Transport's canteen services and its provisions illustrates the lengths to which the company went to provide its employees with meals, from butchering and packing

BFI Stills

Wolfgang Suschitzky (left) filming *Mining Review*

fresh meat for distribution to running fully staffed canteens. The commentary describes London Transport as a 'family' looked after by the 'housewife' – the canteen services – because a good meal 'helps to keep the wheels of London Transport turning'.[28] This is not just a perfect example of the style of these paternalistic sponsored cinemagazines and the content they used in order to put across their message, but also an illustration of the philosophy which underpinned the making of such series as *Cinegazette*. The sponsor companies saw themselves very much as the heads of large families, overseeing, directing and encouraging the other family members through their cinemagazines. *Cinegazette* was produced by the London Transport Film Unit, a part of the London Transport Executive's public relations department. Its internal relations and public relations roles often amounted to much the same thing, especially when British Transport Films took over production in 1950. The cinemagazine was distributed to staff with 16mm projectors (about 100 in the company as a whole), but was also shown at the very works' canteens and social spaces featured in the series itself. Later in the 1950s *Cinegazette* also appeared on children's television as an educational film.

Mining Review was likewise an attempt by the NCB to invigorate the workforce through a newsletter-style bulletin. Memos from NCB headquarters regularly described the series as the film equivalent of the NCB's print magazine *Coal*, and their contents were very similar. Issues featured traditional mining songs, and entertainments such as pigeon fancying, darts and snooker, in an attempt to emphasise the similarities shared by mining communities as disparate as Kent, Durham and Nottingham. The effect intended was 'making people feel part of a great enterprise'.[29] The cinema distribution of *Mining Review* to some major cities and even the West End of London at first seems quite incongruous when the cinemagazine is viewed from this angle. Of course, the priority audience was the miners and their communities, and it was hoped that by showing the series in cinemas, these people would be reached in greater numbers without affecting production in the mines. However, the NCB also saw as vital their responsibility to the nation as the company's shareholders, particularly because of the anti-nationalisation campaigns of 1949 and 1950. *Mining Review*, therefore, also played a secondary role as an animated newsletter to the public in their capacity as part owners of the NCB, showcasing mining talent and the vast investment in modernisation undertaken by the NCB.

Sponsored cinemagazines for advertising

Throughout the 1960s, as larger industrial concerns moved away from prestige and public relations towards more direct advertising in their film output, the cinemagazine once again came into its own. Dunlop used its cinemagazine *Montage* (Dunlop Rubber Co., 1960) to great effect, advertising it as 'eighteen minutes of colourful entertainment with an instructive background', whilst all the time it drip-fed the names of Dunlop's products to the audience.[30] Like the more traditional sponsored cinemagazines, *Montage* featured exciting action sequences and entertaining stories such as shots of motorcycling at the British Experts' Trial and an illustration of the difference between boys' and girls' shoes.[31] However, it also contained purely advertising stories for products such as Polimul, Latex, Gauntlet, Gripsure Gloves and Selflay Tiles.[32] This was a delicate balance to maintain, as one imagines that audiences would not continue to engage Dunlop Film Library if they thought they were being targeted thus too heavily.

The end of the sponsored cinemagazine?

The sponsored cinemagazine felt its sharpest decline with the coming of video in the 1970s. With 16mm no longer the exhibition medium of choice, companies had no need to employ or create a specialist film unit in order to get their messages across. Those few cinemagazines that persisted or were started in the 1970s and 1980s (with the exception of *Review*, formerly *Mining Review*, which ended in 1983) were often, therefore, released on VHS video. It is hard to say why, if there was a VHS market for industrial film in general, as suggested by John Chittock in *Screen Digest*, cinemagazines themselves took such a deadly blow.[33] Perhaps, as 'home video became more common and viewers' options expanded',[34] the decreasing likelihood of audiences seeing several issues of the series (one of the keys to the cinemagazine's success in getting its message across) made the format less viable; perhaps the more casual, in-house method of video production tended to discourage the kind of planning and forethought needed to construct a regular series, as opposed to single, instructional films made when they were needed; or perhaps the coming of video coincided with a change in industry. The 1970s and 1980s did see corporate restructuring and cost-cutting on a large scale on account of industrial decline, recession, and a move away from a paternalistic corporate culture towards a more profit-orientated regime. All of these changes meant that a relatively large film promotion budget, whether to finance a company film unit or to outsource expertise, became a much less viable option to public relations and marketing departments. John Chittock reported a number of 'large UK companies closing down their internal units and switching to using commercial companies' in the late 1970s, and the cinemagazine was often the first production to be cut under this new regime.[35] Thus, just a handful of video-cinemagazines began in the 1970s and 1980s – *Spotlight on Agriculture* (NFU, 1974), *Pipeline* (BP, 1979), *Texaco Video News* (Texaco, 1980), *BICC Balfour Beatty Linkline* (Balfour Beatty, 1981) and *Balfour Beatty Review* (Balfour Beatty, 1987), all short-lived. The 1980s also saw the demise of a giant of the cinemagazine world, *Mining Review,* in 1983, because of the winding up of the NCB. Interestingly, those companies that did bring out VHS cinemagazines during this period seem to have been larger organisations with some environmental impact inherent in their work. The series may well have been an attempt to answer their critics in the same way that the NCB had hoped to in the 1940s.

One should not be tempted, however, to 'characterise sponsored films as specimens of extinct media'.[36] Rick Prelinger suggests that 'it is more accurate to see them as part of a continuum that today includes video and the Internet, the media of choice for corporate and institutional communications.'[37] Indeed, it is through these media that the sponsored cinemagazine continues, albeit greatly diminished. Thus, in the 1990s and beyond, we see *Meat Video Magazine* (British Meat Education Service, 2000) provided free to secondary schools and *Prisons Video Magazine* (Prisons Video Trust, 1991), a self-described 'video newsletter'.[38] The Internet has spawned a great many streamed and downloadable films, or films available for order, along similar lines to the sponsored cinemagazine, such as the streamed *Parkour Video Magazine* (Threesixtyclothinguk and 3B Ramps, 2000), *VHS Link*, now *Link* (The Salvation Army, 1998) and the video podcast *Zigzag* (Massachusetts Institute of Technology 2006).[39]

Despite its decline in the final quarter of the twentieth century, the sponsored cinemagazine has not died; indeed, the advent of the Internet may well be heralding a new boom in the genre, which has evolved throughout the last century, adapting as much to its production and distribution media as to its audience.

Notes

1   Sponsored cinemagazines are credited with (Sponsor, Launch date) on the first mention throughout this article.
2   *Shell Cinemagazine* issue no. 1 (1938).
3   Paul Smith, *British Transport Films – The First Decade: 1949–1959* (http://www.britishtransportfilms.co.uk/history/history1.html; accessed 26 March 2008).
4   *Film User*, vol. 8 no. 94 (August 1954), p. 373.
5   Interview with Peter Pickering, 6 February 2007.
6   Gordon Begg, 'How We Use Films: 6 – At ICI', *Film User*, vol. 8 no. 90 (April 1954), p. 169; H. Donaldson, *Coal Film Makers: An Appreciation* (London: NCB, 1981), p. 2.
7   *Oil Review* issue no. 3 (1951); *Oil Review* issue no. 5 (1951).
8   *Imagery,* vol. 2 no. 22 (March 1950), p. 8.
9   'The Anglo-Iranian Oil Company's Film Show Past and Present Portrayed to a Great Audience', *The Petroleum Times*, 9 January 1953.
10 Ronald Tritton, 'An Indirect Aid to Sales', *Imagery*, vol. 2 no. 3 (September 1950), p. 11.
11 *British National Film Catalogue,* vol. 2 (1964), p. 1.
12 Ibid.
13 Advertisement, *Film User*, vol. 11 no. 123 (January 1957), p. 5.
14 D. A. Gladwell, 'Ingot Pictorial – Four Years' Progress', *Imagery*, vol. 5 no. 3 (Autumn 1953), p. 7.
15 'The Story of Mining Review', *Film and TV Technician* (June 1984), pp. 8–9; Begg, op. cit., p. 170.
16 Gladwell, op. cit., p. 7.

17 Begg, op. cit., p. 170.
18 'Films for the Workers', *Film User,* vol. 6 no. 69 (July 1952), p. 335.
19 Ibid.
20 Howard Marshall, in Frank A. Hoare, 'Modern Methods of Film-Using in Industry,' *Film User,* vol. 6 no. 66 (April 1952), pp. 175–178.
21 Gladwell, op. cit., pp. 8–9.
22 'The Inside Story of Ingot Pictorial – Your Own Cine-magazine', *Ingot* (May 1951), p. 27.
23 *Ingot Pictorial* issue no. 7 (1951); *Ingot Pictorial* issue no. 21 (November 1954).
24 Howard Marshall, op. cit., pp. 176–177.
25 Howard Marshall, 'Film Magazines: Ingot Pictorial', *Imagery*, vol. 2 no. 2 (March 1950), p. 9.
26 'Commentary', *Imagery,* vol. 6 no. 3 (October 1954), p. 2.
27 *Imagery*, vol. 4 no. 1 (Summer 1952), p. 14.
28 *Cinegazette* issue no. 5 (1949).
29 Tritton, op. cit., p. 11.
30 *Film User*, vol. 14 no. 162 (April 1960), p. 165.
31 *Montage* issue no. 6 (1961); *Montage* issue no. 3 (1961).
32 *Montage* issue no. 2 (1961); *Montage* issue no. 6 (1961); *Montage* issue no. 7 (1963).
33 John Chittock, 'The Fall of Industrial Film,' *Screen Digest* (February 1978), p. 29.
34 Rick Prelinger, *The Field Guide to Sponsored Films* (San Francisco: National Film Preservation Foundation, 2006), p. ix.
35 Chittock, op. cit., p. 27.
36 Prelinger, op. cit., p. vi.
37 Ibid.
38 http://www.londonshakespeare.org.uk/othello2/pvm.htm (accessed 4 February 2008).
39 *Parkour Video Magazine* at http://www.pkvm.co.uk/ (accessed 4 February 2008); *VHS Link*, now *Link* at http://www1.salvationarmy.org.uk/uki/www_uki.nsf/vw-dynamic-index/798225548446796780256FE9004D9C6C?Opendocument (accessed 4 February 2008) and *Zigzag* at http://libstaff.mit.edu/amps/zigzag/ (accessed 4 February 2008).

MAKING TRACKS: NEWSREELS, CINEMAGAZINES AND THE RAILWAY INDUSTRY

Steve Foxon

From the earliest years of cinema the railways in Britain used film as a promotional tool, and pre- and especially post-nationalisation they made regular use of the cinemagazine format. Film archivist Steve Foxon, historian of British Transport Films, gives the background history to series such as Events, Cinegazette, Rail Report *and* The Way Ahead.

Today railways carry more passengers than ever before and yet news stories generally consist, at best, of a report on a new operating company's policy or, at worst, inaccurate reports of tragedy or an 'anorak' jibe levelled at an enthusiast. To the twenty-first-century viewer the idea of a self-proclaiming, positive news record of the year's events of the local railway company must seem a foreign concept. Yet there was a time when our railway companies were extremely adept at representing themselves on the screen.

Industrial newsreels and cinemagazines have never had a glamorous existence compared to their journalistic, entertainment-driven counterparts, yet the very existence of the first railway film unit is largely due to the American newsreel companies and their work. Though the individual railway companies of Great Britain had used film for promotional and advertising purposes almost right back to the birth of the cinema, the existence of an official railway film unit did not come about until the early part of 1934.

After the successful 1933 American and Canadian tour of the London Midland and Scottish Railway's (LMS) *Royal Scot* train, a large amount of newsreel film poured into the company's Euston headquarters from numerous grateful American newsreel staff who had been given filming facilities at various points along the route of the tour. The LMS press and public relations office of the day had already made photographs and lantern slides available as a means of external advertising, publicity and to some extent internal training, but had not considered films up to this point. The influx of this inflammable film stock prompted a suggestion to assemble all the silent film material together into a thirty-minute film. Encouraged by Bill Brundell, writer and later editor of the LMS magazine, and with the blessing of the publicity-minded chairman Sir Josiah Stamp (later Lord Stamp), the plan was approved. With the help of a local projector supplier and a keen projectionist, a 35mm show using a portable 'Ironhouse' projection box was given one Sunday morning to LMS staff and their families at St Pancras town hall. This was so successful that a repeat screening had to be arranged and the idea of an official railway film unit was born.

The LMS film unit started out in a small way as a division of the Publicity and Advertising department and initially produced silent travel-promoting films which would then be made available for screening through various non-theatrical film libraries. Yet the desire to produce a greater quantity of films led to an association with the Topical Press Agency, whose Commercial and Educational Films department was commissioned to produce sound films for advertising and training purposes.

Events

During the 1930s, the LMS was the largest transport undertaking in the world, not only running a railway but also several major British docks and ports, passenger and freight shipping services, an air service, a fleet of road vehicles and literally thousands of horse-and-dray carts. It would be impossible for one film to cover all these activities so it was agreed that a yearly magazine-style news film, in sound, should be produced to chart the success of the company. Simply entitled EVENTS OF 1935, this twenty-minute two-reeler used the vibrant newsreel style to feature a new diesel rail car, the launch of new steamers for the Clyde, Heysham–Belfast shipping services, the Silver Jubilee of Transport at Euston, the construction of new stations, the naming of locomotives and the opening of new facilities. It set the pattern for the *Events* series of yearly cinemagazines that was considered an integral part of the LMS film unit's screening activities, and it would go on to be used at nearly all of the comprehensive touring film shows organised and carried out by the advertising department to complement the filmmaking activity.

EVENTS OF 1936 followed in a similar fashion, with more locomotives being named, more ships for the Clyde, the best-kept station awards and the first all-steel signal post. The magazine was again attached to a touring programme, much to the delight of the chairman, Sir Josiah Stamp, whose staff, it was claimed, 'could now feel part of the bigger picture and wider organisation'. The chairman's support and belief in the use of film was key to the success and longevity of the unit and it is no coincidence that Sir Josiah Stamp appears in a leading role in no less than seven of the twelve stories featured in EVENTS OF 1937. Keenly aware of the value of publicity, he believed that it was good for staff to see him at the forefront of the

Frame stills from CORONATION SCOT *Events*, 1937

The Railway Film Archive

company activities and not just a name controlling them from an office in London. Many of these stories were locomotive naming ceremonies, one of which was carried out by Winston Churchill. In this 1937 issue, Sir Josiah names the Patriot class locomotive 5524 *Blackpool* at Blackpool station. In front of an audience of railway and council dignitaries he is then presented, to his surprise, with the Freedom of the Borough. 'Surely one of his most treasured possessions', the narrator exclaims.

It is the final item in EVENTS OF 1937 which is perhaps the most famous magazine item produced by the LMS film unit: CORONATION SCOT, the launch of Sir William Stanier's blue-and-silver streamlined Coronation class locomotives. This item was produced, directed and narrated by John Shearman and employed the bold idea of intercutting newsreel footage of the 1937 Coronation procession in London with shots of the first of a new breed of streamlined locomotives constructed at Crewe. Edited with great effect to the accompaniment of Elgar's 'Pomp and Circumstance' March No. 4 and William Walton's 'Coronation March', the film works well, and as crowds cheer at the passing of the Royal Coach, a smaller group of railway staff cheer as the new streamlined locomotive makes its way out of the workshop. There are some historic shots of the locomotive designer William Stanier himself, the driver Tom Clarke on the now famous *Princess Elizabeth* and *Coronation Scot* runs, and impressive aerial shots of the 114 mph record run. CORONATION SCOT was later separated from the cinemagazine and used as a film in its own right. It is considered by some to be on a par with the GPO's NIGHT MAIL (1936), which was facilitated by the LMS the previous year. John Shearman later commented, 'My only regret is that the film is not in colour!'

EVENTS OF 1938 was released in January 1939 but by the outbreak of war in September the LMS Advertising department had other things on its mind. EVENTS OF 1939 was abandoned, the film unit was closed and its staff left the company to join the fighting forces. Sir Josiah Stamp, who had been such a great advocate of the use of the pre-war cinemagazine format, never had the opportunity to see his film unit re-form after the war or to see how the use of film would help to serve a postwar nationalised transport system. Sadly he, his wife and children became casualties of one of the first air raids over London, suffering a direct hit on their family home.

Following the cessation of hostilities the railway companies found themselves both physically and financially crippled from the effects of war, and it was not until 1947 that the LMS felt it had something to shout about. Through a close relationship with the English Electric company the LMS had spent significant time and money in developing a new diesel-electric locomotive that would revolutionise the British railway industry, and a large part of EVENTS OF 1947 (the only postwar magazine the LMS produced) was dedicated to diesel-electric locomotive No. 10000. Nationalisation was now inevitable and the LMS was determined to tell the world that this new diesel locomotive was a product of that company.

Cinegazette

The year 1947 also saw the start of a new cinemagazine series, *Cinegazette*, produced by London Transport and contracted out to Academy Pictures. *Cinegazette* was a twice-yearly newsreel-style production, with each issue containing around three items covering different aspects of London Transport's activity. Each activity, it was claimed, was vital to the successful running of Britain's largest urban transport undertaking, and the company felt that its legions of customers should be told about them. This non-theatrical audience of staff and the general public were kept informed of a wide variety of transport issues ranging from tube train overhaul to lost property, the lubrication of trolleybus overhead wiring to testing wider buses. Even cake production at the Croydon Canteen Food Production Centre had an airing. These screenings took place via the vast network of clubs, church groups, societies, institutes and London Transport's own touring cinema vans, with some items even finding their way onto BBC children's television as early as March 1952.

The two magazines of 1947 compared train comfort with that of the modern bus, and looked at staff canteens, a new radio network, the longest service record for night staff, the opening of the Central Line extension, night-time bridge replacement work and finally, with an effort to keep the stories human, staff sports news. The *Cinegazette*s for 1948 carried on in similar vein; there would, however, be a new sponsor paying Academy's fee. When the Transport Act of 1947 came into effect on 1 January 1948, it brought together, with the exception of the airlines BOAC and BEA, the railways, roads, canals and London Transport under one nationalised umbrella known as the British Transport Commission (BTC). The BTC provided new opportunities for the use of films in the service of a national industry and in 1949, a Films Section of the commission was established in the department of the Chief Public Relations and Publicity Officer as a result of two investigations.

The first made a thorough examination into the use of films by the separate elements of the Commission for the twenty years prior to nationalisation, including the LMS Railway and London Transport Films. The second carried out an evaluation of the film activities of other British industries, both private and nationalised, so the Commission might benefit from the experience of the Shell Oil Group, the National Coal Board, Imperial Chemical Industries and the Gas Council, as well as the Central Office of Information. The result was British Transport Films

(BTF), an amalgamation of what already existed but with widened scope to cater for the work of the other elements now forming part of Britain's very first nationalised transport authority. It was destined to be the biggest industrial film unit in Britain and was led by the renowned documentary filmmaker Edgar Anstey, a protégé of the 'father' of documentary, John Grierson.

By 1949 Anstey had built up a creditable reputation in the world of documentary filmmaking and represented short film production on the Cinematograph Film Council. It was this impressive record that persuaded J. H. Brebner, chairman of the BTC's Public Relations Co-ordination Committee, to appoint him Producer in Charge in May 1949. By 1951 BTF was sufficiently organised to take control of the production of series such as *Cinegazette*, which was previously contracted outside of the film unit. The first *Cinegazette* produced by BTF for what was now known as the London Transport Executive was OPEN HOUSE, *Cinegazette* issue no. 9. This was a single-subject issue focused on the many English country houses now open to the public and within reach of the London Transport network.

Without doubt the most deliberated *Cinegazette* is THE ELEPHANT WILL NEVER FORGET, *Cinegazette* issue no. 12 released in 1953. It described the last week of London's trams, which had taken place the previous July and represented a shift in BTF style. BTF had a policy that its films would be about the new and exciting; they were to lead staff and public into a new transport age which had little or no room for nostalgia. This film was intended and authorised only as a record of the passing of (what was considered then to be) an outdated mode of transport. Anstey therefore quickly dismissed director John Krish's idea to turn the shoot into a story in which the travelling public are seen to mourn the loss of an old friend. Krish was disappointed but undeterred and went ahead with his idea, using the roll-ends donated by other cameramen. The editing is said to have taken place during the midnight hours. Krish never made another film for Anstey and it would be another twenty-four years before he directed another film for BTF, which again proved controversial although for very different reasons. Ironically, after Krish's departure from BTF following completion of THE ELEPHANT WILL NEVER FORGET, the film turned out to be one of BTF's most requested titles and is still extremely popular today.

The year 1957 saw the last of the London Transport *Cinegazette*s with A CENTURY OF BUSES, *Cinegazette* issue no. 16. This described a parade in Regent's Park including some of the old horse buses and first petrol buses, with members of present-day staff enjoying a day out in the costumes of the period. Examples of London Transport's present fleet culminated in the Routemaster, London's bus of the future. In 1958 analysis of audience returns for the series of

*Cinegazette*s revealed that 67,947 people viewed a cinemagazine from the series in the month of March alone – extremely impressive for a news magazine concentrated solely on London and the surrounding area.[1]

Report on Modernisation

With BTF fully in control of all transport-themed filmmaking the *Report on Modernistation* series was created to chart the modernisation of the British railways. Filmed in colour and each with a running time of about twenty minutes, it marked a new style of cinemagazine for the railways. This was not a record of the

BTF Film Unit on location for *Rail Report* c. 1970

The Railway Film Archive

year's achievements; these films were about what could be achieved and what was being achieved: a forward-looking series for a forward-looking future.

The FIRST REPORT ON MODERNISATION was released in 1959 and subsequent reports appeared at roughly yearly intervals, with a short production break in 1962 to experiment with a new style, or when something significant was taking place. FIRST REPORT ON MODERNISATION looked at the results of the far-reaching 1955 modernisation and re-equipment plan for British Railways. As the modernisation scheme progressed, its effects became increasingly apparent in every aspect of railway work throughout the regions: in track improvements, in electrification and signalling; in new depots, marshalling yards and stations; in the latest coaches and traction units and in the railway training schools. It was these visible signs of progress that the camera examined as the commentary interprets 'their greater significance for the future'.

The SECOND REPORT ON MODERNISATION continued in the same vein, describing the moving of a hillside to make a new marshalling yard; express freight trains that carried complete loads of oil, limestone, cars and frozen foods; griddle cars and Blue Pullmans, roadrailers and driverless trucks. By 1961, the THIRD REPORT ON MODERNISATION took a gritty and far less glamorous stance, taking a frank look at inefficiencies within the system and how the railways were losing money. The magazine talked of how many of the present-day railway problems were created during the years of competition between the various railway companies prior to nationalisation. For example, we hear of the incomprehensible story of a journey of freight from a small goods yard in Sheffield and how it spends the most part of a day travelling around Sheffield to get to a destination just a few hundred yards from where it started.

The Way Ahead (Wyvern)

The Transport Act of 1962 established the British Railways Board as successor to the British Transport Commission. Its function was, broadly, to provide a railway service in Great Britain, and as such the Board had a vast range of responsibilities. One of these responsibilities was to inform British Railways employees of developments within the industry. They did this in part by sponsoring a new style of cinemagazine, to be produced by BTF, called *The Way Ahead*.

The Way Ahead began as a localised news-based cinemagazine for the Midland region of British Railways, and was described as *The Way Ahead (Wyvern)* series, Wyvern being the mythical dragon-like creature adopted as the symbol for the Midland Railway (later part of the LMS and eventually British Railways Midland Region). More akin to magazine programmes of today, the series was presented and hosted on screen by Huw Thomas, already a well-known BBC announcer and popular ITN newscaster. Thoughtful editing spliced human stories which profiled railwaymen such as Alex Wishart, checker at St Pancras goods department and secretary of the British Amateur Wrestling Association, with key progress reports and developments in the region.

Six editions of the *The Way Ahead (Wyvern)* were produced in 1962, and the intensive schedule of planning, shooting and editing kept some freelance staff in employment for a full year as well as frustrating the rest of the unit working on 'proper' films by using equipment they needed. The year 1963 would see a more ambitious programme for the series on a national scale.

THE NORTH EASTERN GOES FORWARD

During 1959 Anstey employed his former boss John Grierson as a freelance at BTF. Grierson, who had just spent a year searching for a new purpose in the documentary field, was asked to go to the north of England and test the ground for a film on the modernisation of the railways. Modernisation had taken a strong hold in the North East and new marshalling yards, modern diesel traction and colour-light signalling were just a few of the new technological advances taking place on the railway system. Grierson accepted the challenge with gusto and proudly presented his findings to Anstey with the proclamation, 'There is not one film that can be made, there are twelve!'[2] Unable to finance the ideas Grierson came up with, the proposals were shelved, but an opportunity arose to make use of part of Grierson's plans when in 1962, already aware of the *Report on Modernisation* and *The Way Ahead (Wyvern)* series, the North Eastern Region of British Railways requested a film dedicated to the changes taking place in its area.

The result was a one-off production that helped to shape the style of later issues of *Report on Modernisation*. Running for twenty minutes and basking in Eastmancolor, THE NORTH EASTERN GOES FORWARD (1962) showed the building of new marshalling yards, the improvement of passenger and freight facilities and the design of modern aids for speed and safety on the track. It made good use of Grierson's original ideas and helped the staff of the division keep pace with rapidly developing social and industrial needs and achievements of the North Eastern Region.

The Way Ahead (National) and Rail Report

The year 1963 brought a new change to *The Way Ahead* format; now it would be for all regions and known as *The Way Ahead (National)*. The series had a rather complicated structure, pairing national stories with individual stories made for each region of British Rail. Thus, the Southern Region would view the same national stories as the Western Region, but each would also view its own local stories as part of the same issue.

Only four editions were produced, covering some forty-seven separate stories, marking the busiest and most productive time for BTF. Costing a staggering £59,663 to produce and distribute, it was considered a valuable and successful communication channel with railway staff. Interestingly, staff were allocated time off from their duties and were expected to watch the films at one of the many canteen or mess room screenings. It was estimated that a total of 284,000 people saw the series, but with high production and distribution costs plus the cost of relieving staff of their duties to take time to see the films it was clear that this method of communication could not be maintained.[3] A rethink was called for and the answer was found in a revamped *Report on Modernisation* based on the styles laid out in THE NORTH EASTERN GOES FORWARD.

BTF Film Unit filming RAILWAYS CONSERVE THE ENVIRONMENT *Rail Report* issue no. 11, 1971

The Railway Film Archive

By 1965 the SIXTH REPORT ON MODERNISATION had become the catchier *Rail Report* 6: THE GOOD WAY TO TRAVEL. It extolled the best in new railway thinking, the newest of materials and how the most modern methods were now being employed to make sure that British Rail became the undisputed 'good way to travel'. The new *Rail Report*s seemed to bode well with staff and film unit, and it was said of *Rail Report* 7: SPEED THE PAYLOAD that 'the annual film in the now seven years old series has proved increasingly popular with all types of audience, it now provides, with the disappearance of *The Way Ahead* series, our main channel of film communication with the staff.'[4]

Rail Report 11: RAILWAYS CONSERVE THE ENVIRONMENT, released in 1971, was the only issue in the series intended for a cinema circuit release and for the occasion it was treated to a coat of Technicolor. The year 1970 was European Conservation Year and the entire issue was devoted to examples of what railways in Britain were doing to help conserve and improve the environment. The conversion of former railway property – including the Roundhouse at Camden – is shown, while former trackbeds yield nature trails for children and training runs for racehorses.

Rail Report 12: THIS YEAR BY RAIL, released in 1972, showed technical developments at British Rail that would take the company right through the decade: new freight loads, air-conditioned carriages, an ultrasonic test-train for checking the permanent way, a lecture train, and a new station for motorists – all part of the railway scene in the 1970s. However, on completion it was felt that the format of a yearly magazine was no longer the favoured channel for communicating with staff and in line with many industrial organisations (the National Coal Board excepted) television was fast becoming the favoured medium.

In 1980 (six years after Edgar Anstey had retired from the unit) *Rail Report* was given a brief reprise when, over coffee at British Railways headquarters, it was decided to combine various unused short topics and produce a new addition to the series. Taking an altogether different approach, *Rail Report* 13: ON TRACK FOR THE 80s takes a more reflective view on what the future was to hold for the industry in the next decade. It featured a review of innovation and development within British Rail and its businesses and included modernisation of freight facilities and service to new companies, progress of the Bedford–St Pancras electrification project, paved track and permanent way maintenance, Sealink's *Galloway Princess*, Seaspeed's SRN4 hovercraft, and the research department's magnetically levitated vehicle. It also included preserved steam locomotive-hauled specials, a concept that would have been out of the question in the forward-looking unit of Anstey's time.

For a while it was touch and go as to whether *Rail Report* 13 would ever be completed. The cinemagazine was in rapid decline and the future of the film unit remained uncertain, along with other industrial film units, in the coming video age. BTF soldiered on until 1984, even optimistically chalking up on the proposals board a *Rail Report* 14, but the sad truth was that the film unit's time had come and it only continued as a small video unit, BTF Video. By this time many of the senior members of staff had retired and with them the age of the rail cinemagazine.

Notes

1   'Monthly Audience Returns', BTF internal document, March 1958, (S. Foxon Collection).
2   John Grierson, letter to Edgar Anstey, 'Notes on the Modernisation of British Railways', 1959 (BFI Special Collections).
3   A. J. Potter, 'Production Costs and Returns', BTF internal memo, 1963 (S. Foxon Collection).
4   Edgar Anstey and A. J. Potter, 'The Ad Hoc Film Programme Committee – Proposals for 1967', BTF internal document, 7 November 1966 (S. Foxon Collection).

RECONCILING POLICY AND PROPAGANDA: THE BRITISH OVERSEAS TELEVISION SERVICE 1954–1964

Linda Kaye

For decades, British taxpayers have paid their government to produce thousands of films about themselves for overseas distribution that they have never seen or heard of. At their height in the 1960s, hundreds were produced and distributed each month by the government's Central Office of Information. In the first of two essays examining the development and production of official film and television magazine series from 1954, Linda Kaye explores the problematic engagement of the British government in the art of national projection.

In the early 1960s the Australian Broadcasting Corporation broadcast a weekly five-minute programme in its early evening slot, which was so popular that when its presenter, Noeline Pritchard, was married in 1963, a special edition was produced showing scenes of her wedding and reception.[1] The series was called *This Week in Britain* (1959–1980) and each week reports would be delivered on aspects of contemporary Britain ranging from LONDON SHOE WEEK (1961) to WOMEN IN PARLIAMENT (1964). This was not a commercial enterprise. The series was financed by the British government and produced by its Central Office of Information (COI) as part of an unprecedented expansion in film production that would see Britain projected, in a myriad of different languages, into living rooms across the world to a global audience of millions (Table 1).[2] Many of the strategies developed as a result of this possess a contemporary resonance, including the dissemination of material as unattributed items within television schedules and the development of a recognisable cohesive image of Britain, or nation brand, repackaged for different 'territories'. This remarkable volume of material, produced purely for overseas distribution, has retained an extraordinary invisibility over the years, consistently dipping below the academic radar.[3] This has led to the perception that government film production, from the demise of the Crown Film Unit in 1952, was preoccupied with public information films while the projection of Britain overseas faded as the Overseas Information Service (OIS), starved of funds, entered a period of decline.

69

TABLE I Overseas Television Service magazine series 1954–1964

	Release Date	Distribution
Transatlantic Teleview	1954–1958	USA
Commonwealth Teleview	1957–1958	Canada and Australia
Viewpoint	1957–1960	Canada
Telerama Britanico	1958–?	Latin America
Topic [Meet the British]	1958–1959	USA
British Calendar, later *Calendar*	1959–1969	USA and Commonwealth
Dateline Britain	1959	Canada and Australia
People and Places/Arab Televiews	1959–1960	Middle East
Portrait	1959–1965	Middle East and Africa
Report from London/Persian Televiews	1959–1960	Middle East
This Week in Britain	1959–1980	Latin America, Commonwealth and Middle East
Middle East Newspots/Letter From London	1960–1969	Middle East
Moslems in Britain	1961 and 1964	Middle East
Ticket to London	1963	Australia and Canada
London Line	1964–1979	Commonwealth, Africa, Latin America and Middle East

In fact, by 1964 the Overseas Information Service had emerged as a revitalised force since Suez had catalysed a reversal of its fortunes in 1957, while the volume and nature of television material it created finally answered Sir Stephen Tallents' plea, made over thirty years earlier, that Britain fully engage in 'the art of national projection'.[4] Tallents, then Secretary of the Empire Marketing Board, had argued that this work could not be left solely to government or private enterprise since the nature of each would compromise it and proposed the establishment of a 'school of national projection' occupying the borderline between the two.[5] Indeed, the process of mastering this art proved to be a problematic one for the OIS. Although the British government had previously made excursions into the field of 'national projection' through film, most notably through the work of the Empire Marketing Board and the British Council, the production of a clear and cohesive image of Britain for the small screen eluded the organisation for most of this period. Indeed it was so preoccupied with the production and distribution of this material that its actual impact on the audience was neglected. Although the receptivity was gauged through size and placement for, example, no attempt was made to measure the actual effect these programmes might have on the viewer.[6] Through an examination of the output of television series produced by the Overseas Television Service, or propaganda as contemporaries termed it, this article will look at why the OIS could not effectively deliver policy until 1964 and the hard lessons learnt that finally enabled it to do so.[7]

Policy of national projection – a hollow commitment

On 1 April 1946 the Central Office of Information materialised as the peacetime successor to the Ministry of Information (MOI), heralding the emergence of a centralised organisation for the production and dissemination, through all media, of official information overseas. Under this system the three separate Overseas Departments – the Foreign Office, the Commonwealth Relations Office and the Colonial Office – each acquired their own information service and would commission or 'sponsor' their publicity from the COI, an agency that effectively acted as a producer. The COI was one of three 'agents' that supported the overseas information work of the Departments, the others being the External Services of the BBC and the British Council. These Departments and agencies, together with the Board of Trade, were collectively known as the Overseas Information Service (OIS), the main aim of which was articulated in February 1946, '… to ensure the presentation overseas of a true and adequate picture of British policy, British institutions and the British way of life'.[8] However, this commitment to a policy of national projection in the decade following the end of the Second World War proved to be a hollow one.[9] Although the policy and structure were in place, the OIS was subject to such financial cuts in the late 1940s and early 1950s that implementation was virtually impossible and medium hit hardest was film.

Although moving images were used to an unprecedented degree by Attlee's government in the provision of information at home, very little was made specifically for the projection of Britain overseas, the exception being the cinemagazine *This Is Britain* (1946–1951) sponsored by the Board of Trade.[10] By the early 1950s government film production had virtually ground to a halt as a result of recommendations made in 1951 by a ministerial committee under the chairmanship of Lord Salisbury. The COI budget for the financial year 1952–1953 was set at £1,653,000, a 30% decrease on the previous year and less than half the amount enjoyed at its peak postwar production in 1948–1949 (Table 2).[11] The brunt of this was borne by the COI's Films Division, with the closure of its film production arm, the Crown Film Unit, accounting for the majority of the redundancies. By 1953 the Films Division, now merged with Exhibitions, was functioning with a skeleton staff and the production of films reduced to a trickle. As the COI noted:

During this year [financial year 1952–1953] Films Division had experienced a difficult and rather painful transition from a major and widespread operation in conjunction with Crown Film Unit and with a principal emphasis on Home publicity to a much smaller though still very important operation carried out without the assistance of a film production unit and with emphasis largely on Overseas publicity.[12]

However, this change of emphasis was more about the total demise of films for home publicity than the first salvo of a campaign informed by the stringencies of the Cold War. No new films for overseas distribution were produced between April 1952 and April 1953, although five were commissioned.[13]

TABLE 2 Total COI expenditure 1945–1946 – 1964–1965

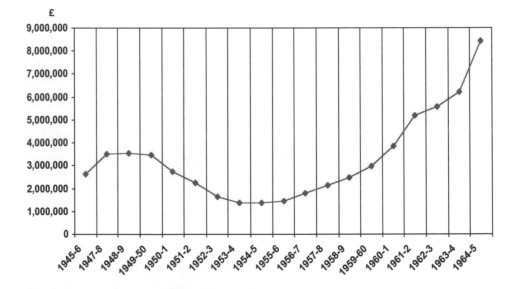

Drogheda: a blueprint for implementation

Days after the Crown Film Unit had ceased to function, an answer to a parliamentary question set in motion a series of enquiries that would provide the justification and template for the implementation of a policy of national projection. It was Anthony Nutting, Parliamentary Under Secretary of State at the Foreign Office, who announced in the House of Commons on 2 April 1952 an internal review of the OIS, stating

> It is high time, in my view, that an enquiry was made into the political aspects of this field. We have, therefore, already taken steps to invite the departments concerned … to consider the whole range of our overseas information services from the political and strategic aspects.[14]

The resulting report argued that it had '… established the necessity for, and the advantages of, efficient overseas information work, on both political and strategic – and indeed on economic grounds'.[15] The aspect that could not be settled internally was the degree to which it should expand and the finance required for this. Following its recommendation the government appointed an independent committee in October 1952, chaired by the Earl of Drogheda, to assess the work of the OIS and make recommendations for future policy.

The findings of the Drogheda Report, published in April 1954, signalled a fundamental shift in the attitude of government to the role of overseas information work. It identified two major failings with the OIS, one a direct consequence of the other. The first was '… the lack of a generally accepted body of principles serving either to justify their [OIS] existence at all or to define their potentialities', which had been propagated by the continued polarised public discussion surrounding it.[16] This had in turn fostered an ambivalent attitude within government to information work resulting in little long-term planning or financial commitment to the OIS, the second failing. The Service itself estimated that it was currently doing half the work achieved in 1947.[17] The wording of the committee's summary reveals that they initially shared this ambivalence and reflects the degree to which the information services still constituted a source of controversy within the public and private circles.[18]

> The conclusions have been forced upon us by sheer weight of evidence. At first we were inclined to be skeptical of the value of activities which are still comparatively new and have been the subject of much criticism. Moreover, we could not but feel suspicious of this invasion by Government of a field which in the not very distant past could be left to non-official agencies. Nevertheless, we have found it impossible to avoid the conclusion that a modern Government must concern itself with public opinion abroad and be properly equipped to deal with it.[19]

The members seem to reach this conclusion almost against their will and their conversion to the cause of the OIS was as much the result of field trips made to assess the impact of information work overseas as the evidence heard in London. While tracing the haphazard history of the British Information Services (BIS) to an attitude of mind of a 'people who instinctively dislike the idea of self-advertisement', they acknowledged that governments now had to explain, justify and defend their actions to a global audience, a process fuelled by the establishment of organisations such as the United Nations and, more importantly, by the increasing use of mass communications to do this.[20] This was '… no longer a field that could be left to non-official agencies.[21] Indeed, it stated that the information services must now be regarded as part of the normal apparatus of diplomacy, playing an essential role in support of Foreign, Commonwealth and Colonial policies. Moreover, this work 'should be done well, continuously and on an adequate scale', otherwise it would be better not to do it at all.[22] It finally made the astute observation that there was no further room for vacillation, and indeed, if this continued, it would prove detrimental to British interests abroad, possibly the only fact that would shake Britain out of its instinctive dislike for self-advertisement. More importantly it recognised the difficulty in assessing the impact of this work, that its significance is most notable when its presence has been reduced or removed entirely.

Suez and the global rise of television: catalysts for the implementation

The Drogheda Report had provided for the first time '… a comprehensive blueprint showing how the Information Services worked, why they were necessary, and suggesting the directions in which they needed to be developed'.[23] It effectively demonstrated that policy could only be implemented through expansion and it set out the cost. Over the next couple of years implementation of Drogheda's recommendations were subject to exactly the same prevarication they sought to guard against and only required renewed urgency when Britain's standing within the world 'community' suffered as a result of Suez. Internal reports, such as the 'four-day blackout' of news, together with the popular perception that Britain failed to communicate her position adequately to the world, focused the government on providing the structure and means for a more responsive information service.[24] The necessity of national projection was recognised in 'direct response to a downturn in foreign perceptions' and was designed to re-establish an acceptance within the international community.[25]

The man charged with carrying these recommendations out was Charles Hill, who was appointed Chancellor of the Duchy of Lancaster and Co-ordinator of Government Information Services in January 1957. He candidly describes how he was '… washed into the Cabinet by the turbulent waters of Suez. The enterprise had failed; everybody was smarting under the sting of defeat and, naturally enough, the search for scapegoats was on … Those who had supported or tolerated the venture … did not take long to find [one] – the information services … Suez is a perfect example of this "blame the spokesman" technique.'[26] Hill used his position to re-examine the details of Drogheda's recommendations, published in Overseas Information Services White Papers of 1957 (Cmnd. 225) and 1959 (Cmnd. 685), and obtain the means to implement them.[27]

We delude ourselves if we think that in a fiercely competitive world British virtues are so obvious as not to need expert presentation. Our ideas, our policies and our objectives can only become known if we organise the telling – and this costs money.[28]

Charles Hill not only made recommendations, he used his position as Cabinet minister to fight the Treasury to ensure that this expansion of the OIS, and the COI in particular, materialised. The budget for the OIS as a whole rose from £10 million in 1954 to £20.8 million in 1962, although only half of this represented expansion with the rest eroded by inflation.[29] Of this, the money available for the COI rose from £539,500 in 1954–1955 to £1,341,550 in 1959–1960.[30] The expenditure of the COI as a whole underwent an even greater increase from £1,380,000 in 1954–1955 to £6,203,000 in 1963–1964.[31] Of this a substantial amount was apportioned to the Films Division (later Films and Television Division) with its budget rising from £170,750 to £1,530,000 over this period (Table 3).[32]

TABLE 3 Total COI film expenditure 1954–1955 – 1964–1965

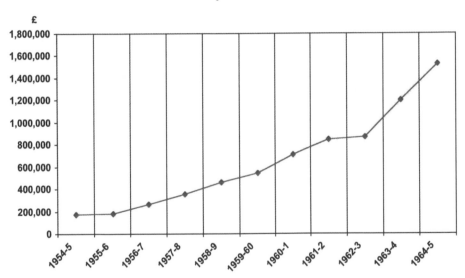

If Suez had provided the 'push' to present Britain overseas then the global rise of television from the early 1950s supplied not only the 'pull' but the prime medium for the expression of it. The Drogheda Report had not only been quick to recognise the detrimental impact of a drastic reduction in film production: 'During the recent cuts films suffered more than any other activity and we believe that their position should be restored,' but also noted the increasing importance of television as an 'outlet' for films, particularly within the United States'.[33] It recommended the establishment of film officers in Washington, Chicago and Los Angeles as well as an additional one in New York to 'handle television', boldly stating, '... now is the time to establish a footing in this new field.' These thoughts, however, were not confined to the committee of enquiry. As they were finalizing their report, an ad hoc committee convened by the Board of Trade were discussing at some length the issue of a 'British presence' on overseas television. Early in 1954 Frank Lee of the Board of Trade brought together representatives of the Overseas Departments and the COI primarily as a result of a despatch from Archibald Nye, the United Kingdom High Commissioner in Canada, on the use of UK material by the Canadian Broadcasting Corporation (CBC) in November 1953.[34] In it he outlined the slow decrease in the percentage of UK films broadcast by the CBC in the face of growing demand. He argued:

> Our challenge must come now, or the web spun across the border will become too strong to be loosed. Television is a major and dynamic force inevitably tending to draw Canada away from the United Kingdom and the Commonwealth. It reaches whole families in countless homes – especially the young people – with a power that no other information medium possesses … The stakes are so high that I seek to enlist your interest and influence in order that this problem should be resolutely tackled and mastered. Every day that passes without the United Kingdom being able to offer what is needed adds to the strength of the United States in Canada. This is a problem which cannot wait.[35]

Initially the committee saw this primarily in commercial terms – how to increase the general volume UK television material exported to Canada – and different courses of action, including a scheme proposed by the BBC, were outlined in a report with the aim of stimulating this. By March 1955, however, the forum for this discussion had shifted to the Overseas Information Services (Official) Committee. The issue was now regarded essentially as an 'information exercise', as the emphasis shifted from providing an income to generating a British presence on the small screen. By this stage two factors had been recognised and generally accepted within the Overseas Departments. The first was the potential of television as a tool of propaganda. Joe Garner of the CRO noted in 1954 that 'T.V. is a quite new medium, penetrating every home in a far more direct way and, in the years ahead, is likely to be the most potent influence on public opinion in all countries of the world.'[36] The second was that the concerns raised by Nye were no longer confined to Canada, but were rapidly acquiring an international dimension. Commenting on the imminent arrival of television in Hong Kong, Singapore and Kingston in 1954, C. Y. Carstairs of the Colonial Office highlighted the importance of a steady supply '… of acceptable material of British flavour – otherwise the "message" of this most powerful medium will be virtually entirely American'.[37] By 1957 these concerns were addressed and the argument to increase the provision of official British films for television won.

> In many countries there is no early prospect of television supplanting sound broadcasting, sound remaining the main broadcasting medium. Nevertheless, television is an immensely powerful medium of growing scope and importance and our information services must take full advantage of its opportunities. The demand for television material of all kinds ... is growing fast and we must expect competition from other countries in meeting it. While it is too early to define a hard and fast policy, expansion should begin now ...[38]

To this end the COI would substantially increase its television activities to ensure that an hour of British material should be available to principal television stations around the world each week. The COI reported that it intended to quadruple the number of films adapted or specifically made for television by 1958 as its expenditure on this material rose from £25,000 to £110,000.[39]

By 1957 the British government was fully committed to policy of national projection and through expansion of the OIS established the machinery to propagate this, most significantly through the production of television material for overseas distribution. However, the successful implementation of this required more than the provision of additional resources. The development and output of the Overseas Television Service from 1954 would reveal fault lines in the structure of the OIS which would seriously compromise its ability to deliver the programmes demanded by this policy for many years.

Phase I: Foreign policy and propaganda (1954–1958)
Transatlantic Teleview, Commonwealth Teleview

In April 1954 Charles Dand, Director of the Films and Publications Division of the British Information Services in New York, proposed a series of 'interview-magazine[s] on film', *Transatlantic Teleview*, to be broadcast across the United States.[40] Using the intermediary of the interviewer, American people would become '... more familiar with our leading political and economic personalities ...' and more informed '... about our attitudes to current international problems and ... our own domestic problems which affect our relationships with the US and other countries.'[41] He envisaged that British political leaders would cease '... to be only a name or somebody far off but a person with whom they (the American people) have had a personal contact, somebody who has actually been in their homes'. The transformation of this idea into, initially, three thirteen-minute films took four months, involving the sponsoring department, in this case the Foreign Office, the COI and the production company.

Robert McKenzie, then foreign editor of *Picture Post*, was the face of the *Televiews* and later *Viewpoint*. These series dealt primarily with political issues by means of a single interview with one or two people, often conducted in their homes. In *Trans-atlantic Teleview* the informality of the setting complemented the ease with which McKenzie would discuss, cigarette in hand, 'Questions the Americans are asking about Britain', with people drawn from across the political spectrum. Subjects included the role of trade unions with Vic Feather, Secretary General of the Trades Union Congress; the future of Jamaica with its Chief Minister, Norman Manley; and Britain's colonial policy with A. Lennox-Boyd, Secretary of State for the Colonies.[42] Many of these series, particularly the *Televiews*, shared the same content although the approach adopted by the interviewer was slightly different in each.

Charles Dand also identified the format that would form the main output of the Overseas Television Service – the cinemagazine or magazine film.

> It is our view that what we are most in need of for U. S. television use is not the usual type of documentary film on subjects of lasting interest … but inexpensive films with a short life on subjects of topical interest in the political and economic relationships of the United States and the United Kingdom.[43]

These short film series, which presented topical material in a magazine format, were not an innovation prompted by the arrival of television. Cinemagazines as a genre had been a popular opening element in the British cinema programme since *Pathe Pictorial* in 1918. Indeed the format had been successfully utilised by the British government during the Second World War with magazine series such as *Worker and Warfront*.[44] However, the element that made them particularly attractive to the COI at this point was the flexibility of the magazine style, enabling it to cross over between cinema and television. As John Maddison of the COI noted in 1957, the perception within the organisation was that:

> While the spectacular growth of TV is enormously increasing its importance as an outlet for information films, overseas *non-theatrical* distribution, through film-lending libraries, mobile cinema vans and so on, established by BIS over the past fifteen years, will remain, certainly for a very long time to come, an essential instrument in projecting Britain abroad. The COI's aim is therefore to provide as great a proportion as possible of films suitable for television and non-theatrical use.[45]

Later, magazine series such as *This Week in Britain* were essentially produced as films, distributed through different media.[46]

The magazine series identified closely with its audience through the representative voice of the presenter, and later direct inclusion of audience members themselves. This helped it to communicate the ordinary, mundane and even technical information in an easily digestible form and more importantly, on a regular basis. This was particularly appropriate for television where '... the TV audience is subject to a greater degree of continuity and repetition of content and message, and this is important from our point of view'.[47] The series element was also an important factor for the 'hard-pressed' information officers tasked with persuading television stations to broadcast the material.

> The consensus of evidence in favour of the superior value of series against single films is conclusive and much can and should be done to plan our programmes in terms of series of some coherence in length, treatment and subject matter ... It is also apparent that television is less amenable than is the theatrical or non-theatrical film programme to the integrity and inviolability of the individual film.[48]

The magazine format could provide an entertaining visual drip-feed to inform, promote and persuade and this, together with the relatively cheap and rapid nature of production, would make it an ideal tool for national projection.

Within the OIS both *Transatlantic Teleview* and *Commonwealth Teleview* were viewed as successful, both in terms of what was produced and the extent of distribution achieved.[49] In the United States there were around 400 television stations, primarily commercial, operating at the beginning of 1955 and it was up to the individual information officers to make contact with television station managers and effectively syndicate the material. It was certainly hoped by BIS New York that a placement of between 150 and 200 stations could be achieved for *Transatlantic Teleview*, given its content, although the COI thought this optimistic.[50] By the end of January 1955, the first issue of *Transatlantic Teleview* was placed through the regional officers of BIS New York with around fifty stations.[51] Within a year the monthly release schedule was to around 150 stations, representing around 38% of the total stations available.[52] The estimated audience in 1956 was between 10 and 20 million.[53] Although the series successfully communicated what BIS New York required, it was less so in the projection of a nation, presenting Britain through a succession of politicians and other figures of authority who proceeded to explain political and economic points. While these programmes established the principles of an effective format of communication via the small screen, what they conveyed were essentially aspects of Foreign Office policy rather than a government policy of national projection.

The reason for this lies in the structure of the OIS itself, where policy was controlled by the individual Overseas Departments and separated from the machinery designed to propagate it. This was one of its defining characteristics and the main element that differentiated it from its predecessor, the Ministry of Information, which had had responsibility of overseas policy as well as the production of 'information'. Prior to 1946 the Foreign Office had argued successfully for the retention of policy by the Overseas Departments but the dangers inherent in this were recognised at Cabinet level when it was concluded that:

BFI/COI

Noeline Pritchard, presenter of *This Week in Britain* c. 1962

The projection of Britain abroad required the deliberate formulation of a comprehensive theme. Neither the Foreign Office alone, nor all the overseas departments together could discharge this work. It followed that the formulation of policy for overseas publicity must be conducted inter-departmentally and under the direction of a Minister.[54]

By the mid-1950s, the minister had long gone and an emaciated OIS had become increasingly insular in the face of repeated cuts in expenditure. Although expansion would provide the necessary machinery to deliver propaganda, it could only work effectively if lubricated by a great deal of coordination, directed at Cabinet level. This was the role Charles Hill was brought in to play in 1957. Although he referred to his role as Chancellor of the Duchy of Lancaster as 'Information Coordinator' he was really doing more than initiating a period of expansion and restructuring – he was attempting to rectify a basically dysfunctional institution. Initially this followed the pattern of development etched out by the home information services and was '… carefully worked out in the English way, as a result of trial and error'.[55]

Phase 2 – Propaganda informing policy? (1958–1959)
Dateline Britain, Topic, Viewpoint, Telerama Britanico

The second phase of development was characterised by experimentation with the formula established by the two *Televiews,* both of which were replaced in 1958. *Topic,* also known as *Meet the British* (1958–1959) took the place of *Transatlantic Teleview* on American television while *Dateline Britain* (1959) and *Viewpoint* (1957–1960) replaced *Commonwealth Teleview* in Canada and Australia, the only Commonwealth countries with television networks at this time. At this point sponsorship for the series remained quite separate with the Foreign Office funding material for the United States and Latin America, while the Commonwealth Relations Office sponsored programmes destined for Canada and Australia. All these magazine films followed roughly the same format, with each issue focusing on an aspect of contemporary Britain through a series of interviews with presenters encouraged to adopt a more informal approach that was felt to be more appropriate for television.[56] In the series *Dateline Britain* the Canadian couple Bernard Braden and Barbara Kelly introduced viewers to very diverse aspects of British life from British advances in science in TOMORROW IS ANOTHER WORLD to the teenage population in FACE OF YOUTH.[57] Across the border it was Joan and Julius Evans who in *Topic* explored a number of different issues ranging from children's cinema to Northern Ireland.[58] As national television stations expanded across Latin America, a new series was developed – *Telerama Britanico* (1958–?) – for this territory.[59] This news magazine initially consisted of a single topical story and was distributed with a commentary in both Latin American Spanish and Brazilian Portuguese. With few local production services in operation, demand for free content from any source was high and it was this that the British government sought to satisfy.

The pattern of gradual uptake by television stations in the United States experienced by *Transatlantic Teleview* repeated itself with *Topic*. Initially, on its release in 1959, it was only booked by forty-nine stations, thirty-three commercial and sixteen educational, but by October 1960, 129 stations had transmitted the entire series, with a further two broadcasting it, one booking it and eight repeating it. Of these 101 were commercial and thirty-nine educational, with an estimated audience of eleven million.[60] In Canada the distribution arrangement was different, with *Dateline Britain* and *Viewpoint* carried by the CBC. *Dateline Britain* was a networked show, carried on the CBC trans-Canada network, and was therefore also available to private stations taking certain CBC programmes. Although it was a current affairs programme shown on a Sunday afternoon a '… substantial number of Canadians must have seen one or more of the programmes.'[61] *Viewpoint* was a series of filmed contributions to CBC's own series, also called *Viewpoint*, which was shown on a daily basis after the evening news bulletin to a larger audience.

In 1958 the production of television material by the COI had more than doubled following the prioritisation of expansion set out in Hill's 1957 White Paper. However, this rapid expansion exposed a series of fault lines within the OIS that militated against the more rapid and cohesive approach demanded by the policy now being implemented by government. The two that proved the most severe at this point ran through the COI and the individual information services of the Overseas Departments. The COI had recognised early on that its own terms of reference made it impossible to produce films rapidly, that is, within a matter of weeks. John Grierson, Controller of Films, commented in 1950, 'McN's [N. F. McNicoll, Director of Films] memorandum is a valuable reminder … of the shortcomings of the COI terms of reference, as and if events assume urgency. Of this we have all been aware, with one or two of us holding the minority view that events have never been other than urgent and the COI terms of reference have accordingly been basically inadequate from the outset.'[62]

The whole process of producing a government film was a complex and bureaucratic one. Policy was controlled by the Department, which often limited the creative actions of the film company and compelled the COI to act as a mediating force between the two. Once the initial proposal for a film was accepted, the COI was briefed as to the requirements and would commission a treatment. There would then be a series of discussions between the COI and the writer, and once this was completed, the COI would discuss possible amendments with the Department. Once satisfied, the Department would sign it off and agree a budget. A production contract would be offered to a company with this three-way process of consultation then repeated at the rough-cut and final-cut stages. Delays were often incurred because the information officers within the Overseas Departments had no responsibility for specific productions and staff turnover was relatively high. Thomas Fife Clark, Director General of the COI from October 1954, while noting the successful operation between the Foreign Office and the COI with *Transatlantic Teleview*, observed that 'this policy control, which has to be reconciled with the needs of the medium in terms of presentation, is especially difficult to operate when the material is topical and the pace must be fast.'[63] With some series, such as *Topic*, the speed with which the films had to be made compromised the COI's position as an 'agency', forcing it to take over both as producer and director from contracted companies and effectively moving towards 'direct production'.[64] Furthermore this strict delineation between the policy function of the Overseas Departments and the production role of the COI was consistently cited to disclaim responsibility for the films produced in this period. By invoking its neutral 'agency' role, Fife Clark deflected any comments on COI films by stating that the responsibility for them ultimately rested with the Departments.[65] The Departments claimed that they did not have the expertise to judge them and this was devolved to the COI.[66] The production companies wanted more say in what was made but were basically prevented by the other two.[67]

The fact that policy effectively followed rapid expansion and engagement with a new medium revealed a second major fault line – inconsistent interpretations of policy within the Departments themselves. With series such as *Dateline Britain* the content and presentation were moving steadily towards a picture of Britain but the uneven quality of this series and others reflected uncertainty about what should be communicated and how television should convey this. One of the most controversial issues of *Dateline Britain* was the first, FACE OF YOUTH, which attempted to portray the whole spectrum of British teenagers stretching from the coffee bars of Soho to the life of a debutante who interviewed by the author Colin Wilson.[68] Although approved by the Commonwealth Relations Office in London before its broadcast, it initiated a dialogue between Donald Kerr, the Director of UKIS in Ottawa and later Overseas Controller of the COI, and Alistair Scott of the CRO in London, which highlights the existence of fundamental differences of intent and expression within the information services.

In his report on *Dateline Britain* Kerr states: '… our job is to present hard information to Canadians and not to entertain them, except when a little entertaining can smooth the way for presenting much hard information,' indicating a relatively narrow view of what was to be communicated. This, in his eyes, is at odds with the material produced. He goes on to note that:

> Any assessment of this sort of programme must be related to the objective. If the objective was to open the door of the C.B.C. to future T.V. opportunities then the series was an almost unqualified success. If the objective was to present mainly entertainment and a background sketch (not picture) of Britain, the series was reasonably successful. But if the objective was to present hard information, even in sketch form, of modern Britain, then the series had only a limited success.[69]

The priority for Kerr was to communicate certain points of policy, the medium of which happened to be television. His concern here was that BIS was being swept up by demand for television material and in satisfying it, it was losing sight of what the material, in his view, should be doing. For Alastair Scott, however, the intention was very different. It was 'to present an impression … rather than an exposition of some aspects of official policy':[70]

> I disagree with … his definition of 'hard information'. It seems to me very important that overseas peoples should have some 'hard information' in film terms about what British people are feeling and thinking in their everyday occupations. What he calls 'hard information' in my view is adequately dealt with in the other media, and the film is a medium above all which can present a 'personal' view of Britain and the British.[71]

The problem was that these individual interpretations of policy coupled with Departmental concerns had resulted in series that were inconsistent in style and content, effectively presenting fractured facets of Britain. As the potential global audience expanded over the next five years the content became more constant, resented in a format that could be repackaged for different audiences.

Phase 3: Propaganda reflecting policy (1959–1963)
This Week in Britain, British Calendar, Middle East Newspots (Letter from London), People and Places, Report from London, Ticket to London, Portrait

By 1960 the 'interview magazine' series such as *Topic* were replaced with a 'low cost news magazine series' called *British Calendar*, later *Calendar* (1959–1969) and this marked a shift in content and style that would be replicated in established areas of

84

distribution such as the United States and new 'territories', such as Africa and the Middle East.[72] *British Calendar* closely mirrored the traditional cinemagazine format with each issue comprising around six stories linked by a commentator. The content was a mix of political stories, scientific innovation and lifestyle items, some of which were acquired from the two British companies still producing newsreels at this time, Associated British-Pathe and British Movietone, and some from the supplier of news for the ITV commercial channel, Independent Television News. Increasingly items were shot by a dedicated film crew, established as part of a small unit, operating under the title 'In Britain Now', within the Television and Newsreels division of the COI with a remit to produce topical 'news background' material.[73] At first *British Calendar* was issued on a monthly basis, but by July 1961 it was flown to New York every fortnight, and from mid-1964 every week. In 1963 it achieved a 'record distribution' of 115 stations.[74] Occasionally single items were extracted by BIS New York and placed within news programmes such as 'Today'.[75] Although designed specifically for the United States, *British Calendar* was also broadcast in Canada and Australia and gradually seemed to infiltrate the format of *Telerama Britanico*.[76] These versions had a title sequence stating 'British Information Services present British Calendar – A News Magazine From Britain and the Commonwealth', whereas the version for the United States was re-voiced and contained no credits.[77] Up to this point every programme distributed in the United States, Canada and Australia had effectively declared its origin. It is more likely this change was the result of demands from information officers and station managers for more 'unobtrusive' material than a conscious decision taken within the OIS.[78] Nevertheless this represents a significant change in how these programmes were disseminated and possibly received: the audience might now think these items were produced by the station itself.

This technique of dropping unattributed official British material into television schedules was certainly adopted for what was to be the COI's longest-running series, *This Week in Britain* (1959–1980), initially piloted in Latin America. These five-minute films were '… intended for programming with local television newsreels and will provide an item of interest from Britain, topical if possible, but of a "behind the headlines" character rather than newsreel'.[79] Initially *This Week in Britain* was produced in two versions, Latin American Spanish and Brazilian Portuguese, each of which was introduced by a 'woman reporter', Leda Casares and Madalena Nicol respectively. By July 1960 a weekly schedule was established and its distribution spread to Cuba and Columbia (September 1959), Honduras (May 1960), Costa Rica and Mexico (July 1960) and Panama (November 1960). This rapid take-up led to the creation of five further versions in the course of 1960 and established a system of 're-versioning' series that would provide a formula to meet the demand of a rapidly expanding global market in the early 1960s. There were two separate versions for Canada and Australia (and the Commonwealth in general), presented by women such as Ann Forsyth and Noeline Pritchard, with a 'standard English' edition for New Zealand, east and west Nigeria, India and Southern Rhodesia. In October Persian and Arabic versions were produced for weekly distribution to Beirut and Tehran by mid-November.

This Week in Britain was particularly popular in Australia where it was networked through the Australian Broadcasting Corporation and shown at the peak hour of 8.25 pm on Saturday evenings, with *British Calendar* getting 'very good use' by several commercial stations.[80] By the following year fifteen-minute compilations of back issues of *This Week in Britain* were produced to meet demand not only from television, with new country stations starting up, but non-theatrical outlets as well.[81] By 1961 the user reports from Canada stated that twenty-two stations used *British Calendar* on a monthly basis and thirty-nine *This Week in Britain*, describing the scale of distribution in the country, with *British Television News*, part of the COI news provision, as 'impressive'.[82] This success was mirrored in Latin America where, for example, it was shown at a similar time in Mexico and on 80% of the television channels in Sao Paulo.[83] By 1963 the Television and Newsreels Division would claim that '[*This Week in Britain*] is now one of the world's most widely seen television news programmes'.[84] *Telerama Britanico* complemented *This Week in Britain* with stations usually carrying one or the other, and in some cases both. In both the Middle East and Africa, these series were placed with all the stations and often repeated.

This Week in Britain was the fourth series to be produced for the Middle East in eighteen months. Two that served as forerunners to it were *People and Places* (1959–1960), a series of thirteen-minute films in Arabic, and *Report from London* (1959–1960), which contained similar content but was presented in Persian. The format was identical in each, with a male presenter, Ali Nour or Hannah Jamil (Arabic) and Hussein Darabaghi (Persian), introducing a single story from Britain.[85] By the following year these seem to have been amalgamated into a single new series, *Middle East Newspots*, later known as *Letter from London* (1960–1970), which was transmitted alongside *This Week in Britain*. Earlier, in June 1959, the Foreign Office had approved the first in 'a new series of Arab Televiews'. *Portrait* (1959–1965) was a series of fifteen-minute films each showing a different occupation followed in Britain and these effectively bucked the trend towards a more 'news magazine'-orientated format. The pilot, dubbed in Persian, featured the work of a bricklayer in Harlow New Town, and later issues would feature a watchmaker and

BFI/COI

Ann Forsyth, presenter of *This Week in Britain* c. 1962

a lorry driver.[86] *Portrait* was another series that would rapidly be produced in different language versions – English, Hindi and Arabic by May 1960, and, in this case, visually adapted for specific audiences in Africa as well as the Middle East. It was:

> … an example of a technique increasingly used in our television production of making films which appear to have been tailored for a specified territory but which, in effect, are mass produced for many territories … The versions for Nigeria feature a Nigerian artist who is seen in the introduction to the film and subsequently with the subject of the film. Similarly an Indian artist is seen in the Indian version – but the bulk of the shooting is common to all versions.[87]

By December 1962 *Portrait* formed part of the schedule for the new Kenyan television service, as well as being used non-theatrically in Ghana and Uganda.

Although most series produced by the COI had a multi-use function, some were very specific, such as *Moslems in Britain* (1961 and 1964), which was only produced in Arabic for distribution in the Middle East. These twenty-eight minute films took an in-depth view at the lives of Muslim communities in Cardiff and Manchester through interviews in Arabic conducted by Gemal Kinay.[88] A further two, focusing on Liverpool and Sheffield, were scripted but never shot and it seemed like the series would be very short-lived. However, in 1964 two further films, PEOPLE and PLACES, were produced along more thematic lines.[89]

The development of this more cohesive image of Britain was underpinned by restructuring within the OIS that took place during this phase and proved particularly effective in two main areas. The first was far greater coordination throughout the organisation, primarily facilitated by the committee established by Hill in 1957. This met on a regular basis, initially twice a week, to coordinate the work of the different overseas information departments and the COI and helped to catalyse and consolidate changes that were already taking place within Departments. For example, within the Foreign Office the 'operations' side of the information service was gradually given greater responsibility and recognition resulting in the formation by the early 1960s of the Information Executive Department, within which was established a section with sole responsibility for film and television. This acted as an important liaison between the COI and the Foreign Office to ensure the overseas posts had what they required. The second area concerned the COI and the increasing level of autonomy it experienced in its relationship with the departments. It could now, for example, communicate directly with Foreign Office posts to receive feedback on programmes without having to go through London. The expansion of the COI in both numbers and experience also shifted the weight of initiative in programme development from the Departments. For example, Raylton Fleming was instrumental in the creation of *British Calendar,* while another COI staff member, Roseanne Brownrigg, proposed *Telerama Britanico* in 1958.[90] Series such as *This Week in Britain* were now jointly sponsored by the Departments and this, together with the regularity of these 'running services', led to a more hands-off approach, with approval required at the script and sometimes only the show copy stage.

These measures contributed to a greater understanding and confidence or, as Marett terms it, 'forbearance', within the OIS during this period and the television material produced reflects this increased adhesion within the organisation. Britain was now presented in a consistent format, 'the news magazine', tailored to suit a diverse international audience. Although the portrayal of the nation was no longer a fractured one it was, however, still split. What emerged from this regular transmission of topical stories were two Britains, or more accurately, two Englands (very few stories moved over the two borders), one modern, the other traditional. These aspects would finally coalesce in 1964 through the distinctive contemporary style of *London Line*, providing a mode of national presentation that still resonates today.

Phase 4: The reconciliation of policy and propaganda
London Line

London Line was the COI's first studio-based magazine programme produced at the Granville Studios in Fulham, London. It was jointly sponsored and made in four versions for weekly distribution: one version for the 'Old Commonwealth', Australia and Canada; one for the 'New Commonwealth', primarily the newly independent states of Africa and the Caribbean; as *Aqui Londres* for Latin America and an Arabic edition *Adwa Wa Aswat*. As the title suggests most of the topical content was centred on London, something which had been prefigured in earlier series such as *Report from London, Letter from London* and *Ticket to London*. A general issue would contain primarily cultural stories, many featuring live music and scientific breakthroughs mixed in with interviews. Although there was some crossover of content, many stories were specifically designed for the target audience of each edition. For example, one of the earliest issues of *London Line* (New Commonwealth version) featured an interview with the Reverend Ogundura, a parish priest from Nigeria working in Britain, together with a music item from Mike Falana and the African Messengers.[91] Above all, the style of London Line was completely contemporary, reflected in the studio, the presenters and most evocatively in its title sequence, which was specifically foregrounded. These sequences were particularly important since they were repeated on a regular basis and effectively functioned in a similar way to an advertisement, distilling Britain into a single package lasting around twenty seconds. Designed by Eddie Newstead, the *London Line* titles utilised the latest techniques of graphic design to present a rapidly cut collage of black-and-white illustrations including a London street map, Nelson reflected in a woman's sunglasses, television sets, tower blocks and the Beatles, culminating in the words 'London Line African Correspondents Reporting From London'. Here contemporary London represents Britain, the traditional is presented in a modern guise and all content has a 'progressive' aspect. This change in style also reflected an appreciation of the changing nature of its audience. Through television the government was crossing boundaries of literacy and reaching a much wider audience both geographically and perhaps more importantly generationally. *London Line* was a programme designed to appeal to children and teenagers as well as their parents. In 1954 Drogheda had stated that the role of the OIS was to influence 'the opinion makers'. Within a decade the British government was producing programmes designed, consciously or subconsciously, to influence the opinion-makers of the future.

By 1964 a cohesive visual presentation of Britain as a modern and progressive nation was being delivered through magazine series to millions of television sets around the world. In many ways this image, centred on contemporary aspects of London but rooted in British heritage, represented a visual integration of govern-ment's view of Britain articulated in 1957: '… a people proud of the past but living in the present and confident of the future'.[92] It is an ethos which continues to remain at the heart of the 'promotion' of Britain today.[93] This integrated projection of the nation not only reflected the fact that the OIS now functioned more efficiently but also that the OIS had finally come in from the cold, its role now understood and accepted in Whitehall. 'If they [OIS] were being expanded, this was not through the blind workings of Parkinson's Law, but as the result of a deliberate policy of the government of the day, based on a series of exhaustive enquiries, first by the officials concerned, then by an independent body of private citizens, and finally by Ministers.'[94] This ensured the continuous production of magazine series for overseas distribution well into the 1990s with productions such as *The Pacemakers* (1969–1971), *Living Tomorrow* (1969–1983), *Perspective* (1983–1996) and *UK Today* (1989–1995).

Conclusion

In 1957 a decade of arbitrary cuts levelled at the Overseas Information Service came to an end as the British government, in the wake of Suez, belatedly realised the value of national projection and the necessity of investing in it. If the push of Suez compelled the government to implement this policy, it was the demand generated by the global expansion of television, and the fear that the United States might satisfy it, that pulled it into projecting Britain through this new medium. The process of realising this policy proved to be a problematic one as the struggle of the OIS to convey a cohesive image of Britain on the small screen mirrored its own endeavour to overcome inherent dysfunctional aspects within the organisation. Essentially these revolved around the distinct separation of an often inarticulate policy from the machinery designed to propagate it and were eventually reconciled through a high level of coordination, rooted in an appreciation that staff required a basic level of understanding of both the message and the medium. It had taken the government many years to learn this lesson and it was one that would be repeated on a regular basis for decades to come, as both coordination and understanding were allowed to lapse.

Although this period saw Britain fully engaged in the art of national projection, the process of mastering it is still ongoing, as the recent independent review on public diplomacy led by Lord Carter of Coles bears testimony to.[95] The recognition by Lord Carter of the vital role of a coordinated infrastructure, designed to support both a clear articulation of policy and the means to deliver and assess it, indicates that an end to this cycle of relearning might be in sight. Ironically the place occupied by bodies such as the Public Diplomacy Board and the Public Diplomacy Partners Group is very close to the borderline advocated by Tallents over seventy years ago.[96] However, the role of moving images within the delivery of this is an ambivalent one. Although the Foreign and Commonwealth Office has a dedicated television news vehicle in British Satellite News, its Film and Television Unit is rarely utilised, with the full potential of this medium in the integrated digital delivery of information lost.[97] It remains to be seen whether these mechanisms for increased coordination will promote a shared understanding that goes beyond that of 'common purpose'.

Notes

1   The National Archives of the UK (TNA): Public Record Office (PRO) INF 8/41 February 1963, p. 1. Broadcast times from http://televisionau.siv.net.au/tvguide.htm (accessed 24 January 2007).

2   See Table 1 Overseas Television Service magazine series 1954–1964. The data for most of these film series can be found on the British Universities Newsreel Database at http://www.bufvc.ac.uk/cinemagazines. This has been constructed from a variety of sources including production documents at The National Archives, London, and on microfilm at BFI Archive Footage Sales and the BUFVC, COI index cards and film catalogues. It is these sources that are cited in relation to specific issues since very few of these film series still survive. Those that do are held at BFI Archive Footage Sales and the BFI National Archive, London.

3   Although British government information policy and film production in the early years of the COI, generally from 1946 to 1951, has been analysed, most notably by Martin Moore, *The Origins of Modern Spin: Democratic Government and the Media in Britain, 1945–51* (London: Palgrave MacMillan, 2006); Mariel Grant, 'Towards a Central Office of Information: Continuity and Change in British Government Information Policy, 1939–51', *Journal of Contemporary History*, vol. 34 no. 1 (1999); Albert Hogenkamp, *The British Documentary Movement and the 1945–51 Labour Governments* (Ph.D. thesis, Westminster College, Oxford, 1991); and Alan J. Harding, 'The Closure of the Crown Film Unit in 1952: Artistic Decline or Political Machinations?', *Contemporary British History*, vol. 18 no. 4 (2004), little was specifically been written about overseas information policy and propaganda post-1952, with the exception of 'Power, Public Opinion and the Propaganda of Decline: The British Information Services and the Cold War, 1945–57' in Philip M. Taylor, *British Propaganda In The Twentieth Century* (Edinburgh: Edinburgh University Press, 1999) until quite recently with works such as James R. Vaughn, *Failure of American and British Propaganda in the Arab Middle East, 1945–57* (London: Palgrave Macmillan, 2005) and 'A Certain Idea of Britain: British

Cultural Diplomacy in the Middle East, 1945–57', *Contemporary British History*, vol. 19 no. 2 (2005) and Alban Webb, 'Auntie Goes To War Again: The BBC External Services, the Foreign Office and the Early Cold War', *Media History*, vol. 12 no. 2 (2006) signalling a resurgence of interest.

4   Sir Stephen Tallents, *The Projection of England* (London: Film Centre, 1955), p. 38 [originally published Faber and Faber, 1932].

5   Tallents, ibid., p. 40.

6   The existence of this statistical evidence, collated from the inconsistent feedback from posts, has been gleaned from references within reports (see endnote 49 for more details) and virtually none of it seems to have survived.

7   I have used this definition of propaganda, and its delineation with policy, in line with contemporary usage by people such as Robert Marett, Head of the Information Policy Department (1952–1955) and later Assistant Under-Secretary of State (1959–1962) at the Foreign Office.

8   Report of the Committee on Government Information Services, 9 February 1946 CAB 129/7, CP (46) 54. Cited in Taylor, *British Propaganda in the Twentieth Century*, p. 232.

9   Taylor, ibid.

10 For an incisive analysis of the use and re-assessment of film in the provision of information at home see Moore, op. cit., particularly pp. 55–98.

11 See Table 2 Total COI Expenditure 1945–1946 – 1964–1965. These figures are for the *total* net estimate provision of the COI, including all divisions and are taken from Sir Fife Clark, *The Central Office of Information* (London: George Allen & Unwin, 1970), Appendix VI, p. 172.

12 TNA: PRO INF 8/30 April 1953 p. 13.

13 Five in the *Democratic Way* series were given Treasury approval in November 1952.

14 Robert Marett, *Through the Back Door* (London: Pergamon Press, 1968), p. 146.

15 Ibid. p. 147.

16 *Summary of the Report of the Independent Committee of Enquiry into the Overseas Information Services April 1954* [Drogheda Report], Cmd. 9138, p. 4.

17 Ibid. p. 5.

18 The Beaverbrook press was not an advocate of the OIS in the late 1940s. 'The British Council, as is well-known, shares with the Arts Council and the British Information Services the honour of exciting in Beaverbrook and (by infection or instruction) in his newspapers the sort of blind fury which used to make Marshal Goring reach for his revolver when he heard the word "culture"', Tom Driberg, *Beaverbrook* (Hamish Hamilton, 1972), p. 156, quoted in Frances Donaldson, *The British Council: The First Fifty Years* (London: Jonathan Cape, 1984).

19 Drogheda Report, p. 4.

20 Ibid.

21 Ibid. p. 4.

22 Ibid. p. 7.

23 Marett, op. cit., p. 169.

24 *Third Report from the Select Committee on Estimates Together With Minutes of the Evidence taken before Sub-Committee E (Commonwealth Relations Office), Session 1958–59*, p. 106. Taken from the evidence of former Directors of Information in India and Pakistan, Mr J. T. Hughes and Mr R. Samples. Later Thomas Fife Clark, Director General of the COI, refuted that the Information Service was responsible for this, as above, *Sub-Committee F (Central Office of Information), Session 1959–60*, p. 59.

25   Jan Melissen (ed.), *The New Public Diplomacy* (London: Palgrave Macmillan, 2005), p. 9.

26   Lord Hill of Luton, *Both Sides of the Hill*, (William Heinemann, 1964), p. 179.

27   There was a perceptible shift in popular acceptance of national self advertisement by this time with campaigns such as 'Operation Britain'. This was launched by the Advertising Council for Great Britain, a voluntary organisation of advertisers and media owners with the aim of facilitating 'a fresh projection of Britain on a far-reaching scale'. TNA: PRO INF 12/693.

28   Lord Hill, op. cit., p. 202.

29   Marett, op. cit., p. 181.

30   *Third Report from the Select Committee on Estimates Together With Minutes of the Evidence taken before Sub-Committee F (Central Office of Information), Session 1959–60.*

31   Sir Fife Clark, op. cit., p. 172. These figures are net estimate provisions.

32   See Table 3 Total COI Film Expenditure 1954–1955 – 1964–1965. These have been compiled from the *Third Report from the Select Committee on Estimates Together With Minutes of the Evidence taken before Sub-Committee F (Central Office of Information), Session 1959–60* for 1954–1955 – 1959–1960 and from Derrick Knight and Vincent Porter, op. cit., p.118 for 1960–1961 – 1963–1964.

33   Drogheda Report, op. cit., p. 4.

34   TNA: PRO INF 12/681, Nye to Crookshank, November 1953.

35   TNA: PRO INF 12/681. Quoted in 'Final Draft of Export of UK TV Material to Canada – Report of Committee of Officials', p. 3.

36   TNA: PRO INF 12/681, Garner to Dean, 23 July 1954.

37   TNA: PRO INF 12/681, Carstairs to Dean, 24 July 1954. However it did take time for the full impact of television to be recognised. This was still a time when broadcast referred to sound and even five years later the Foreign Office would still warn against over-estimating the importance of the new medium. *Third Report from the Select Committee, Sub-Committee F*, p. 13.

38   *Overseas Information Service*, Cmnd. 225, p. 5.

39   'Projecting Britain – without Projectors', *Film User*, no. 130 (August 1957), p. 334.

40   TNA: PRO INF 6/1976, Dand to Senior, April 1954. Reproduced in full in this volume.

41   Ibid.

42   VICTOR FEATHER, *Transatlantic Teleview* issue no. 4, 1955, TNA: PRO INF 6/1978; NORMAN MANLEY, *Transatlantic Teleview* issue no. 10, 1955, TNA: PRO INF 6/1981 and MR LENNOX-BOYD, *Transatlantic Teleview* issue no. 1, 1954, TNA: PRO INF 6/1976.

43   TNA: PRO INF 6/1976, op. cit.

44   See Erwin F. Erhardt, *War Aims for the Workforce: British Workers Newsreels during the Second World War* (Ph.D. thesis, University of Cincinnati, 1996).

45   TNA: PRO INF 12/683, Maddison to Ballantyne, 1 March 1957.

46   This perception of producing films for television is echoed by John Schlesinger's recollection of making *Monitor* for the BBC in the late 1950s. 'I felt I was making *films* at the BBC ... she [Grace Wyndham Goldie, Assistant Head of Television Talks] would say, "You're making television." And I would say, "No, I'm making a film for television." But she insisted, "No, you're making television." I never have been able to understand the difference.' Quoted in William J. Mann, *Edge of Midnight: The Life of John Schlesinger* (London: Arrow, 2004), p. 154.

47   TNA: PRO INF 12/68, 'COI Television – Report by Mr John Maddison', 2 February 1955, p. 14.

48   TNA: PRO INF 12/681, 'Films For Television Overseas', 1955, p. 7.

49 Although the COI compiled statistical information on distribution and audience figures through formal bi-annual reports and correspondence from the information officers in the field, little evidence of this has survived. The reporting procedures become more formalised and frequent during this period, partly due to recommendations from the Drogheda Report. Bi-annual reports from the major posts were established by 1957, none of which have survived for this period, although they are referred to in the monthly divisional reports. All these survive for the period except 1956 and 1958. They continued until October 1963 when they were replaced by more general progress reports, which no longer survive. These reports were supplemented by correspondence and reports on individual issues, especially at the stage of initial release, a few of which are still extant. There is also evidence from labels inside the film cans ('Please fill in enclosed Audience Statistics form. It is very important to us.') that the COI issued audience statistics forms with prints. However, there is little indication, in both the reports and correspondence, from where the figures derive and to what extent; in the case of television, they take account of repeats in transmission. What there is comes filtered through the monthly divisional reports of the Films Division, drawing a picture of reception, in terms of audience figures, that is a fragmented and coloured one. The monthly divisional reports generally show activities in a positive light. When they were replaced by shorter progress reports in November 1963, Nigel Bicknell of the COI referred to the existing system as '… an example of the established Divisional rivalry making each Division only put its very best face on view'. TNA: PRO INF 8/41, Bicknell to McMillan and Barns, 5 December 1962 [sic].

50 TNA: PRO INF 8/32, January 1955, p. 9.

51 Ibid.

52 TNA: PRO INF 8/32, December 1955, p. 12.

53 TNA: PRO INF 12/683, Fife Clark to Johnstone, 17 July 1956.

54 Minutes of a meeting of the Cabinet committee on the postwar organisation of government publicity, 18 September 1945, CAB 78/37, GEN 85/1. Cited in Taylor, op. cit., p. 232.

55 Marjorie Ogilvy-Webb, *The Government Explains: A Study of the Information Services* (London: George Allen & Unwin, 1965), p. 12.

56 TNA: PRO INF 12/683, Maddison to Ballantyne, 1 March 1957. Referring more specifically to the nature of commentaries John Maddison of the COI notes, 'Commentary is styled to the national or regional audience and is more intimate, casual, ad-libbed or informal than are film commentaries.'

57 TOMORROW IS ANOTHER WORLD, *Dateline Britain* issue no. 4, 1959, TNA: PRO INF 6/840 and FACE OF YOUTH, *Dateline Britain* issue no. 1, 1959, TNA: PRO INF 6/838.

58 NORTHERN IRELAND, *Topic* issue no. 7, 1959, TNA: PRO INF 6/2013 and CHILDREN'S CINEMA, *Topic* issue no. 12, 1959, TNA: PRO INF 6/1361.

59 David Fisher, *Start of Television Services*, http://www.terramedia.co.uk/reference/ TV_service_starts.htm, (accessed 8 February 2008). Some Latin American countries had television by the early 1950s – Brazil (1951), Argentina (1951), Venezuela (1952) and Columbia (1954) – but the main increase came in the late 1950s, as others, such as Peru (1958), Chile (1958) and Ecuador (1959) established services.

60 TNA: PRO INF 8/37, October 1960, p. 14. Initially it was booked by forty-nine stations in the first six months of its release in 1959.

61 TNA: PRO INF 12/786, 'Report on "Dateline Britain" by United Kingdom Information Service, Canada', 1958.

62 TNA: PRO INF 12/295, memo John Grierson to Robert Fraser, Director General of COI, 14 August 1950.

63 TNA: PRO INF 12/683, Fife Clark to Johnston, 17 July 1956, p. 8.

64 TNA: PRO INF 12/683, Langston to Hadfield and Thomas, no date. John Langston, Director of the Films Division, justified the production methods used for *Topic* stating, 'I know of no other way by which we could successfully produce either at short notice or at long television films for overseas than that by which the PCO [Production Control Officer] in charge of each series is in creative charge of the film-making and its associated editing.'

65 *Third Report from the Select Committee on Estimates Together With Minutes of the Evidence taken before Sub-Committee F (Central Office of Information), Session 1959–60*, p. 23.

66 *Third Report, Sub-Committee E*, op. cit., p. 106.

67 *Third Report, Sub-Committee F*, op. cit., p. 218. Memorandum submitted by the Association of Specialised Film Producers included a proposal for the establishment of an Inter-Departmental Planning Board.

68 TNA: PRO INF 6/838, FACE OF YOUTH, *Dateline Britain* issue no. 1, 1959.

69 TNA: PRO INF 12/786, 'Report on "Dateline Britain" by United Kingdom Information Service, Canada', 1959, p. 4.

70 TNA: PRO INF 12/786, Scott to Caplan, 11 February 1959.

71 TNA: PRO INF 12/786, Scott to Langston, 8 April 1959.

72 TNA: PRO INF 8/36, December 1959, p. 27.

73 The establishment of the unit was discussed in the 1959 White Paper and accepted by the Third Committee on Estimates 1960. The COI argued that the unit was required because appropriate stories not covered by existing commercial companies and if so, not necessarily from the angle or within the time desired by government. Although reported as a possible successor to Crown, the scale was smaller and the remit specifically concerned with new provision. 'C.O.I. Want New Government Film Unit', *The Times* 7 October 1960, p. 8, and 'The State as a Sponsor', *Film User*, no. 169 (November 1960), p. 625.

74 TNA: PRO INF 8/41, July/August 1963, p. 9.

75 TNA: PRO INF 8/40, July/August 1962, p. 26.

76 TNA: PRO INF 8/37, November 1960, p. 19. A Latin American version of *British Calendar* was produced for distribution in December. This seems to have been issued as *Telerama Britanico*.

77 *British Calendar*, issue no. 174, 1966.

78 E-mail John Hall to Linda Kaye 23 January 2007.

79 TNA: PRO INF 8/36, February 1959, p. 9.

80 Ibid.

81 TNA: PRO INF 8/40, February 1962, p. 4.

82 TNA: PRO INF 8/38, April 1961, p. 20.

83 TNA: PRO INF 8/38, May 1961, p. 15 and INF 8/39 September 1961, p. 26.

84 TNA: PRO INF 8/41, February 1963, p. 1.

85 *British National Film Catalogue* 1963, p. 21.

86 LORRY DRIVER, *Portrait* issue no. 3, 1960 and WATCHMAKER, *Portrait* issue no. 5, 1960. COI index cards at BFI Archival Footage Sales, London.

87 TNA: PRO INF 8/38, February 1961, p. 1.

88 MANCHESTER, *Moslems in Britain* issue no. 1, 1961 and CARDIFF, *Moslems in Britain* issue no. 2, 1961. TNA: PRO INF 6/1323–4.

89   PEOPLE, *Moslems in Britain* issue no. 3, 1964 and PLACES, *Moslems in Britain* issue no. 4, 1964. TNA: PRO INF 6/1325–6.

90   TNA: PRO: INF 8/36, February 1959.

91   *London Line*, issue no. 4, 1964, TNA: PRO INF 6/1062.

92   *Overseas Information Service*, Cmnd. 225, p. 3.

93   This is reflected in current Foreign and Commonwealth Office publications such as *The UK: A Modern Tradition*. See: http://www.fco.gov.uk/servlet/Front?pagename= OpenMarket/Xcelerate/ShowPage&c=Page&cid=1153392131956 (accessed 8 February 2008)

94   Marett, op. cit., p. 182.

95   Lord Carter of Coles, *Public Diplomacy Review* (2005), http://www.fco.gov.uk/servlet/ Front?pagename=OpenMarket/Xcelerate/ShowPage&c=Page&cid=1007029395249 (accessed 13/2/2007)

96   *Third Report from the Foreign Affairs Committee Public Diplomacy* (June 2006), Cm 6840, p. 4. See: http://www.official-documents.gov.uk/documents/cm68/6840/6840.pdf (accessed 21 April 2008)

97   Carter, op. cit., p. 49.

FOOTBALL, FASHION AND FACTORIES: CONTINUITY AND CHANGE IN THE PROJECTION OF BRITAIN 1964–1975

Linda Kaye

In this article, Linda Kaye looks at the development of Britain's image through the production of official film and television magazine series from the mid-1960s arguing that technical innovation, government information policy and the demands of an international audience led to the re-presentation of traditional themes as well as projecting the margins of British society.

In 1962 George Carstairs concluded his BBC Reith Lecture, in which he had conducted a psychological survey of the state of the nation, with the observation that '… we shall participate most fruitfully in the coming world community if we keep alive a good measure of our eccentricities, our private visions, and our peculiar variations on the pattern of mankind.'[1] In the same year the Central Office of Information (COI) produced *Roundabout*, its first colour cinemagazine series for overseas distribution, destined for South and South-East Asia. Made by Pathe, and later British Movietone, *Roundabout* presented aspects of British life which echoed many articulated by Stephen Tallents decades earlier in his seminal booklet *The Projection of England* – the Monarchy, parliamentary institutions, literature, sport, the countryside, industry – together with particular places and buildings.[2] Staff working on these COI productions condensed these core elements that effectively summed up Britain into one phrase: 'football, fashion and factories'.

This workable template at the heart of thousands of programmes produced by the COI was the result of the British government's policy of national projection. This aimed to generate a British presence on the screens of the world, thereby creating a favourable climate of opinion to support British government policies and increasingly during this period Britain's export drive. However, this nation brand, which sought to present these elements with a contemporary veneer, underwent a subtle metamorphosis during this period.[3] By seeking to portray the modern aspects of Britain over many years, these programmes inevitably drew more frequently from the margins of technology, society and even the national character where these 'peculiar variations' described by Carstairs were particularly ingrained.

MINI BIKE *Living Tomorrow* issue no. 159, 1975

This article will examine the development of the magazine output of the Overseas Information Service (OIS) during this period and through it, explore how the core subjects and values outlined by Tallents were re-presented and supplemented by the eccentricities and innovation valued by Carstairs. Through an analysis of the major series produced it will describe the factors that led to the mediation of this image, including the new colour technology, shifts in government information policy, the restructuring of the COI, and ultimately the changing demands of the audience itself.

London Line (1964–1979)

From 1964 to 1979 Britain's image was becoming gradually saturated in colour as the COI responded to the demands of the marketplace. The COI's first foray into colour was with *Roundabout,* which was produced in Technicolor from 1962. Charles Beauclerk, on whose recommendation the series was produced, had recognised the importance of creating a product that would distinguish itself sufficiently in the already overcrowded market of the cinema programme, and the same reasoning informed the decision to start producing the television magazine series *London Line* in colour in 1966. This expensive technology presented formidable technical challenges and the presentation of content once again highlighted the tensions between the government department formulating the message and the programme makers presenting it to a target audience. These finally precipitated a complete restructuring of programme output and revision of how Britain was projected by the end of the decade.

London Line was the COI's first studio-based magazine programme and had been produced at the Granville Studios in Fulham, London, since 1964. It was made in four versions for weekly distribution: one version for the 'Old Commonwealth', Australia, Canada and the United States; one for the 'New Commonwealth', primarily the newly independent states of Africa and the Caribbean; as *Aqui Londres* for Latin America and an Arabic edition *Adwa Wa Aswat*. It was, however, only the 'Old Commonwealth' version that would make the transition to a colour format by the end of 1966. Although colour transmissions had been operational for some time in the United States, the sale of colour television sets began to take off in 1964 and it was clear that in order to preserve a foothold in this market, programmes would have to be supplied in colour. This was given further impetus by the regular experimental colour television programming undertaken by the Canadian Broadcasting Corporation (CBC) in September 1966.[4] To test the reception of colour television in North America an experiment was conducted during which British Information Services (BIS) in New York received one issue of *Calendar* (a topical magazine distributed from 1960) each month in colour and BIS Ottawa received thirteen programmes of *London Line* in colour. The decision was then taken to produce a colour *London Line* that would serve both the United States and Canada, with additional use in Australia, New Zealand and the Caribbean. Although colour production was expensive, the costs would now be split between the two posts, although BIS New York would bear the brunt of them. Additional finance was also available as a result of the review on the Overseas Information Service carried out by Sir Harold Beeley. His report, published in 1967, recommended the allocation of extra funds for colour to 'maintain our capacity to take the opportunities presented to us in this outstandingly effective medium'.[5]

Although the demand was unequivocal, the production of a colour television series in the context of international distribution was less straightforward. At this point there were three competing television standards, the American NTSC that was also used in Latin America, the French SECAM and the European PAL, and although video-playback equipment was slowly spreading it was expensive both to install and run. The international medium for distribution was still 16mm film, so a system had to be devised which would enable the COI to continue using the existing studio set-up with editing and distribution facilities to produce colour film. The result was 'an ingenious hybrid' – the Gemini system, which basically attached a 16mm film camera to a standard studio black-and-white television camera.

The first programme using this method was filmed in September 1967 and broadcast the same month.[7] However, despite all the extensive consultation between the posts and the COI prior to the launch, within five months BIS New York had concluded that the programme was not likely to fulfil its role in the United States. This led to the establishment of a sub-committee on television overseas under the chairmanship of Mr R. McC. Samples, Assistant Under Secretary of State at the Commonwealth Office, which was charged with examining two main questions. The first concerned the role of government-financed television in the overseas information effort and the second whether the present programmes were the best means of fulfilling it. With regard to the first it stated that:

> Television services should not be directed at overseas targets merely because scope exists to penetrate them. British objectives must in each case be identified, and the potentiality of the television service to further the objective must be assessed, account always taken of the cost of penetration measured against expected return.'[8]

This reflected a change within government regarding the role of information work, first articulated in the White Paper on Representational Services Overseas (Cmnd. 2276), the Plowden Report, published in February 1964. This had emphasised that information work had to be linked to specific policy objectives and '... expressed scepticism of the value of information work of a generalised character such as the "Projection of Britain". It was suggested that where a Projection of Britain campaign was called for, it should be related to specific areas and to our policy requirements in them.' The dissatisfaction of BIS New York with *London Line* seems to rest more with the gradual implementation of this view and a consequent change of information policy than the quality of production: '...to serve effectively the pursuit of high priority information purposes as distinct from generalised projection of Britain'.[9] They wanted material that would convey 'hard information' and identified the form as background material to news and documentaries rather than magazine programmes. The COI argued that the programme was not given the year necessary to establish itself during which time 'harder' material would have been introduced and indeed, had been more successful than expected at this early stage, citing reports from Ottawa and New York which state that it was telecast by more stations and at better times than *Calendar.* In relation to the current proposals from BIS New York it stated in an earlier draft, 'Clearly these approaches have merit but neither is strictly an alternative to the original conception of *London Line,* which, by definition, was intended to appeal to a minority "serious-minded" audience.'[10] Nevertheless, *London Line* was cancelled in the United States from September 1968 and continued for a further six months in Canada, Australia and New Zealand before it was discontinued early in 1969.

Clearly the experience of producing a colour version of *London Line* had raised wider issues concerning the role of television within information policy and more specifically how to produce cost-effective programmes for the needs of different posts throughout the world. This precipitated a proposal for a radical restructuring of television production within the COI with separate series no longer produced by separate units. One unit would supply all magazine series and feature items, thus '...the whole unit is operating in a certain field, and not over the whole range of British activity.'[11] This resulted in the production of packages of magazine series on a single theme rather than a weekly topical series which was primarily informed by colour: '... a major consideration which governs much of the thinking in this paper is colour. Although the pace of the spread of colour television varies from place to place ... colour is happening.'[12] From 1969 virtually all programmes were filmed using colour-negative stock ensuring that whenever a country started to broadcast in colour, some of its first images would be of Britain.

The Enthusiasts (1967) and The Pacemakers (1969–1971)

Early in 1967 work began on a series of six black-and-white profiles entitled *The Enthusiasts.* Each of the programmes was about thirteen minutes long, featuring people at the forefront of their fields. The first of these focused on the rally car driver Stuart Turner; followed by David Attenborough, then Director of Programmes at the BBC, the animal behaviourist Caroline Loizos; Tony Benn, then Minister of Technology; Sandy Dunbar; and the businessman Peter Parker. The format in each case revolved around a studio interview occasionally intercut with location footage. The series was designed for the same market as the colour *London Line* although the form of distribution was a little unusual. In Canada and the United States it was seen as *The Enthusiasts.* In Australia it made up every other issue of the colour version of *London Line.* As a result of the television production restructuring, it was decided to extend the format pioneered by *The Enthusiasts* and produce a new series, *The Pacemakers.*

Between 1969 and 1971 two series of *The Pacemakers* were produced, each consisting of thirteen programmes featuring people drawn from across the spectrum of

British working life. Although the series featured some familiar names such as Glenda Jackson and Colin Chapman, many were 'ordinary' people who strongly advocated the implementation of innovative changes within, say, the National Health Service and education. The idea was to profile 'purposeful and inventive' people who represented a wide range of human activity. This led to stories that focused, for example, on the changing working practice of a local GP with the advent of new health centres and a primary school head teacher implementing a radical new approach to teaching in the light of the seminal Plowden Report of 1967, which questioned the efficacy of a system primarily focused on tests, urging teachers 'not [to] assume that only what is measurable is valuable'.[13] The series moved away from the studio-bound interview format of *The Enthusiasts* to one that was location-based, with the subject often speaking direct to camera. Some people such as the pioneering conservationist Bob Boote and the actress Glenda Jackson literally guided the audience through their beliefs and ideas, whilst other programmes such as BIBA (issue no. 10) relied more heavily on an off-screen narrative.

A Foreign and Commonwealth Office circular to posts outlining the changes to television programmes declared that *The Pacemakers* was a series designed '…to demonstrate that Britain has a valuable fund of knowledge and experience which can be used not only in support of her industry and economic progress but in helping to solve some of the political and social problems of our times'.[14] New developments within Britain were thus conveyed through articulate people who, it was hoped, would enthuse a general audience with their innovative approach to the world. Britain was, therefore, to be seen as a country that nurtured and encouraged different modes of thought which often challenged the accepted orthodoxy and the authority that informed it. However, this approach goes much further than the projection of a progressive Britain and starts to impinge on the personal, the margins of a 'British personality'. All these people to a greater or lesser degree question the status quo and in some cases their portrayal verges on the eccentric. An example of this is a sequence from the first programme in the series, which featured the computer scientist and psychologist Chris Evans. He is shown at work on a typewriter in his back garden, surrounded by a home-made barrier, while his wife mows the lawn and his children play, occasionally crossing this obstacle to show him something. This is by no means conventional behaviour, but the significant point here is that this facet of his personality, and by extension Britain, is portrayed in a positive light. Possibly because eccentricity, as John Stuart Mill noted, is evidence of the strength of a national character:

> Eccentricity has always abounded when and where strength of character has abounded; and the amount of eccentricity in a society has generally been

proportional to the amount of genius, mental vigour and moral courage it contained.[15]

Its inclusion might also convey a more subtle message – that its existence within a society forms one of the touchstones of a democracy that is functioning well.

The Pacemakers was not designed to supplement existing productions but to replace them. The series effectively replaced the colour version of *London Line* and its pattern of distribution reflected this as it reached audiences in Canada, Australia, New Zealand and the Caribbean. It was also produced in a re-edited edition, *No Two the Same*, for the production of language versions, primarily for Japan and French-speaking Canada. The decision to substitute a new package built around a single theme for the more general magazine series meant that programmes such as *Calendar* (1960–1969), *This Week in Britain* (1959–1980) and *London Line* (1964–1979) all ceased production early in 1969. However, both *This Week in Britain* and *London Line* did not entirely disappear; popular versions of each series were maintained. The African version of *London Line* continued until 1979, while a single edition of *This Week in Britain* was continued and produced in two versions: one for Mexico, re-titled *24 Horas,* with subsidiary distribution in Latin America, and another for Australia and New Zealand, with subsidiary distribution in the Caribbean.

These programming changes were driven by three main factors. The first was a change in policy, signalled by Samples, which was an effort to make television provision more effective and included a 'narrowing down' of targets, better field investigation and more pointed placing of material. The second was the ongoing issue of financial expenditure. By 1962 it was estimated that it would cost an additional £65,000 just to maintain the existing television services at a level that would keep pace with the increase in television stations and sets, expanding at an annual rate of around 30%. To extend the distribution of a series such as *This Week in Britain* from its current thirty territories to the eighty territories that now possessed television would effectively mean increasing the number of editions from eight to twenty at an additional annual cost of £100,000. The total provision for the Overseas Television Services provided by the COI was set at £250,000 for the forthcoming financial year, 1962–1963. This in itself represented a substantial increase to the Overseas Departments since the initial cost in 1957 of £110,000. The current production and distribution machinery was also nearing its capacity. By 1964 budgets were increasing in line with costs to ensure consistent provision of the COI's 'running service' of television material but with little expansion and this continued until the late 1960s. Although extra funds had been found for the provision of colour television material on the recommendation of the Beeley Report in 1967, the budget remained fairly static in the following years, representing an effective cut in real terms.

The third factor was a perception that the nature of the demand was changing as television companies sought to introduce different strands of programming and the length of time slots was altered within schedules. This view was consolidated by a trip to investigate the reception of these programmes in Australia, Japan and Canada in May 1969 by John Hall of the Central Office of Information. After meeting representatives from the Australian Broadcasting Corporation, the commercial and the 'country' stations, and showing them paste-up programmes, he was convinced that *The Pacemakers* could occasionally be slotted into burgeoning magazine series such as *Four Corners* whereas the 'country' stations would probably use the entire series.[16] Other posts, such as Ottawa and Bridgetown (Barbados), were enthusiastic about the possibilities of placing this series, a key element of which was its 'timeless' quality that would enable repeated transmission. As a result *The Pacemakers* remained in international circulation well into the mid-1970s. In 1972 the series was still used by all four New Zealand Broadcasting Corporation channels in a regular slot at 6.40 pm.[17] A year later Ottawa reported that it was still responding to continual requests for the series.[18] *No Two the Same* also found audiences in Chile and Malta, although Rio de Janeiro reported in 1973 that an evaluation of COLIN CHAPMAN (issue no. 6) had concluded that there was 'too much dialogue for Brazilian tastes'.[19]

Frontier (1964 and 1969) and Living Tomorrow (1969–1983)

Science and technology made up the second strand to these single-themed magazine series developed in the late 1960s with the production of *Living Tomorrow* (1969–1983) and its 'sister' series *Tomorrow Today* (1969–1974) and *Haçia El Mañana* (1969–?). Initially these series used the same format as *London Line*, a studio-based programme of around four stories led by presenters, to show current scientific developments within Britain. Generally these three series shared the same content, although the running order might change, but the presentation and style was changed to accommodate different audiences. *Tomorrow Today* was presenter-led and designed for English-speaking audiences in, for example, Canada, Australia, New Zealand and the Caribbean. *Living Tomorrow* generally relied on a commentary to link the stories, which could then be dubbed into foreign languages, producing versions for Japan, French-speaking Canada and Portugal, for example. *Haçia El Mañana* was effectively a hybrid, a presenter-led series produced in Spanish for distribution in both Spain and Latin America, where the personalised approach was more popular. These three editions continued until 1974 when

BFI/COI

Filming the Giraffe forklift, *Living Tomorrow* issue no. 233, 1978

Tomorrow Today was dropped in favour of *Living Tomorrow*, probably for financial reasons.

This, however, was not the `first time that science had formed the basis of a series made for overseas distribution. Between 1964 and 1965, a series of fourteen black-and-white films was produced under the title *Frontier*. These films covered a wide range of topics, from radio astronomy and sonic aids for the blind through computers to the hovercraft and the development of antibiotics. Although the series was produced by the COI, film production companies such as Philomel Productions, British Films Ltd and Eyeline Films made the films, using directors including Michael Orrom and Margaret Thomson. The series was not renewed, possibly for financial reasons, until 1969 when a colour version was released along the same line, but it only ran to five films. The decision to produce a science magazine series primarily for television effectively truncated *Frontier* but revealed that a substantial commitment to science was in place by 1968. This was informed by a number of elements. The first was an increasing demand for science content, both in the form of programmes and of separate items that could be used as 'fillers'. For example, in Australia ABC was planning a series of science programmes in the late 1960s which would effectively comprise material drawn from a variety of different sources, providing an opportunity for placement of entire programmes or single items.[20] This was borne out by the use of the series in regular slots in New Zealand and the Caribbean. Bridgetown noted in 1975 that *Living Tomorrow* was an ' ... outstandingly good series which is very well received here and has a regular slot every fortnight. It is then bicycled to St Kitts (for transmission on ZIZ) and Antigua (for transmission on ZAL)'.[21] In other countries, such as Singapore, Kenya and Chile, it was used as a filler but often repeated.

The second revolved around government policy. As the weighting of national projection shifted from one which created a favourable climate of opinion in support of government policies, to one which specifically supported Britain's export drive in the 1960s, the theme of science and technology gained increasing importance. The percentage of the COI's output that contained 'trade promotion' material increased throughout the 1960s until it accounted for more than 60% and continued to remain around this figure well into the next decade.[22] There was a sense that a threshold had been reached here and any further increase would risk a loss of placement. The role of television in trade promotion was examined by the Samples Review, which concluded that although there was evidence of orders placed as a result of programmes they would:

> ... question the extent to which it is productive for programmes to be designed merely for this end. Television is uniquely able to convey the impression of industrial change and modernisation which will contribute directly to trade promotion and this, we believe, should be the guiding principle in COI programming.[23]

With *Tomorrow Today* and *Living Tomorrow,* the COI created series that satisfied the changing demands of information policy and communicated a general impression of modernisation, with many of the stories specifically linked to a manufactured output. There is evidence that these subjects created a great deal of interest among viewers around the world. For example, in 1973 Santiago reported that as a result of *Hacia El Mañana* '... we receive large numbers of enquiries about products mentioned.'[24] By the mid-1970s there was a production secretary within the COI dedicated to answering viewers' letters that arrived as a direct result of *Living Tomorrow*. Generally the requests were for more information concerning a featured item but might come in French or Spanish since the distribution included French-speaking Canada and Latin America. The letters would be sent for translation, the item identified and then a pro forma reply would contain contact information for the company concerned.[25]

This prioritisation of science reflected the Labour government's commitment to funding science and technology as a means of modernising British industry and also to project a gradual reorientation in terms of its international role. This was certainly a view held by Tony Benn, Minister of Technology from 1966 to 1970, who firmly believed that science and technology could provide Britain with the international role she had lost with the Empire.[26] By effectively dedicating the greatest proportion of content to science and technology the overseas magazine output reflected this perception and marked a subtle change in the nation's view of what Britain had to offer the world.

This Week in Britain (1959–1979)

These three shifts in the development of magazine programmes in the late 1960s – the introduction of colour, the use of 'personalities' to communicate innovation and the increasing proportion of content devoted to science and technology – influenced the style and content of the COI's longest-running series, the magazine programme *This Week in Britain*. From 1969 with the production of a single edition, this series started to explore new subject matter and approach traditional content from a different angle. For much of the previous decade *This Week in Britain* had focused on many of the core aspects of Britain identified by Tallents: heritage; culture, particularly fashion; exhibitions/conferences; manufacture and design; science and technology. The majority of stories used traditional elements of the nation either as the focus of the story or the hook from which to examine new developments. An example of this is HARDY AMIES – HEPWORTH (issue no. 461, 1967) in which a menswear collection is followed from the manufacture of the cloth to the catwalk in London. The message here is that at the heart of modern Britain is a tradition that is synonymous with quality, reflecting the melding of contemporary and traditional aspects of Britain that had become the hallmark of the country's image by the mid-1960s.

As *This Week in Britain* moved into the 1970s there were marked changes in the treatment of content. This was mainly the result of feedback from the main distributor of the programme in Australia, the Australian Broadcasting Corporation (ABC). Although the series had an excellent slot, transmitted in Sydney on Tuesday evening at 6.55 pm before the national news when ABC achieved its best ratings reaching 50% of the audience, it was felt the writing and presentation were clichéd

COI

This Week in Britain production team at Somerset House c. 1975

although the subject matter was generally interesting.[27] It was this demand for a more creative approach that informed a different interpretation of traditional content. For example, Kew Gardens is viewed from a tourist perspective in 1961 (KEW GARDENS, issue no. 110) but from a scientific and educational one in the 1970s with KEW RESEARCH (issue no. 672, 1971), STUDENT GARDENERS (issue no. 873, 1975) and KEW SEEDS (issue no. 1077, 1979). This is particularly noticeable in the treatment of British heritage, which shifts from the travelogue approach to stately homes such as Hampton Court, to one that examines them from a restoration angle. Again science and technology provide the key to engaging an audience with possibly familiar material, while other methods can verge on the eccentric with the stories such as LAMP POSTS (issue no. 1092, 1979), which looked at the little-known Museum of Street Lighting, hidden in the depths of Hertfordshire.

There were also distinct shifts in subject matter from 1970, some of which reflect changing concerns within British society, such as a growing interest in conservation. One aspect of this, pollution, provides a good example of how the policy of national projection centred on a progressive Britain renders the content particularly sensitive to these alterations. The subject of pollution does not feature in any *TWIB* until 1970 but from this point on, it occupies at least one issue per year for the next five years. The changing role of women in British society, particularly in relation to work, is another popular thread that starts running through *TWIB* from this time, again signalling a change in attitude that is just starting to register across the country. Many of these stories revolve around a single personality on the cusp of these changes, communicating their own views and beliefs, which were gradually becoming more acceptable. These ranged from the scientist Dr Kit Pedlar on the necessity of a sustainable framework of energy provision (SCIENCE AND SURVIVAL, issue no. 802, 1974) to Erin Pizzey, who revolutionised public thinking about domestic violence and the threat it posed for future generations (ERIN PIZZEY, issue no. 1046, 1979).

One broad area that had barely registered before 1970 and was used increasingly by *TWIB* was social welfare. Although this mirrored changes within Britain in the previous decade, which had essentially seen a shift from charity to social welfare, its inclusion marked the 'profound shift in perception of community work from around 1969'.[28] Some of these stories reflected government initiatives at a local and national level, such as GYPSIES (issue no. 675, 1971), which examined the provision of sites for gypsies by county councils which allowed them to take full advantage of education and social services for the first time, and MEETING WITHOUT BARS (issue no. 813, 1974), which described the experience of families visiting prisoners at the new visitor centre at Wakefield Prison in Yorkshire. However, many of the programmes looked at the activities of organisations that functioned on a voluntary basis, rather than those sponsored specifically by the government, and sought to alleviate social problems, such as increasing social isolation, through community-based solutions. Examples include the pioneering work of a group of solicitors in London to provide people on low incomes with a full range of legal services in NORTH KENSINGTON LAW CENTRE (issue no. 749, 1973), the work of Community Service Volunteers in CAN I HELP YOU? (issue no. 790, 1974) and NACRO (issue no. 838, 1975), which examined the latest initiative from the crime reduction charity NACRO, a national newspaper for prison inmates. These stories revealed aspects of British society such as poverty and crime that had largely remained hidden in the construction of Britain's image in the 1960s. Although they could be perceived as 'negative' they consolidated the image of a progressive Britain through their constructive engagement with problems that could be seen as universal. Indeed, in their pursuit of areas that reflected a modern Britain, the government ironically delved further into the margins of British society in its depiction of the nation. This not only refers to the conditions experienced by sections of the population, but perhaps more interestingly the community-led solutions developed were ideologically at odds with both major parties. For Labour the solution lay with the state while the Conservatives felt it rested with the individual. As a result, many of these stories truly projected Britain, in terms of predicting how the country might develop. By reflecting elements that resided within the margins of our society, they explored the periphery between what might be accepted into the mainstream or what might simply disappear. Essentially these small experiments in living provided a glimpse into the possible futures available to Britain, and many of these forecasts proved to be quite accurate. As Robert Hewison and John Holden observed:

> The belief that people might achieve things together – that solutions would not come from the powers-that-be and the Establishment, but rather from self-help – was very much in the spirit of the times, but was not to become part of mainstream political thinking for another thirty years.[29]

These changes in *TWIB* were primarily generated by demand, specifically from the country where it was most popular, and reflect a gradual change in policy that can be traced back to the consequences of two major enquiries which reported at the beginning of the decade, the Duncan Report of 1969 on overseas representation and the Scott Report of 1970 on the information services. Basically the first resulted in substantial cuts in the staffing of Britain's embassies and high commissions around the world and the second recommended a prioritisation of information work, creating a list of 'top twenty' posts as a means of achieving this. This led to a more 'targeted' approach but also exacerbated a problem that had existed for some time, the tenuous relationship between the COI and the overseas posts, which were effectively the only distribution outlet for the material produced. The Samples Review had noted that there was a general lack of field information and an '… inadequacy at some important overseas posts of resources available for effective placing of material which is produced, after all, at some expense'.[30] Scott also regarded this as a serious weakness and reiterated Samples' recommendation that close liaison between the posts and the COI be maintained by regular consultative visits by the COI. Despite improving relations in the early 1970s this weakness remained, partly as a result of the Duncan cuts which inevitably resulted in a greater volume of work for the remaining staff.

As a report proposing a restructuring of the Overseas Film and Television Service in 1975 noted, television was rarely mentioned in the annual reports from the posts, if at all. The reason for this lay in the fact that it was:

... a difficult medium to use. Unlike the press for which the lines of com-munication are well understood and the results are there for all to see, television is ephemeral and hard to penetrate; instead of a newspaper's single editor, a television station has many 'editors' each with different needs and a tech-nical language that can be incomprehensible to anyone not trained in the medium. Add to this the multiplicity of material that is on offer to station operators, much of it low cost entertainment which makes official material hard to 'sell' and television can become a daunting outlet for an overworked information officer to use.[31]

This informed the decision to move to a more 'modular' form of production that would focus on the production of items rather than programmes that would com-prise a pool of material to draw on, thus providing a flexible response to specific demand. Another important factor here was increasingly limited financial provision. From 1963–1964 the COI/HMSO budgets had declined 18% in real terms, accompanied by a reduction in FCO information expenditure.[32] As a result *London Line* was cut to five minutes and the format changed to a single story, in line with *TWIB*. From this point both series would now occasionally share content but both remained specifically tailored to their respective audiences. For example, *London Line* focused on the experience of Africans living in London with a particular emphasis on education and training opportunities, such as AFRICAN SOCIAL WORKER IN BRITAIN (issue no. 494, 1975), which describes the training given to a social worker at a local authority children's centre. Thus from the early 1970s the emphasis was more on supplying an existing demand than creating one. This meant both these long-running series developed a format that suited the specific demands of their audiences but could only be sustained through consistent feedback from officers and audience. By the late 1970s this had evidently broken down again. In 1979, the same year that *London Line* ceased production, the COI was unaware that *This Week in Britain* had finally lost its prime slot in Australia. With no demand left to supply, the series came to an end in early 1980 after twenty-one years.

Conclusion

Through an examination of the development of television magazine series produced between 1964 and 1975 by the COI, distinct changes in projection of Britain can be traced. The mediation of this image was essentially informed by demand, as the British government sought to differentiate its product in an increasingly com-petitive international television market, by changes in information policy driving a more specific 'targeted' approach and cuts in the Overseas Information Service itself which inevitably led to a concentration on supplying an existing demand rather than creating one.

By the mid-1970s all magazine series were made, and generally broadcast, in colour with a far greater emphasis on science and technology both in terms of actual content and as a means of approaching more traditional subject matter. In the pursuit of a progressive Britain, subjects were increasingly drawn from the margins of British society, reflecting changes that were barely registering across the nation. The people advocating these ideas, and the proposals for their realisation, were often the focus and 'voice' of the programmes themselves. Thus the projection of Britain on the one hand became more narrow, in terms of the higher percentage of content dedicated to science and technology, but on the other much wider, through engagement with broader social problems and attempts to resolve them that conflicted ideologically with the views of the main political parties of the time. By 1964 an image of Britain had been constructed that attempted to meld the contemporary and traditional in Britain. With the passage of a decade this image still adhered to a basic preoccupation with modern aspects of the country but it was far more refined and fluid, projecting a much greater range of possible futures, encompassing social as well as scientific experiments, many of which are now fully integrated within our society today.

In portraying the idiosyncratic with the innovative, the more eccentric dimension within the 'British personality' was positively highlighted, possibly reflecting the inevitable outcome of an established working democracy. This trend to personalise British achievements increasingly illuminated the elements Carstairs had placed such emphasis on in the early 1960s – the peculiar, the curious and the plain eccentric – and it did so without apology. The use of this aspect in the production of official information tapped into a long-standing tradition. The key to its increased use in this period can be found in this anecdote of George Mikes, who dissected the national character in his book *How to Be an Alien*. He recalls how, after its publication in 1946, his 'outspoken' piece was serialised as an anti-British tract by Rumanian Radio, whilst the COI requested permission to translate it for the benefit of Polish refugees settling in Britain.

> 'We want our friends to see us in this light,' the man said on the telephone. This was hard to bear for my militant and defiant spirit. 'But it's not such a favourable light,' I protested feebly. 'It's a very human light and that is the most favourable,' retorted the official.[33]

Notes

1 G. M. Carstairs, *This Island Now: The BBC Reith Lectures 1962* (Harmondsworth: Penguin in association with Hogarth Press, 1964) p. 101.

2 Sir Stephen Tallents, *The Projection of England* (London: Film Centre, 1955), p. 38 [originally published Faber and Faber, 1932]. Extract reproduced in this volume.

3 This nation brand was constructed under the aegis of the different departments that made up of the Overseas Information Service (OIS) and was first seen with the production of *London Line*. For more details on its development see Linda Kaye, *Reconciling Policy and Propaganda: The British Overseas Television Service 1954–1964* in this volume. The OIS consisted of the Overseas Departments of the Commonwealth Relations Office, the Colonial Office and the Foreign Office together with the Board of Trade, which held responsibility for policy, and three 'agents' which propagated the material demanded by it, the Central Office of Information, the British Council and the External Services of the BBC.

4 David Fisher, *Terra Media*, http://www.terramedia.co.uk/Chronomedia/years/1966.htm (accessed 12 February 2007).

5 Cited in Frances Cockburn, 'Proposals for Restructuring the Overseas Film and Television Service' (3 October 1975). Copy at BUFVC.

6 The system is described in 'The Gemini System', by Adam Leys. Attachment in e-mail Adam Leys to Linda Kaye, received 13 December 2006.

7 The National Archives of the United Kingdom (TNA): Public Record Office (PRO) INF 6/1145.

8 TNA: PRO INF 12/1295 'Report of the Sub-Committee on Television Overseas', 31 July 1968.

9 Ibid.

10 Ibid., draft copy.

11 TNA: PRO FCO 26/182 'Overseas Television Production – Proposals for a New Programming Structure for the Financial Year 1969/70', p. 4.

12 Ibid., p. 11.

13 D. Gillard, 'The Plowden Report', *the encyclopaedia of informal education*, http://www.infed.org/schooling/plowden_report.htm. Last updated 28 December 2007 (accessed 28 March 2008).

14 TNA: PRO FCO 26/183 Circular from B. R. Curson to all posts 3 February 1969.

15 John Stuart Mill, *On Liberty*, cited in Mervyn Horder's introduction to Edith Sitwell, *English Eccentrics* (London: Folio Society, 1994).

16 John Hall, 'Report on Television in Australia, Japan and Canada February–March 1969', p. 16.

17 TNA: PRO INF 18/15 Annual Service Reports Wellington.

18 TNA: PRO INF 18/10 Annual Service Reports Ottawa.

19 TNA: PRO INF 18/11 Annual Service Reports Rio de Janiero.

20 Hall, op. cit., p. 4.

21 TNA: PRO INF 18/2 Annual Service Reports Bridgetown.

22 'Report of the Sub-Committee on Television Overseas', op. cit.

23 Ibid.

24 TNA: PRO INF 18/12 Annual Service Reports Santiago.

25 Conversation with Maureen Irving, Production Secretary for *Living Tomorrow* (1976–1979), December 2006.

26 ANTHONY WEDGWOOD BENN, *The Enthusiasts* (issue no. 4, 1967, viewed at Film Images, London 2006). The argument here is that Britain maintained a technological lead internationally through the lost Empire.

27 John Hall, op. cit., p. 6.

28 Robert Hewison and John Holden, *experience and experiment – The UK Branch of the Calouste Gulbenkian Foundation 1956–2006* (Calouste Gulbenkian Foundation, 2006), p. 60.

29 Ibid.

30 'Report of the Sub-Committee on Television Overseas', op. cit.

31 Frances Cockburn, op. cit.

32 TNA: PRO INF 12/1360 'Programme Analysis Review on the Projection of Britain Overseas', paragraph 5.3.2.

32 George Mikes, *How to Be an Alien* (Harmondsworth: Penguin, 1966), Preface to the 24th Impression, pp. 7–8.

EVE'S FILM REVIEW AND PATHE PICTORIAL CORRESPONDENCE

One of the few surviving box files from the Pathe periodicals department is a shabby green box entitled 'Eve and Pictorial Correspondence 13 October to 6 November 1928' (part of the BUFVC's British Pathe Paper Archive). Reproduced here, in their entirety, are a selection of Pathe letters and memos, primarily from the editor Fred Watts together with extracts from a variety of correspondents. They range from Herbert Chapman manager of Arsenal Football Club, noting his player's qualms about facing the camera, to women keen to suggest stories or follow up tips seen on Eve's Film Review.

Requests to film stories for Eve's Film Review *and* Pathe Pictorial

> 17th Oct. 1928
> H. Chapman, Esq. Secretary,
> Arsenal Football Team,
> Avnell Road,
> Highbury, N.5.
>
> Dear Sir,
> We should be glad to have an opportunity of sending down one of our Cameramen to take a short film of your Team in training. We wish to get same for our PATHE PICTORIAL – the well-known Weekly Interest Film.
>
>   Would you kindly let the writer know when we could have the pleasure of sending down.
>
> Yours faithfully,
> Editor.
> PICTORIAL & EVE'S FILM REVIEW

Reply from Herbert Chapman
On 18 October 1928 Herbert Chapman, the 'Secretary-Manager' of Arsenal replied noting that '… unfortunately, our players have very strong views as to standing for

filming. I think the better thing would be for you to have a talk with me before you come down.'

PICTORIAL EDITORIAL

Miss White.

Accts.Dept.

15th Oct. 1928.

FW/RS

Dear Madam,

Will you kindly add the following fees to this week's salaries:-

Mr.Gordon.   Sunday. 14th Oct. Empire Marketing Board Film.
..............£1.1.0.
Debiting COMMERCIAL SECTION accordingly.

Mr.TAMPIERI.   Sunday. 14th Oct. City Scenes........£1.1.0.

Debiting PICTORIAL accordingly.

Friday. 12th Oct. Reville Fashions, Studio.
Mr.Gordon.....................................10/6d.
Mr.Farmer.   ....10/6d.
Mr.Wagniere.   ....10/6d.
Mr.James.   ....10/6d.
Mr.Williamson.   .... 7/6d.
Mr.Wallder.   ....10/6d.
Mr.Perrin.   ..... 7/6d.

Debiting EVE'S FILM REVIEW accordingly.

Mr.Mellow.   Saturday. 13th Oct...Projecting Film at
Russell Hotel,(India Rubber Type Co's Film).
.......................10/6d.

Sunday... ditto.........£1.1.0.

Debiting COMMERCIAL SECTION accordingly.

Yours faithfully,

Editor.
PICTORIAL & EVE'S FILM REVIEW.

P.S.Mr.F.Bourne. Overtime - working until 3 p.m. on Saturday
13th inst., on Gazette Postcard Service.
Debiting GAZETTE accordingly.

A letter to the Accounts department listing additional fees to be added to the weekly salaries, 15 October 1928

17th Oct. 1928
A. Barritt, Esq.
The Secretary,
Blackburn Rovers Football Team,
Ewood Park.
Blackburn

Dear Sir,

We should be glad to have an opportunity of sending down one of our Cameramen to take a short film of your Team in training. We wish to get same for our PATHE PICTORIAL – the well-known Weekly Interest Film.

Would you kindly let the writer know when we could have the pleasure of sending down.

Yours faithfully,
Editor.
PICTORIAL & EVE'S FILM REVIEW

Reply from A. Barritt
A. Barritt was far more accommodating than Herbert Chapman, replying on 5 November that a Pathe photographer might '…call here any Tuesday morning about 11am when I will arrange for him to take photographs you require.'

6th Nov. 1928
A. Barritt, Esq.
Secretary,
BLACKBURN ROVERS FOOTBALL & ATHLETIC CO. Ltd.,
Ewood Park.
Blackburn

Dear Sir,

We beg to thank you for your letter of yesterday's date, and our representative will call upon you at 11a.m. next Tuesday – 13th inst.,

Yours faithfully,

Editor.
PICTORIAL & EVE'S FILM REVIEW

19th Nov. 1928
A. Barritt, Esq.
THE SECRETARY,
BLACKBURN ROVERS FOOTBALL TEAM,
Ewood Park.
BLACKBURN

Dear Sir,
Just a line to advise you that our Mr. Gordon will be on your ground tomorrow,
Tuesday morning to complete the little picture which he started last week.

Thanking you for your kind assistance.

Yours faithfully,

PICTORIAL & EVE'S FILM REVIEW DEPT.
FIRST NATIONAL PATHE LTD.

26th Oct. 1928
Miss TAMARA
Wood Green Empire
Wood Green

Dear Madam,

Our Representative saw your Act last evening, and we should be pleased if you
would allow us to take a short film of same. This would be for inclusion in our
well-known "EVE'S FILM REVIEW".

As this film is shown all over the country it is almost needless to say the
publicity that must accrue from a film of this nature.

Perhaps you will give the writer a call on the matter.

Yours faithfully,

Editor.
PICTORIAL & EVE'S FILM REVIEW

Letters notifying individuals that stories relating to them had been released

25th Oct. 1928
Miss Trefusis-Forbes.
Bell-Mead Kennels
Haslemere

Dear Madam,
We are pleased to advise you that the film we took of your Dandy Dinmonts is included in today's EVE'S FILM REVIEW No: 386. I feel sure you will agree it looks very well and we have mentioned both your name in the title and Haslemere.

Yours faithfully,

Editor
PICTORIAL & EVE'S FILM REVIEW

25th Oct. 1928
Mr. Morris,
British Fur Trade Alliance,
63 Queen Victoria Street
E.C.4.

Dear Mr. Morris,
The first part of the FUR FILM we took with your assistance, is released in today's EVE'S FILM REVIEW No: 386.

Yours faithfully,

Editor.
PICTORIAL & EVE'S FILM REVIEW

Correspondence relating to the supply of material to and from the Pictorial department.

On 16 October 1928 Aron Hamburger, in his capacity as director of British Polychromide Ltd, wrote to Fred Watts requesting permission from First National Pathe '... to reproduce some of your "Eve" posters containing reference to Poly-chromide ... to use in [these] connection with press notices of our recent private exhibition'.

18th Oct. 1928.
A. Hamburger, Esq.
Messrs. British Polychromide Ltd.
99 Charlotte Street
W.1.

Dear Mr. Hamburger,
With reference to your letter of the 16th inst., we would like to have something more definite as regards information in what way these posters would be used, etc.

Kindly let us have more details on the matter.

Yours faithfully,

Editor.
PICTORIAL & EVE'S FILM REVIEW

17th Oct. 1928
Monsieur A. Letrange
38 Rue Tronchet
Paris

Dear Mr. Letrange,
I have now had an opportunity of carefully examining the film of RUFFIN FUR MODES. To say the least, I am surprised that such a poor Fashion film should be taken by you!

The Modes themselves, with the exception of about two coats are hardly worth looking at. The mannequin is certainly one of the worst I have ever seen so far as her looks are concerned, and the film has been taken under poor conditions as regards light – judging by the print you sent.

I may be able to use about 30 or 40 feet but I really cannot understand you, with your experience of our requirements sending such a poor specimen of a Mode. I should be glad to have your comments on my letter.

Yours faithfully,

EDITOR
PICTORIAL & EVE'S FILM REVIEW

18th Oct. 1928
Monsieur A. Letrange
38 Rue Tronchet
Paris

Dear Mr. Letrange,
We are today dispatching you cut positive – length 38 feet 2 MAISON RUFFIN
– Mode No: 1054". Kindly cut the negative to match and hand to Pathe Cinema,
together with our Official Order herewith No: F 212, and also the details as to
colours and sections.

Thanking you,
Yours faithfully,
EDITOR
PICTORIAL & EVE'S FILM REVIEW

In October 1928 Walter C. Mycroft, Scenario Editor for British International
Pictures Ltd, wrote requesting some library footage, specifically '... a shot of an
Indian train? We want about 12 ft for a picture now being edited ... [and] ... a shot
or two of a liner at sea – preferably a P. & O. or a Orient liner.'

Extracts from letters sent by members of the public

On 13 October 1928 Phyllis Chambers (Miss) wrote from Cheltenham suggesting
the following idea for *Eve's Film Review*. 'Everyone knows the annoyance of being
what people describe as a 'dirty walker,' yet some folks can, on the muddiest day
manage to get through without a splash ... this is usually put down to the peculiarity
of the walk, would it not be possible to film whether this would be practicable ...
I thought I would just give you my idea and how you could be very useful to my
sister "Eves"!'

On 16 October 1928 Florence Horton, who had previously been filmed by Fred
Watts, wrote from Cardiff to ask some advice about starting a career in the film
industry.

'... I have also asked the "Daily Mail" to forward on to you 2 large Photographs
of myself ... I am enclosing a small Photograph of myself in Bathing Suit. Mr
Watts as you can see I am reducing to suit fashion. I won 2nd Prize with this
picture as an "advert" advertising "Bourn[e]mouth" for Health and Beauty ... I

would not ask you but I am thinking of buying a house up London somewhere. What do you think of Romford or ought I to live more central? Considering I wish to try & get work in the City? I am thinking of writing to Gibbs Dentifrice, Wapping, as they were very generous over the "heads". I was wondering if they

FW/RS
PICTORIAL
    EDITORIAL
        DEPT.   17th Oct. 1928.

Miss Florence Horton,
    5 Cambridge Street
        Grange.
            Cardiff.

Dear Miss Horton,

            I certainly was surprised to receive
your letter of the 16th inst., and had wondered why
and where the photograph of yourself had come from.

            Regarding you getting on the films,
as you will appreciate, no doubt, there is very little
chance of you getting any engagements living in Cardiff.

            On the other hand, knowing what
a precarious living the films provide for artists, I
would not take the responsability of advising you to
come to London, as this is a matter purely for yourself.

            If you do decide to come to London,
I will certainly be pleased to see you, and to render
you what assistance I can, but I certainly would not
dream of living at Romford, which is very out of the way.

            We are constantly making advertising
films for all kinds of people, but do not know the Tooth
Paste people whom you refer to.

            Kind regards from Mr.Farmer and myself,

                Yours sincerely,

                    Editor,
                PICTORIAL & EVE'S FILM REVIEW.

Reply from Fred Watts to Florence Horton, 17 October 1928

BUFVC

would advertise on a film for the teeth & give me a chance in the advert. What do you think of it Mr Watts? ... The Publicity Films are doing this sort of thing & the firm who advertised a tooth paste last week had a young lady film actress cleaning her teeth, and it said "The Beauty of her smile". Well I am sure I could smile much nicer than that & my teeth are miles in front of hers ...'

On 18 October 1928 Ronald Eldridge, a fifteen year old boy, wrote stating that he wished '... to take up Cinematography as a career. I have studied the subject a little, and should prefer to be a cameraman. Have you any vacancy which I could fill, and thus work my way up to that position.'

2nd November 1928.
Miss L. Renaham
Walsingham

Dear Madam,
We thank you for your letter and enclose herewith instruction leaflet on How to Make Crystalised Flowers.

We regret we have no leaflet to send you regarding Feather Buttonholes. Your kind remarks regarding our EVE'S FILM REVIEW are greatly appreciated.

Yours faithfully,

Editor,
PICTORIAL & EVE'S FILM REVIEW.

On 19 October 1928 the manager of the Brighton Grand Hotel Company Ltd wrote, on the recommendation of Pathescope Ltd, to outline a story he thought might be of interest.

'... there was a PARROT and KITTEN here which played and BOXED together, also a very large M[A]CCAW and large TOMCAT which occasionally boxed together. The smaller parrot, also does peculiar tricks and turns somersaults on the perch, and if you would like to take a film of them, I shall be glad to hear from you ... As a matter of fact, I intended writing to you about this a few weeks ago, as the kitten is now getting on the "large" side and will soon be too big to play with the parrot, I am afraid.'

THE MAGAZINE FILM

Edgar Anstey

In this article Edgar Anstey, who had just been appointed Producer in Charge of British Transport Films, acknowledges the difficulty of defining the magazine film as a genre before going on to argue its value in the face of criticism 'by the aesthetes'. He describes the elements that have contributed to its success and those that need to be addressed if the magazine film is to develop in the future.

By the time this is in print it is likely that the Central Office of Information will have put into production a regular screen magazine in the same class as the *March of Time* and *This Modern Age*. It will be under the supervision of Stuart Legg, and will fall within the administrative parish of John Grierson in his capacity as C.O.I. Controller; so that we may expect the new release to show some of the characteristics of the old Canadian *World in Action* series which Gierson and Legg, in their Canadian National Film Board days, developed into *March of Time*'s first serious rival.

The *genre* has been known by a variety of names and never neatly defined. It is a combination of Press leader and feature article translated into pictures and sound. Let us for simplicity (and stressing regularity of appearance rather than content) call it the magazine film. In attempting an examination of accomplishments and status, I should begin perhaps by renouncing any claim to objectivity. As a practitioner who has been responsible for items in both the *March of Time* and *This Modern Age*, I am likely to be more conscious of aim than achievement. At any rate I am expert in the good intentions with which the paths of screen journalism have always been so lavishly paved. For these films have – first and foremost – been films of purpose; they have had something to say of more consequence than the manner of the saying. And they have survived nearly fifteen years of criticism by the aesthetes.

There is something of a paradox in that the preponderant importance of content has not prevented the form of the magazine film from becoming individual and immediately recognisable whatever the subject-matter. This may or may not demonstrate that quick-fire picture and vigorously didactic commentary provide the only means of bringing to the screen direct sociological and political comment. Certainly it is the most constantly effective means yet devised. Yet let us not ignore the likely limitations of a film form that so frequently eschews the full-blooded screen creation of people, place and mood in favour of illustrated phases. At its infrequent best this type of film can achieve a counterpoint of word and image rising near to poetry; it is of consequence that it more often rivals a lantern lecturer over-anxious about a last train home.

Let us try to recall some of the outstanding magazine films. Do you remember, for example, *Inside Nazi Germany 1938*, *Nazi Conquest No. 1* and *King Cotton*, all from *March of Time* in its hey-day? They were made in the two years immediately prior to the war, and no films did more to arouse public (and official) opinion to a belated awareness of the power of film as a sharp instrument of sociological and political comment. The weight of the argument as expressed in commentary would find its emotional overtone in picture; or sometimes the cold objective comment of an unremarkable shot would be given pulsating life by the turn of a commentary phrase. I shall never forget the grim, proud climax in *Rehearsal for War* (how sadly prophetic were the *March of Time* items of that period), when an account of the steady retreat of the Loyalist forces in the Fascists' Spanish Rebellion was brought to a halt by the ringing, defiant sentence, 'Then came Madrid.'

Generally the trick was to create a counterpoint between sound and image. The favourite exhortation of Louis de Rochemont, *March of Time*'s inventor and for many years its producer, was 'Never call your shot,' meaning that precious commentary wordage should never be squandered upon what was already sufficiently obvious to the eye, that commentary should always add some new idea, should be complementary to the image and not alternative to it. Commentary, as de Rochemont understood it, was to contribute what was impossible to the unaided picture, whether that contribution took the form of ideas or feelings. Too often to-day one hears commentary that is merely descriptive of the scenes portrayed, or sees images which merely illustrate in a pedestrian manner ideas that already have complete and self-sufficient existence in the narrator's words.

Like others of the more experimentally-minded producers (notably John Grierson and Basil Wright), Louis de Rochemont is a great editor in his own right. He had an eye for the foot of picture wherein lies the instant of maximum eloquence; and can cap it with just the word of commentary or phrase of music which will bring the idea or emotion home to the target of all good editors – the human stomach. Yet I am not sure that Stuart Legg, in a shorter run with his *World in Action* series, did not achieve enough hits in the solar plexus even to rival de

Rochemont. I call to mind in particular *And Now the Peace* – the best boost the United Nations has ever had – and *Churchill's Island*, a film about Britain which came at a time in the war when our friends overseas were anxious to hear that there was life and a few kicks still left in poor old Britannia.

The World in Action combined in its editing shrewd political insight with what often was sheer brilliance in the selection of the appropriate images. And selection was an especially true description of the process, for Stuart Legg employed – often of necessity – a very high proportion of library material originally photographed for quite different purposes. He combed the film vaults of the world for material of historical value, or scenes which seemed to symbolise or dramatise some mood or emotion of significance to his audiences. The other side of the medal is that the photographic quality of the *World in Action* series was, on the whole, low, and sometimes shots seemed over-familiar – an inevitable consequence of using so many duplicated scenes.

Yet for my money coherence and vitality of exposition is more to the point of the magazine film than beautiful photography. Ideally one employs both, and this has sometimes been achieved by the *This Modern Age* series, notably in *Palestine Problem*; but in other releases of the new magazine, editing has been loose and undynamic, and the consistently beautiful photography has given us a kind of travelogue of ideas rather than an integrated conception of the theme. The editors of *This Modern Age* could well devote some study to the precision of the ideological and emotional relationship between word and image achieved in the early *March of Time* items. The more so since they are undoubtedly seeking and finding a higher degree of precision in their commentary wording than the *genre* has yet experienced. Moreover, *This Modern Age* is showing healthy signs of being less stereotyped in its camera-work than the older magazines. *March of Time*, for example, has been traditionally opposed to the use of camera movement except on those occasions when it is virtually unavoidable. It was argued that shots in which the camera moved required to be left too long on the screen if they were to make their point, and this would interfere with the brisk, staccato manner of cutting which was held to be obligatory in screen journalism. *This Modern Age* had demonstrated the validity of a slower tempo for certain purposes, and there has been a consequent gain in the freedom and power of the camera.

It appears to me, however, that if the magazine film is to develop beyond its present stage (and it has been stuck there all too long), more is required than eloquent counterpoint in the editing and a new freedom for the camera.

Let us look back to the origins of the *March of Time* in 1927–28. During those years Louis de Rochemont and Jack Glenn were making for the U.S. Navy a series of recruiting films. They were not documentaries in the generally accepted sense of that word, but consisted of short acted stories played against the real background of the Navy. Subsequently the same team made *March of the Years* in 1933, and began work on the first experimental issues of *March of Time* in 1934. The first release was made in 1935.

During this whole period the idea of 're-enactment' was not lost. More importantly the creation of character by script analysis and screen synthesis was not regarded as the exclusive prerogative of the feature fiction film. In such early *March of Time* items as *Father Divine*, *The Lunatic Fringe*, *Fiorella La Guardia* and *Father Divine's Deal*, leading personalities of America were re-created on the screen with understanding and often with delightful humour. These were tiny screen biographies; they were full of the life and warmth of real people. All of them were directed by de Rochemont's first associate, Jack Glenn, and there is no doubt that they represented a important part of the original de Rochemont-Glenn conception, a part which has now been quite lost. To-day the magazine film has become a medium for the editor rather than the director. The shooting is rarely imaginative and the characters are eliminated rather than interpreted.

It may be argued that two reels are too short to create character, and some support for such a thesis may perhaps be seen in the fact that Louis de Rochemont now devotes most of his time to documentary story films of feature length like *Boomerang*. Yet I remain unconvinced that characterisation cannot play its part in our magazine films. Jack Glenn used often to create character in a single scene, and I suspect he would be doing it still if these films were coming out of film-makers' heads and hearts and not off assembly lines. Of course, you may argue that people, characters, have no business mixing in with the sociology of the magazine film, anyway. In that case we must be prepared to find them soon deciding they have no business in the audience either.

Penguin Film Review no. 9 (May 1949), pp. 17–21.

The National Archives holds material, including scripts and production notes, used in the production of Mining Review *and can be can be found in COAL 30 and COAL 32. This is one item from COAL 32, a memo written by Clifton Reynolds in November 1948 describing the present position of* Mining Review *and proposals for its future development. It contains a list of all the cinemas in Britain receiving copies of* Mining Review *at the time.*

Previous References:
PR/M(48)4, Item 41
PR/P(48)17
PR/P (48)34
2nd November, 1948.
NATIONAL COAL BOARD
PUBLIC RELATIONS COMMITTEE
"MINING REVIEW"
(Memorandum by Mr. Clifton Reynolds for consideration
by the Committee at their Meeting to be held at 3.30 p.m.
on Friday, 5th November, 1948)

INTRODUCTION
1. "Mining Review" has, since the beginning of 1948, been built up into a regular monthly newsreel forming a film with aims parallel to those of the magazine "Coal". It constitutes a medium of communication between the National Coal Board and the mining and non-mining public.
2. At their meeting on 19th May the Public Relations Committee authorised expenditure of £8,000 upon four additional issues of "Mining Review" to maintain distribution on a monthly instead of a quarterly basis during 1948.

    I now seek authority to produce "Mining Review" monthly during 1949. I have to seek this authority in advance of the main Public Relations Branch budget for 1949, for unless continuity of the series which we have been at pains to build up, is to be broken, a contract must be places without delay with the producing film company. This will, in the first place, make possible completion of the work which has already been begun, on the authority of Sir Arthur Street, on the issue for January, 1949.

PURPOSE

3. "Mining Review" is intended to inform the miners of developments in their industry and by relating the practice and experience of one area to another to break down narrow regional insularity. It aims in addition to record major events concerning the mining community and to raise the morale and prestige of the miner, while at the same time showing him the vital part he plays in relation to the rest of the community. It has not, in the past, been primarily designed as a recruiting medium, but there has been evidence in some parts of the country that in raising the prestige and morale of the British miners, "Mining Review" has a beneficial effect on recruitment. One of the advantages of an established information vehicle like "Mining Review" is that it can be used as occasion arises as a medium for running campaigns on specific subjects such as dirty coal.

DISTRIBUTION

(a) Commercial

4. "Mining Review" has an automatic monthly release on the Associatied British Cinemas circuit and is also shown in Odeon and Gaumont British circuit cinemas, as well as in many Miners' Welfare halls and other independent cinemas. In all, some 245 cinemas, mainly in mining areas, exhibit the newsreel. (A list of cinemas in Divisions where "Mining Review" is shown is appended.) Through this commercial distribution "Mining Review" reaches approximately two million people in mining areas every month.

(b) Non-commercial

5. In addition, "Mining Review" is widely shown on 16 mm. projectors to Colliery Consultative Committees and to schools and youth clubs by the Board's Divisional Recruitment Officers. Education Branch also use it regularly at E.V.W. training camps.

Copies of "Mining Review" have been demanded by British Embassies overseas and it is now also being distributed abroad by the Foreign Office. Excerpts from it are being sent to America by the Central Office of Information and negotiations are proceeding with the "March of Time" for their acquisition of certain items.

COST

6. The direct production costs of each issue of "Mining Review" are £1,600. To this must be added the cost of printing sufficient copies to meet the regular monthly theatrical release and the despatch charges which bring the total monthly cost of the newsreel to £2,000.

    It will be recalled that at the meeting of the Public Relations Committee in May, Sir Arthur Street said that he and Sir Joseph Hallsworth had been favourably impressed by "Mining Review", and he wondered if it would not be possible for the Board to make a charge for distribution. Investigations have been made into this matter, and because of its present greatly improved technical standard, the chances of receiving some financial return for "Mining Review" are now greater. Preliminary negotiations are being carried on [sic] on our behalf by the present Production Company with Eros Film Distributors. It still remains to be seen, however, whether exhibitors will be prepared to pay for a production which is obviously sponsored.

RECEPTION

(a) Outside the industry

7. Since "Mining Review" has been taken over and run directly by the Board, favourable comments have been received from the Film Trade press, the Director of Documentary B.B.C. Television Service, and the Controller of the Films Divisions of the Central Office of Information who has described it as the best industrial newsreel he has seen.

    Favourable comment was also received in the Coal Trade press, particularly on the August edition of "Mining Review" which, within a few days of the publication of the Board's Annual Report, showed a short film history of the Board's first year. Reports from cinema managers indicate that the "Mining Reviews" are also well received by non-mining sections of their audiences.

(b) Within the Industry

8. As a result of a recommendation by the National Consultative Council, "Mining Review" has been successfully shown at Colliery Consultative meetings, especially in the Northern and South-Western Divisions. The Board's Education Branch feel that "Mining Review" is of considerable value as a medium of industrial education; and the Secretary of the N.C.C. thinks it can be used to encourage the best use of the Consultative machinery.

DIVISIONAL VIEWS

9. A teleprint was sent to Divisional Secretaries asking what value they attached to "Mining Review" as a means of :-

    (a) stimulating recruitment;

    (b) enhancing and maintaining the prestige of the miner in the public eye and consequently his morale;

    (c) from time to time conveying information to the mining community on certain aspects of the Board's work and policy.

They were informed that the cost was of the order of £2,000 a month.

West Midlands and North-Eastern Divisions thought the results did not justify the expense. East Midlands and South-Eastern Divisions thought that "Mining Review" had some value for some or all of the purposes mentioned above but that the cost was excessive. Scottish, Northern and North-Western Divisions were strongly in favour of "Mining Review" being continued. South Western Division have not yet replied.

CONCLUSION

10. The value of industrial newsreels to disseminate information and to foster production and industrial morale has been recognised by the Ministry of Supply and other Government Departments who have sponsored such series as "Worker and Warfront" and "Britain Can Make It", which were shown extensively to factory audiences. The London Transport Executive have recently embarked on a cine-magazine. But no industrial newsreel other than "Mining Review" has ever secured distribution in commercial cinemas whence the Board monthly receive thousands of pounds worth of free screen space and reach an audience of two million people. To reach an audience of this size at a cost of £2,000 means that it costs less than a farthing to reach any one individual. This low cost per head of "Mining Review" compares very favourably with similar costs of other publicity media.

11. It is suggested that the continuity of this series, which we have been at some pains to establish, should not be broken and that this monthly newsreel should be continued next year.

12. I therefore recommend the Committee to authorise the expenditure of £24,000 on the production of twelve issues of "Mining Review" during 1949.

C. G. Reynolds
Distribution
As for PR/P(48)33.
Revised
APPENDIX A to PR/P(48)34.

DISTRIBUTION OF "MINING REVIEW"

SCOTTISH DIVISON ……	…	41 Cinemas
NORTHERN DIVISION …	…	36 Cinemas
NORTH-EASTERN DIVISION..	…	24 Cinemas
NORTH-WESTERN DIVISION	…	25 Cinemas
EAST MIDLANDS DIVISION	…	23 Cinemas
WEST MIDLANDS DIVISION…	…	25 Cinemas
SOUTH-EASTERN DIVISION…	…	2 Cinemas
SOUTH-WESTERN DIVISION.	…	58 Cinemas
UNCLASSIFIED	… …	11 Cinemas
	TOTAL:	245 Cinemas

APPENDIX B to PR/P(48))34.

DISTRIBUTION OF "MINING REVIEW"

SCOTTISH DIVISION:

The Odeon Cinema, Airdrie; The Odeon Cinema, Coatbridge; The Odeon Cinema, Hamilton; The Odeon Cinema, Motherwell; The Regal Cinema, Kilmarnock; The Regal Cinema, Kirkcaldy; The Regal Cinema, Coatbridge; The Rex Cinema, Motherwell; The Regal Cinema, Hamilton; The Plaza Cinema, Wishaw; The Regal Cinema, Falkirk; The Ritz Cinema, Cambusland; The Picture Theatre, Bellshill; The Pavilion Cinema, Motherwell; La Scala Cinema, Hamilton; Picture House Cinema, Coatbridge; The Cinema, Wishaw; The Pavilion Cinema, Falkirk; The Gaumont Cinema, Alloa; The Rialto Cinema, Kirkcaldy; The Picture House Cinema, Brighton Polmont; The Miners' Society, Harthill, Lanarks.; The Regal Theatre, Shotts.; The Windsor Cinema, Carluke; The Whitburn Cinema, West Lothian; The Picturehouse Cinema, Stirling; The Cinema, Glen Boig; The Western Theatre, Methil, Fife; The Hayweights Cinema, Musselburgh; The Star Theatre Cinema, Glencraig; The Picture House Cinema, Prestonpans; The Gourock Picture House, Glasgow; The Gothenburg Picture House, Kelty; The Cinema House, Tillicoultry; The Cinema House, Uphall, West Lothian; The Globe Cinema, Buckhaven; The Miners' Cinema, Douglas; The Picture House Cinema, Sanquhar; The Victory Cinema, Portobello; The Pavilion Cinema, Airdrie; The Picture House Cinema, Polmont.

TOTAL: 41 Cinemas

NORTHERN DIVISION:

The Scala Cinema, Gateshead; The Pavilion Cinema, Newcastle; The Gaumont Cinema, Wallsend; The Scala Cinema, South Shields; The Boro' Cinema, North Shields; The Hippodrome Cinema, Middlesbrough; The Picture House Cinema, West Hartlepool; The Alhambra Cinema, Darlington; The Palace Cinema, Sunderland; The Odeon Cinema, Bishop Auckland; The Empire Cinema, Darlington; The Odeon Cinema, Darlington; The Odeon Cinema, Gateshead; The Odeon Cinema, Middlesbrough; The Odeon Cinema, South Shields; The Odeon Cinema, Stockton; The Odeon Cinema, West Hartlepool; The Corn Exchange Cinema, Alnwick, Northumberland; The Prince of Wales Cinema, Bedlington; The Miners' Welfare Cinema, Linton, Morpeth; The Welfare Institute, Morpeth; The Empress Cinema, Lanchester, Co. Durham; The Ritz Cinema, Horden Colliery; The Shotton Colliery Cons. Comm., Shotton Colliery; The Empire Cinema, Murton; The Miners' Cinema, Sedghill, Northumberland; The Haymarket Cinema, Newcastle; The Elite Cinema, Middlesbrough; The Forum Cinema, West Hartlepool; The Ritz Cinema, Gateshead; The Ritz Cinema, Sunderland; The Savoy Cinema, South Shields; The Ritz Cinema, Wallsend; The Rex Cinema, Consett.; The Majestic Cinema, Benwell; The Globe Cinema, Stockton.

TOTAL: 36 Cinemas

NORTH-EASTERN DIVISION:

The Ritz Cinema, Leeds; The Shaftsbury Cinema, Leeds; The Gaiety Cinema, Leeds; The Ritz Cinema, Bradford; The Ritz Cinema, Barnsley; The Ritz Cinema, Huddersfield; The Hippodrome Cinema, Sheffield; The Playhouse Cinema, Dewsbury; The Ritz Cinema, Brighouse; The Regal Cinema, York; The Ritz Cinema, Keighley; The Regal Cinema, Wakefield; The Albion Cinema, Castleford; The Regal Cinema, Halifax; The Whitehall Cinema, Rotherham; The Picture House Cinema, Doncaster; The Alambra Cinema, Barnsley; The Odeon Cinema, Rotherham; The Odeon Cinema, Barnsley; The Empire Cinema, Barnsley; The Empire Cinema, Wakefield; The Gaumont Palace Cinema, Doncaster; The Princes Cinema, Barnsley; The Carlton Cinema, Wakefield.

TOTAL: 24 Cinemas

NORTH-WESTERN DIVISION:

The New Victoria Cinema, Preston; The Gaumont Cinema, Ashton; The Gaumont Cinema, Oldham; The Palace Cinema, Leigh; The Odeon Cinema, Barrow; The Odeon Cinema, Warrington; The Odeon Cinema, Bolton; The Odeon Cinema, Burnley; The Odeon Cinema, Chorley; The Palladium Cinema, Morecambe; The Regent Picture House Cinema, Nelson; The Broadway Cinema, Eccles; The Regal Cinema, Leigh; The Ritz Cinema, Rochdale; The Ritz Cinema, Warrington; The Savoy Cinema, St. Helens; The Palace Cinema, Ashton/Makerfield; The Capitol Cinema, Bolton; The Ritz Cinema, Wigan; The Palladium Cinema, Oldham; The Regal Cinema, Rochdale; The Odeon Cinema, Accrington; The Miners' Institute, Rhos, Wrexham; The Majestic Cinema, Wrexham; The Odeon Cinema, Wrexham.

TOTAL: 25 Cinemas

EAST MIDLANDS DIVISION:

The Odeon Cinema, Alfreton; The Odeon Cinema, Chesterfield; The Gaumont Palace Cinema, Derby; The Ritz Cinema, Clipstone Village; The Ritz Cinema, Pilsley; The Ritz Cinema, Whitwell; The Empire Cinema, Long Eaton; The Metro Cinema, Newton, Derby; The News Theatre, Nottingham; The Plaza Cinema, Bolsover; The Windsor Cinema, Nottingham; The Electric Cinema, Grassmoor, Chesterfield; The Savoy Cinema, Leicester; The Trocadero Cinema, Leicester; The Carlton Cinema, Nottingham; The Regal Cinema, Derby; The Grand Cinema, Mansfield; The Regal Cinema, Chesterfield; The Ritz Cinema, Scunthorpe; The Rex Cinema, Radcliffe-on-Trent, Notts.; The Regent Cinema, Riddings, Derby; The Regent Cinema, East Kirkby, Notts.; The Empire Cinema, Nottingham.

TOTAL: 23 Cinemas

WEST MIDLANDS DIVISION:

The Tower Cinema, West Bromwich; The Savoy Cinema, Walsall; The Olympia Cinema, Darlaston; The Majestic Cinema, Stoke; The Empire Cinema, Longton; The Savoy Cinema, Newcastle/Lyme; The Capitol Cinema, Hanley; The Odeon Cinema, Bloxwich; The Odeon Cinema, Ashton/Lyme; The Picture House Cinema, Walsall; The Queens Cinema, Wolverhampton; The Criterion Cinema, Dudley; The Regent Cinema, Hanley; The Empire Cinema, Hanley; The Hippodrome Cinema, Stoke; The Coliseum Cinema, Burslem; The Gaumont Cinema, Wednesbury; The Picture House Cinema, Willenhall; The Scala Cinema, Wolverhampton; The Royal

Cinema, Dordon, Tamworth; The Alexandra Picture House, Chesterton; The Palace Cinema, Audley; The Tivoli Cinema, Hednesford; The Scala Cinema, Blidworth; The Ritz Cinema, Nuneaton.

TOTAL: 25 Cinemas

SOUTH-EASTERN DIVISION:
The Odeon Cinema, Kings Wood; The Odeon Cinema, Deal.

TOTAL: 2 Cinemas

SOUTH-WESTERN DIVISION:
The Olympia Cinema, Cardiff; The Olympia Cinema, Newport; The Castle Cinema, Merthyr; Gracie's Banking Cinema, Annan; The Workmen's Hall, Blaengwynfil; The Welfare Association, Kenfig Hill; The Workmen's Hall Cinema, Abergwynfi, Port Talbot; The Workmen's Hall Cinema, Caerphilly; The Workmen's Hall Cinema, Garndiffaith; The Workmen's Hall Cinema, Gartl Terr, Bedlinog; The Workmen's Hall Cinema, Gilfach Goch; The Workmen's Hall Cinema, Abercynon; The Workmen's Institute, Penrhiwceiber; The Rern Hill Workmen's Institute, Treherbert; The Park and Dale Hall, Treorchy; The Kenfig and Pyle Cinema, Pyle; The Miner's Welfare Association, Glynneath; The Public Memorial Hall, Crynant, Neath; The Welfare Hall, Cefn Cribwr; The Lady Windsor Workmen's Institute, Ynysbwl; The Welfare Hall, Cribbuw, Bridgend; The Fernhill Workmen's Hall, Treherbert; The Workmen's Hall Cinema, Abertridwr; The Welfare Association, Pyle; The Workmen's Hall Cinema, Ynishir; The Hippodrome Cinema, Llanelly; The Miners' Welfare Association, Cwmllynfell; The Workmen's Hall, Mardie, Rhondda; The Workmen's Hall, Bedlinog; The Cinema, Clydach Vale; The New Theatre, Maesteg; The Olympia Cinema, Ogmore Vale; The Coliseum Cinema, Abergavenny; The Workmen's Hall, Tredegar; The Miners' Cinema, Markham; The Playhouse Cinema, Llanhilleth; The Workmen's Cinema, Uplands, Swansea; The Memorial Hall, Penclawdd; The Princes Theatre, Bedlinog; The Empire Cinema, Cardiff; The Coliseum Cinema, Newport; The Palace Cinema, Cinderford; The Odeon Cinema, Bedminster; The Odeon Cinema, Bristol; The Capitol Cinema, Cardiff; The Odeon Cinema Newport; The Odeon Cinema, Tredegar Hall, Newport; The Odeon Cinema, Port Talbot; The Odeon Cinema, Sketty; The Odeon Cinema, Taibach; The Odeon Cinema, Llanelly; The Odeon Cinema, Cardiff; The Palladium Cinema, Midsomer Norton; The Miners' Cinema, Lynemouth; The Welfare Hall, Ammanford; The Ambassador

Cinema, Bristol; The Regent Cinema, Taibach, Port Talbot; The Workmen's Hall, Llanbradach.

TOTAL: 58 Cinemas

UNCLASSIFIED CINEMAS:
The Welfare Society, Eastfield, Harthill; The Orion Cinema, Midhurst Sussex; The Capitol Cinema, Mill Hill, N.W.7; The Palace Cinema, Brentwood, Essex; The Orion Cinema, Burgess Hill; The Savoy Cinema, Egham, Surrey; The Orion Cinema, Hassocks; The Palace Cinema, Rainworth; The Welfare Society, Douglas Water; The New Cinema, Aylesham, Kent; The Plaza Cinema, Hastings.

TOTAL: 11 Cinemas

The National Archives holds a variety of production documents and associated material in INF 6 related to selected magazine series made by the British government, through the Central Office of Information (COI). This memo held in INF 6/1976 is from Charles Dand, Director of British Information Services in New York, to the Foreign Office in April 1954. In it he outlines the genesis of the first television magazine series produced by the COI, Transatlantic Teleview.

Copy
(PS 2454/110)
BRITISH INFORMATION SERVICES
30 Rockefeller Plaza
New York 20, N.Y.
Reference for reply
M541/Policy
April 12, 1954.

Dear Miss Senior,

Will you please refer to your letter PG 14514/1 of March 8 about film interviews for American television and Mr. Mullard's request PS 2454/110 of April 8 for a reply.

2. Since this reply was unlikely to be in time for the Overseas Film Committee meeting on April 13, I cabled: "YOUR PS 2454/110 LETTER IN BAG PROPOSES THREE FILMS FOR BIS RELEASE ON TELEVISION NOVEMBER JANUARY MARCH UNDER TITLE TRANSATLANTIC TELEVIEW STOP EACH THIRTEEN MINUTE MAGAZINE OF THREE INTERVIEWS WITH LONDON PERSONALITIES ONE OF SEVEN MINUTES ON A POLICY TOPIC TWO OF THREE MINUTES EACH ON LIGHTER SUBJECTS ALL STRAIGHT INTERVIEWS COST SHOULD NOT EXCEED £1500 MAXIMUM STOP NO NETWORK ARRANGEMENTS YET."

3. We have given the whole question further consideration in the light of your suggestion that you might be able to produce a series of items over a number

of years. We are wondering what the possibilities may be for the following idea which I have discussed with my fellow-Directors and which they all think I should submit to you for urgent consideration. The reason at our end for the urgency will emerge later.

4. It is our view that what we are most in need of for U.S. television use is not the usual type of documentary film on subjects of lasting interest which take a long time to produce and are usually expensive but inexpensive films with a short life on subjects of topical interest in the political and economic relationships of the United States and the United Kingdom. Of course, we want a supply of long-range films suitable for television medium (1) to inform the American public about our attitudes to current international problems, and to explain to them our own domestic problems which affect our relationships with the US and other countries; and (2) to make them more familiar with our leading political and economic personalities so that when they read about them or their speeches they have a mental picture of them, a recollection of their voices, and some idea of their characters. Television steadily assumes more and more importance as a medium for the expounding and explaining of policies and if people are given the opportunity of <u>seeing</u> a British political leader expound a policy matter, not only do they pay more attention to what he is saying on that occasion but they form an impression of him which gives them a continuing interest in his subsequent pronouncements because he has ceased to be only a name or somebody far off but a person with whom they have had a personal contact, somebody who has actually been in their homes.

5. We have not yet been able to arrange with the networks for their initiating at the London end interviews with politicians and other leaders. We shall continue to pursue this possibility but whatever comes of it we feel that BIS should also be able to offer interviews on film in the following form.

"Transatlantic Teleview"

6. This would be a 13-minute film magazine.

7. Each issue would be made up of a 7-minute interview with a British expert or authoritative speaker on some subject which is of policy importance in Anglo-US relations and two 3-minute interviews on non-policy topics related to interesting developments or happenings in British industry, science and technology, culture, sport, entertainment, social welfare. The interviews could be straight and unadorned or could be illustrated where appropriate with film or other visual material. The essential feature of the interviews, however, should be that they appear to be conducted <u>across the Atlantic by one of the</u>

regular staff of each TV station. In this way each station, however, small, can appear to its local viewers to have had the enterprise to arrange interviews with prominent persons in London and to have the means of linking up Cedar Rapids, Iowa, or Easton, Pennsylvania, with London so that questions seen and heard as being put by a well-known interviewer in Cedar Rapids seem to be answered by a personality in London.

8. We are confident this device will make a strong appeal to a very large number of the 370 local TV stations and presents no technical difficulties to any station able to use a live speaker and pieces of film in the same programme. The method would be: the questions are put to the interviewee in London by a person off-screen. They are then cut off the sound-track and silent pauses substituted. The questions are supplied in a script with the film to the TV station and the local interviewer on the TV screen puts them in his own voice and is answered immediately in picture and sound by the personality in London. Thus any small-town station director can have the local distinction of seeming to chat TV-wise across the Atlantic with London politicians, actresses, sportsmen, etc.

9. We should like to suggest that you try to give us three issues of this "Transatlantic Teleview" for release in November, January and March of the current year.

10. The method of distribution could be: if issues were being prepared for November, January and March in the current year, one or more prints of the film could be supplied by October 15, say, to each Information Officer and Consul who would have from then until the end of December to get the issue shown on many TV stations in the area as possible. The next issue could be sent on December 15 and the process repeated. If the October issue had gone out of date by then, it would be withdrawn. If not, it could go on being used as long as there were stations to take it.

11. It should be possible for the COI to prepare an issue and send the negative here by air in not more than four weeks. If the Foreign Office agreed topics and the policy item questions with us by September 15 for the November issue (and similarly for following issues) it should be possible to carry out the above time-table. It should not be difficult for us to agree in September on a policy item (and a treatment of it) which would remain valid for three months. If anything went out of date for any reason, it would not be difficult to withdraw an issue.

12. Film interviews as described above need not be expensive to make. There would seem to be no reason why any issue should cost more than £500 and it might be possible to do it even more cheaply. The idea would seem to be one

which could readily be "sold" to stations in advance of production and if we had a reasonably favourable response to preliminary soundings we should like to persuade you not only to give us three issues in the current year but to budget for an issue per month in the following year. Whether the money should be spent in 1955–56 could be determined by the results obtained from the November and January issues.

13. There are three advantages to us in the scheme as outlined:

    (1) The subjects, the interviewees, the questions and the answers are all under British control which they could not be if we rely entirely on interviews made by the networks for their own purposes. (To obviate any distortion of the policy interviews by the substitution by a local interviewer of slightly different and possibly angled questions, we should propose to ask all stations to sign an undertaking that the questions would be put in the form provided by us.)

    (2) A network programme is never carried by more than a proportion of the stations. With the help of our special device we have an opportunity of having our interviews carried by all the stations which have defined local areas and are not competing with one another for the same public (there are probably 300 of these). Stations affiliated to a network do not necessarily carry all the more serious material the network puts out. We feel the device would induce them to carry our "Teleview" and put it on at a good viewing hour of the day. Moreover, we cannot expect more than an occasional network interview originated in London. The device should ensure regular use by all stations at whatever frequency of issue we can afford to provide. (One station director to whom I broached the idea said at once he would be prepared to find time once a week but we are not so ambitious – for the present, at least).

    (3) The proposed method of distribution could bring our regional information offices and consulates into direct regular contact with TV stations in their areas and through it relationships could be established which might make it easier to have other films shown, talks arranged, etc. We feel there are wide and long-term advantages to be gleaned from this method of distri-bution in building up goodwill towards Britain on the part of local stations in difficult areas which no amount of network programming would provide. A network interview has the advantage of speed of distribution but it remains remote and impersonal, so far as the local station is concerned. We feel, too, that many local audiences, particularly in the less friendly areas, will pay more attention to an interview in which a known local man appears

to be taking part than they will be similar interviews which are carried out wholly at a distance from them.

14. We should be glad to have your reactions to the proposal as speedily as possible because I am going on a tour of our depositories starting on May 2 in which I shall be talking to quite a number of TV station personnel and I should like to try this scheme on them. I do not wish to do so, however, if there is no possibility of money being available for two or three experimental issues this year or if you see other objections.

15. It may be that an interview-magazine on film of the kind proposed could be used for televising in other territories. We should like to suggest, however, that special consideration be given to our scheme in view of its simple form and low cost and the arguments we have presented. I have discussed it with the Regional Information Officers in Chicago and Boston, both of whom are warmly in favour of it.

16. We are facing a growing competition in the television field from free films offered to stations by industrial and other sponsors. There is strong pressure from some of our regional people that we should also offer films for free use by TV stations. I propose to inquire more fully into the position on my forthcoming tour. The question is a large and complex one with many ramifications which will all have to be most carefully considered. If I find, however, that there seems to be a strong case for re-consideration of our present policy in regard to TV rental fees, are you at all likely to be prepared to allow us to offer the proposed "Televiews" on a no-charge basis?

17. We hope to have ready for release at the end of this month four series of thirteen films each for television composed of existing films and re-edits. They are under the titles: "All on a Summer's Day"; "Diversion"; "See and Enjoy" and "Science Quest and Conquest". The promotion material should be ready in about a week's time and it will give you full particulars. These four series are in addition to the "Impact" and child welfare series about which we have been corresponding.

18. I am sorry this letter will not reach you in time for the Overseas Film Committee meeting tomorrow but I did not see Mr. Mullard's letter about the meeting until late on Saturday morning and the idea for the "Teleview" scheme was finally discussed and formulated only last week.

Yours ever,

(signed) C. H. Dand.

THE PROJECTION OF ENGLAND

Sir Stephen Tallents

These three extracts from Stephen Tallents' seminal booklet The Projection of England, *originally published in 1932, summarise the case for national projection and describe the elements that should be incorporated into England's image overseas, many of which are still intrinsic to Britain's nation brand.*

England has always held herself aloof from the world's opinion. She can no longer afford that indifference. Her responsibilities as a world state, as the European partner in a great Empire, and as a trading community with world-wide interests, alike demand that she should set herself to throw a true and modern picture of her qualities on the screen of the world's mind.

This pamphlet is a plea for the deliberate study of a new art – the art of national projection – which should embrace all the modern forms of communication, from the printing press, the wireless and the cable to the film and the exhibition, but in which every individual citizen has a part to play.

***

If we want to know what material England should project, it is wise to ask ourselves what are the English characteristics in which the outside world is most interested. It is an entertaining pursuit – this breaking up of the fame of England into its primary colours. At one end of the spectrum are to be found, I suppose, such national institutions and virtues as:

The Monarchy (with its growing scarcity value)
Parliamentary Institutions (with all the values of a first edition).
The British Navy.
The English Bible, Shakespeare and *Dickens.*
('What marked and striking excellence,' wrote Gerard Hopkins to Patmore nearly fifty years ago, 'has England to show to make her civilization attractive? Her literature is one of her excellences and attractions … This is why I hold that fine works of art … are really a great power in the world, an element of strength even to an empire.')

In international affairs – *a reputation for disinterestedness.*
In national affairs – *a tradition of justice, law and order.*
In national character – *a reputation for coolness.*
In commerce – *a reputation for fair dealing.*
In manufacture – *a reputation for quality.*
(How agreeable it was, only last summer, to read of the two astute merchants of Eastern Europe, who were found to be selling their native cloth at a fantastic price by the simple device of calling it English!)
In sport – *a reputation for fair play.*

At the other end of the spectrum might be found such events as the *Derby* and the *Grand National*, the *Trooping of the Colour*, the *Boat Race, Henley, Wimbledon,* the *Test Matches,* and the *Cup Final.* But between these two extremes comes a medley of institutions and excellencies, which every man may compile for himself according to his humour and his ingenuity. My own list would include:

Oxford and *St. Andrews.*
Piccadilly, Bond Street, Big Ben and *Princes Street, Edinburgh.*
The *English Countryside, English villages,* the *English home* and *English servants.*
The *Lord Mayor of London.*
The *Times, Punch,* and the *Manchester Guardian.*
The *Metropolitan Police* and *Boy Scouts.*
The *London omnibuses* and *Underground Railways.*
Football and *Foxhunting.*
English bloodstock and *pedigree stock.*
The arts of *gardening* and of *tailoring.*

Of some such elements as these is the standing raw material of England's esteem in the world composed. There should be added to them all those achievements which by a sudden stroke place England from time to time on the world's screen and win her there a favourable reflection. Of such are England's speed records by land, sea and air, Miss Johnson's flight to Australia and Squadron Leader Hinkler's magnificent crossing of the Atlantic to Africa. Striking actions and events such as these need, it may be said, no deliberate projection. Yet among them are some at least of which the excellence could have been enhanced to our advantage in distant eyes, if the arts of national projection had lent them skilled support. How many people in the world, for example, know that Lindbergh's flight, for all its unmatched brilliance, was not the first crossing of the Atlantic by air? How many Canadians, with the news reels of the United States continually before their eyes, know that not all the athletic championships of the world are held by America? Not are the materials for England's projection to be found in England alone. Just as a skilled English workman likes to see and to read about the working conditions of men engaged in tasks comparable with his own, so the Canadian or the Australian farmer is interested to learn of the conditions of other farmers, working under different conditions of other farmers, working under different conditions but encountering the same ultimate problems of soil and weather and animal welfare. So too the native of Africa enjoys pictures of other peoples not too far removed from his own manner of living. To satisfy this universal desire of men and women to see and read of the conditions of their fellows, England can summon up the infinite variety of her Empire's resources, and bring that material, however indirectly, within the compass of her own projection.

So much, by way of illustration rather than catalogue, for the more familiar and traditional of the raw materials which can be used in the projection of England. I suspect that the briefest study of our new art and its requirements would disclose a treasure of less familiar excellencies, better fitted to-day than many of these to be flashed upon the screen of a new world. I suspect also – so utterly does our memory of the England of yesterday becloud our perception of the England of to-day – that the same study would discover the need of a preliminary projection of England to herself.

***

I have claimed that England, reluctant through she seems, must master that art in fulfilment alike of her needs and her responsibilities. Let us consider what those needs and responsibilities are.

In the first place it is essential for England as a world power that she should be able to make herself known to her fellows. Peace itself may at any time depend upon a clear understanding abroad of her actions and her motives. International co-operation is vital; and it is ultimately dependent not merely upon the excursions of statesmen from capital to capital – great though the value of such visits be – but upon a good understanding of each other by the peoples of the world. If we are to play our part in the new world order, we need to master every means and every art by which we can communicate with other peoples. The need is specially urgent between ourselves and the other parts of the Empire. We are experimenting together in a novel political organization, in which are joined together peoples most widely separated from each other in space and in character. Good communications are plainly a first essential for its successful working. On this ground pre-eminently we need to be able to project overseas a full and true presentation of England. We need that ability all the more because it is certain that, if we do not undertake the task ourselves, others will be found to undertake it for us, not always with truth nor always with sympathy.

The Projection of England by Sir Stephen Tallents (1955 edition) dust jacket and pp. 13–18

TELEVISION LOOKS AHEAD, *This is Britain* issue no 42, 1950

BFI/COI

A-Z OF BRITISH CINEMAGAZINES

This directory lists each cinemagazine series alphabetically by title with (where known) release date, a brief history, producer, sponsor, production company, archive (where viewing copies are available) and source of the data. For most of these series the details of each known issue and story can be found on the British Universities Newsreel Database (BUND) at http://www.bufvc.ac.uk/cinemagazines.

ABCA MAGAZINE

Dates: 1943 and 1946

History: *ABCA* [Army Bureau of Current Affairs] *Magazine* was a series of black-and-white films, each lasting around ten minutes, looking at postwar issues such as EDUCATION (issue no. 3), TOWN AND COUNTRY PLANNING (issue no. 5) and COAL (issue no. 7), all released in 1946. However, one issue, possibly the first, was produced in 1943, directed by Ronald Riley, with music composed by William Alwyn. The film credits state that it was produced for the Directorate of Army Kinematography under War Office auspices.

Sponsor: Army Bureau of Current Affairs/War Office

Production company: National Interest Picture Productions Ltd

Archive: Imperial War Museum Film and Video Archive

Source: *British Film Yearbook* 1949–50, p. 361; Imperial War Museum online catalogue

AC-DELCO MAGAZINE

Dates: 1957–1962

History: *AC-Delco Magazine* was a public relations tool for AC-Delco, a company that mainly produced parts used in the manufacture of automobiles. Issues featured the manufacture and use of parts such as thermostats, ignition coils and radiator pressure caps. It appears that just three 16mm issues were made, lasting between 22 and 30 minutes each and released in 1957, 1960 and 1962. The first two issues were made in black and white and the final one in colour.

Sponsor: AC-Delco

Production company: Stanley Schofield Productions

Original distribution: 16mm on request

Source: *British National Film and Video Catalogue* Retrospective File; *Film User* no. 230 p. 719 (December 1965)

ACE CINEMAGAZINE

Dates: 1937–1938

History: *Ace Cinemagazine* was made and distributed by Ace Films Ltd It began in July 1937, with 26 one-reelers with punning titles. Each issue was made up of several seemingly unconnected items on themes ranging from manufacturing techniques and dance routines to nature studies and jokes. The series ran for seventy-nine issues with the last, PULLING THE WIRES, released in August 1938. This final issue featured electric cable manufacture, French poodles, easy-to-make musical instruments, early mechanical instruments and some traditional peasant dances.

Production company: Ace Films

Original distribution: National cinema distribution

Source: *Monthly Film Bulletin; Today's Cinema; Kinematograph Weekly*

ANNUAL FILM MAGAZINE

Dates: 1959 and 1965

History: *Annual Film Magazine* appears to have been a regular round-up of events made for the East African Railways and Harbours Administration. It featured stories on railway and harbour construction, and royal visits to East Africa.

Sponsor: East African Railways and Harbours Administration

Production company: Gateway Films

Source: *Film User*, BFI Film & TV Database

ARCHITECTURAL NEWSREEL

Dates: 1971–1979

History: *Architectural Newsreel* was a colour series produced by the Central Office of Information (COI) for the Building Research Establishment. It was aimed at architects and the building trade in general, and each issue featured a single story, for example SPECIFYING STRUCTURAL TIMBER and FIRE RESEARCH.

Producer: Central Office of Information

Sponsor: Building Research Establishment

Production company: Keith Z. Ord & Co.

Archive: BFI Archive Footage Sales

Source: COI production files held at BUFVC

AROUND THE TOWN

Dates: 1919–1923

History: *Around the Town* was first trade-shown at the Shaftesbury Pavilion, London, on 30 October 1919. The production company, Around the Town Ltd, was co-directed by Aron Hamburger, inventor of the Polychromide colour process (in 1918) and later director of British Polychromide Ltd. National distribution of the series began on 8 December 1919 (London having received the first

Around The Town issue no. 105, 1921

issue on the 4th) and the series was 'exclusively controlled' and distributed by the Gaumont Company Ltd.

Around the Town began as a 750-foot reel released once a week, described as 'varied interest' but with an emphasis on the arts and literature. Its first slogan was 'Beauty and Celebrity Everywhere'. The 'town' mentioned in the title was most definitely London – a number of the early issues began with scenic tours of parts of the city, and the advertising material often featured outlines of the London skyline behind its central images. The implied intention of the cinemagazine in this advertising was to allow the public a glimpse into 'society'. The series was initially well-received by the press as a novelty in cinema programmes, *The Times* commenting that *Around the Town* was 'visualizing gossip columns ... so popular of late' (*Kinematograph Weekly*, 27 November 1919). As well as its usual fare of fashion, sports, science and theatre, *Around the Town* ran a beauty competition in 1920 – 'The Golden Apple Competition' – whose winner, Winifred Nelson, subsequently appeared two minor British movies. This was followed by a Screen Joke Competition in 1921. This self-promotion may well have been aimed at combating the new competition that *Around the Town* itself was facing in the guise of Pathe's new cinemagazine, *Eve's Film Review*. In 1921, *Around the Town*'s slogan was changed to 'The Original and Best Weekly Review', presumably as a poke at their new rival. At this point Gaumont also chose to emphasise the appeal that *Around the Town* had for men as well as its predominantly female audience. In addition, its 1921 advertising campaign focused on the 'prestige' merited by its coverage of the great and good. In 1922, Gaumont went one step further in attempts to increase consumption of *Around the Town*, launching a poster competition in association with the *London Evening News* with a first prize of £1,000. Gaumont announced its intention to continue producing and distributing *Around the Town* in *The Bioscope* of 4 January 1923, boasting that 'Everybody who is Anybody is screen-interviewed in *Around the Town*'. This, however, was not be, and *Around the Town* was no longer mentioned in the trade press after 1923. This could be connected to the fact that Mr H. T. Redfern, editor and secretary of *Around the Town* since his demobilisation in 1919, left Gaumont in January 1923. The move seems to have coincided with bigger changes in the structure of *Around the Town*'s parent company, as January 1923 was also the date that Messrs Bromhead took sole control of the Gaumont Company Ltd. The last issue of *Around the Town* that we have a record of was released on 5 July 1923.

Production company: Around the Town Ltd

Original distribution: National cinema distribution through the Gaumont Company

Archive: BFI National Archive

Source: *Kinematograph Weekly*; *The Bioscope*

BABCOCK REVIEW

Dates: 1956

History: *Babcock Review* was a compilation of stories from Babcock & Wilcox's other cinemagazine, *Home and Away*.

Producer: Film Producers Guild

Sponsor: Babcock & Wilcox Ltd

Production company: Technical & Scientific Films

Original distribution: 16mm copies on request from Babcock & Wilcox

Source: *Imagery* vol. 8 no. 2 (October 1956); Scottish Screen Archive online catalogue

BALFOUR BEATTY REVIEW

Dates: 1987–1988

History: *Balfour Beatty Review* was a short-lived video magazine of the company's activities.

Sponsor: Balfour Beatty

Source: *Marketing Video Library Catalogue* 1990

BEHIND THE SCENES

Dates: 1953

History: *Behind the Scenes* was sponsored by the Gas Council of Britain and made by Film Workshop. It ran for six issues during 1953; each issue featured several stories with some connection to gas, including cooking and heating demonstrations, and also boasted a celebrity guest.

Sponsor: Gas Council

Production company: Film Workshop

Archive: BFI National Archive

Source: *Film User*; BFI Film & TV Database

BELADUNA

Dates: 1953–c.1958

History: *Beladuna* was produced specifically for audiences in Iraq by the Iraq Petroleum Company. *Beladuna* issue no. 2 (1953) is a typical example of an early issue, featuring a visit to the Ain Zallah oilfield, a Baghdad cotton factory and the corn harvest in northern Iraq. Later ones seem to have favoured themed formats such as MODERN MEANS OF TRANSPORT (1954).

Sponsor: Iraq Petroleum Company

Production company: Iraq Petroleum Company Film Unit

Original distribution: Iraq

Source: BFI Film & TV Database

BICC BALFOUR BEATTY LINKLINE

Dates: 1981–1984

History: A video magazine of the company's activities.

Sponsor: Balfour Beatty

Source: *Marketing Video Library Catalogue* 1990

BOROUGH GAZETTE

Dates: 1948–1953

History: *Borough Gazette* was intended as public relations for Slough County Council. It recorded major events in the town and was issued on an annual basis. Frank Taylor made *Borough Gazette*, using his own equipment to film the magazine whilst the Council met additional expenses. His budget for 1953 was £150, which was largely spent filming local celebrations for the Coronation.

Sponsor: Slough County Council

Production company: Frank Taylor, Council photographer

Source: *Film User* no. 88 p. 85 (February 1954)

BRITAIN CAN MAKE IT

Dates: 1945–1947

History: *Britain Can Make It* was a successor series to the Ministry of Information's *Worker and Warfront*. It was produced by Paul Rotha's company, Films of Fact, for the Ministry of Information and then its successor, the Central Office of Information (COI). Its intention was to promote British industrial achievement and design in a postwar age. There was a major public exhibition on design entitled 'Britain Can Make It' which opened in London in September 1946, but the film series preceded it and seems to have had no association with it. *Britain Can Make It* was issued monthly, with three items per issue, some of which were shared with the COI's other cinemagazine *This Is Britain*. There were eighteen issues in all, each around ten minutes in length.

Producer: Ministry of Information/Central Office of Information

Sponsor: Ministry of Supply and Board of Trade

Production company: Films of Fact

Original distribution: Worldwide

Archive: BFI National Archive

Source: *Central Film Library* catalogue 1949; *Documentary News Letter, Monthly Film Bulletin*

BRITISH ATOMIC NEWS

Dates: 1956–1957

History: *British Atomic News* featured the contribution to Britain's nuclear energy programme of four companies: Costain–John Brown, Van Moppes, Morgan Crucible and Edwards High Vacuum.

Production company: B. Charles-Dean/British Atomic News

Source: *Film User* no. 113 p. 125 (March 1956); BFI Film & TV Database

BRITISH CALENDAR

Dates: 1959–1969

History: *British Calendar* was produced by the Central Office of Information (COI) for the Commonwealth Relations Office and the Foreign Office, primarily for distribution in the USA and English-speaking countries of the Commonwealth such as Australia. Initially this 13-minute 'cinemagazine for television' was flown to New York on a monthly basis, but by July 1961 it appeared fortnightly and from mid-1964, every week. Occasionally the stories in the US version would differ from those in the Commonwealth one. The suffix 'A' identifies these issues. From October 1964 the series' name was changed to *Calendar* but the format remained the same. This usually consisted of about seven topical stories and was generally more political in scope than other cinemagazines produced by the COI. Sometimes issues were produced with a single story, such as TRINIDAD INDEPENDENCE (issue no. 42,

Title frame from *Calendar* 1965

BFI National Archive/COI

August 1962), and from 1966 one issue per month was produced in colour as demand grew for colour material. Distribution to the USA stopped in September 1967 when *Calendar* was replaced by *London Line (Colour Series 2)* and the series itself ceased production in February 1969. Initially the production company was British Movietonenews Ltd but certainly from issue no. 124 (1965), the contract had passed to Kay (West End) Laboratories Ltd.

Producer: Central Office of Information

Sponsor: Commonwealth Relations Office and Foreign Office

Production company: British Movietonenews Ltd/Kay (West End) Laboratories Ltd

Original distribution: Commonwealth and the USA

Archive: BFI Archive Footage Sales and BFI National Archive (*Calendar* only)

Source: Production files (INF 6) and COI monthly divisional reports (INF 8); COI catalogue cards; film copies

BRITISH SCREEN TATLER

Dates: 1928–1931

History: *British Screen Tatler* was conceived as a sister cinemagazine to the newsreel *British Screen News*. It was made by British Screen Pictures and distributed every Monday for two years. The series' name, reminiscent as it is of the print magazine *The Tatler*, suggests that British Screen Pictures had aspirational aims in mind for its content. This seems to have been borne out in the subjects covered by the reel, such as 'Home Hints'. The series also featured regular episodes of the cartoon 'The Adventures of Little Nibs'.

Production company: British Screen Pictures

Original distribution: National cinema distribution

Archive: BFI National Archive

Source: *Kinematograph Weekly*; *The Bioscope*

BRITISH SPORTING PERSONALITIES

Dates: 1959–1962

History: This series of ten films, made between 1959 and 1962, was the first produced by the

Title frame from *British Sporting Personalities* 1961

Central Office of Information (COI) to focus on contemporary personalities. Each of the nine-minute films centred on the life of a particularly successful British sportsman or -woman. These included the swimmer Judy Grinham, John Surtees, Pat Smythe, Mary Bignal Rand, Stanley Matthews, Courtney Jones and Doreen Denny, Peter May and Derek Ibbotson. The production company for the first three issues was Anvil Films Ltd and then the contract passed to Associated British Pathe. There is no evidence that this cinemagazine was dubbed into any other language, so the distribution, given the sponsors, would have been to the USA and English-speaking countries of the Commonwealth and colonies.

Producer: Central Office of Information

Sponsor: Colonial Office, Commonwealth Relations Office and Foreign Office

Production company: Anvil Films Ltd/ Associated British Pathe

Original distribution: USA and English-speaking countries of the Commonwealth and colonies.

Archive: BFI Archive Footage Sales and BFI National Archive

Source: Production files (INF 6); COI catalogue cards; *Films from Britain* 1964–1965

BUTLIN NEWS

Dates: 1966

History: *Butlin News* (sometimes referred to as *Butlin Movienews* by Butlin's advertisements) was described by Butlin's Ltd as a local newsreel. It was shot by cameramen at each of the holiday camps during the season, as a weekly roundup of camp sports and other activities. The series was the successor to *Butlin's Holiday Magazine* and despite its repackaging as a newsreel, it retained much of its character as a cinemagazine. Shown at Butlin's holiday camps during the summer season, it achieved an average weekly audience of some 80,000 people.

Sponsor: Butlin's Ltd

Production company: Butlin's Ltd

Original distribution: Shown on 16mm at Butlin's holiday camps during the summer season

Source: *Film User* vol. 20 p. 481 (September 1966)

BUTLIN'S HOLIDAY MAGAZINE

Dates: 1958–1962

History: *Butlin's Holiday Magazine* was produced periodically and looked at the activities of the various Butlin's holiday camps around Britain. Typical stories include camp sports, beauty contests and new facilities, such as the chair lift at Ayr.

Sponsor: Butlin's

Production company: Associated British Pathe

Original distribution: Available free of charge on 16mm from Department F, Butlin's

Source: *Film User*, BFI Film & TV Database

CALENDAR *see* BRITISH CALENDAR

CARROUSEL BRITANICO

Dates: 1963–1974

History: *Carrousel Britanico* was a cinemagazine produced by the Central Office of Information (COI) for the Foreign and Commonwealth Office. Following the successful launch of the Technicolor cinemagazine *Roundabout* in South and South-East Asia in May 1962, it was decided to pilot a similar magazine for distribution in Latin America in December of the same year. This series was designed for cinema and non-theatrical distribution and was issued as *Carrousel Britanico* in Latin American Spanish and *Carrossel* in Brazilian Portuguese. Following the positive reception for the pilot, the first bimonthly issue was released in July 1963 and continued on this basis until June 1974. Each issue carried topical stories about developments in Britain and the Commonwealth, as well as items with a particular focus on Central and South America. Initially *Carrousel Britanico* was made by Associated British Pathe but in 1970 the contract passed to British Movietonews with issue no. 44, released in October 1970.

Producer: Central Office of Information

Sponsor: Foreign and Commonwealth Office

Production company: Associated British Pathe/British Movietonews

Original distribution: Latin America

Archive: BFI Archive Footage Sales

Source: COI catalogue cards; production files (INF 6) and COI monthly divisional reports (INF 8); COI production files at BUFVC

CINEGAZETTE

Dates: 1947–1957

History: *Cinegazette*, also known as *Cine-Gazette* or *London Transport's Cine Gazette*, was conceived as a series to promote the work of the London Transport Executive both to its staff and the wider public. The first issue, produced by Academy Picture Corporation and released in 1947, was a mixture of recent technological developments and staff sporting news. The series was shown to staff in cinema coaches and by mobile units, and also to members of the public through mobile units and exhibition displays. There was no regular distribution network for the series, and it seems that there was also no regular production schedule – the series was just released periodically.

From the third issue onwards, it was Academy Pictures' intention that issues would have a more formal structure. Each issue was to have a set pattern: a main item on an aspect of London Transport activities; a 'Round and About' feature for staff; and an item of interest to the general public. However, this pattern was only applied sporadically, being interspersed with single-story issues.

When British Transport Films (BTF) took on film production for the entire transport network, it also took on the production of *Cinegazette,* for which it is credited from issue no. 11 onwards. The film unit, under the direction of Edgar Anstey, continued with single-story issues, rather than the pattern set by Academy Films. This format seems to have been especially successful from a distribution angle, as several of the later issues were shown in cinemas or televised by the BBC. These include some of the most famous films made by BTF, such as THE ELEPHANT WILL NEVER FORGET (issue no. 12, 1953) and DO YOU REMEMBER? (issue no. 14, 1955). The final issue of *Cinegazette,* issue no. 16, was released in 1957.

Sponsor: London Transport Executive

Production company: Academy Picture Corporation/British Transport Films

Original distribution: 16mm showings to staff and the public.

Archive: London Transport Museum and BFI National Archive

Source: London Transport Museum; BFI Film & TV Database; *British National Film and Video Catalogue* Retrospective File

CITY SIDELIGHTS

Dates: 1951–1958

History: *City Sidelights* was a periodically produced series focusing on Glasgow. Each issue included several stories ranging from Christmas activities and the production of bibles to a catering school and the Glasgow School of Art. Five issues were produced between 1951 and 1958, each lasting around fifteen minutes.

Production company: Elder Film Productions

Archive: Scottish Screen Archive

Source: Scottish Screen Archive online catalogue

CIVIC MAGAZINE

Dates: 1956–1957

History: *Civic Magazine* was sponsored by Dagenham Borough Council to promote its activities. The only reference to it notes the intention to produce it for the municipal year 1956–1957. It was anticipated that it would last ten minutes and cost £100.

Sponsor: Dagenham Borough Council

Production company: Dagenham Co-operative Film Society

Source: *Film User* no. 115 p. 230 (May 1956)

COLONIAL CINEMAGAZINE

Dates: 1945–1949

History: *Colonial Cinemagazine* was produced by the British government's Colonial Film Unit for distribution throughout the British colonies. Each black-and-white issue lasted about ten minutes and featured around five items. Most of the stories focused on Africa, and Nigeria in particular, with the occasional story dedicated to countries such as Fiji.

Producer: Colonial Film Unit

Sponsor: Colonial Office

Production company: Colonial Film Unit

Original distribution: British colonies, primarily Africa

Archive: BFI National Archive

Source: BFI Film & TV Database

COMMONWEALTH REVIEW

Dates: 1964–1965

History: *Commonwealth Review* was a series of black-and-white 13-minute films made by the Central Office of Information (COI) and sponsored by the Commonwealth Relations Office for distribution in Commonwealth countries. Each issue consisted of about seven stories 'concerning Commonwealth personalities and events in Britain, and general activities in all countries of the Commonwealth' (*Films from Britain* 1964–1965). Kay (West End) Laboratories produced *Commonwealth Review* issue no. 5 and was probably responsible for the entire series of thirty-nine issues, which only ran from 1964 to 1965.

Producer: Central Office of Information

Sponsor: Commonwealth Relations Office

Production company: Kay (West End) Laboratories

Original distribution: Commonwealth
Archive: BFI National Archive and BFI Archive Footage Sales
Source: *British National Film Catalogue; Films from Britain* 1964–1965; COI catalogue cards; film copies

COMMONWEALTH TELEVIEW

Dates: 1957–1958
History: *Commonwealth Teleview* was a series of black-and-white 15-minute films made by the Central Office of Information (COI) and sponsored by the Commonwealth Relations Office for broadcast in Canada and later Australia. It was designed, as its opening titles state, to present 'The Commonwealth to The Commonwealth'. Within Canada it was 'presented by arrangement between the United Kingdom Information Service and the Canadian Broadcasting Corporation'. The first issue was released in January 1957 and a further fourteen issues were produced over the next two years. Each issue concentrated on a single story, such as the future of the Commonwealth, the radio telescope or the role of art in the community. *Commonwealth Teleview* was usually presented by Robert McKenzie, who would explore the topic through an interview with a single prominent personality such as the Earl of Home (issue no. 1). Other presenters such as Ted Morrisby would conduct a series of interviews to give an idea of, for example, industrial relations within a British factory (issue no. 14).

This format drew heavily on the one already established by *Transatlantic Teleview* and indeed many issues shared the same material. NEW TOWNS, for example, is the subject of *Transatlantic Teleview* issue no. 21 and *Commonwealth Teleview* issue no. 2. However, the approach for each was slightly different, slanted to their specific audiences.

Producer: Central Office of Information
Sponsor: Commonwealth Relations Office
Production company: Independent Television News/Worldwide Pictures
Original distribution: Canada and Australia
Archive: BFI Archive Footage Sales and BFI National Archive

Source: Production files (INF 6) and COI monthly divisional reports for 1957 (INF 8); *Overseas Film Library* catalogue c. 1957, COI catalogue cards; film copies

COUNTRY MAGAZINE

Dates: 1947
History: *Country Magazine* was part of Triumph's production of 'substandard' silent films. The series was designed to show unusual shots of wildlife as well as rural places and people.
Sponsor: Triumph
Production company: Triumph
Source: *Film User* no. 3 p. 93 (January 1947)

DATELINE BRITAIN

Dates: 1959
History: *Dateline Britain* was a short-lived series of four films produced by the Central Office of Information (COI) and sponsored by the Commonwealth Relations Office for distribution on television in Canada. This was done in association with the Canadian Broadcasting Corporation with the first issue, FACE OF YOUTH, broadcast in February 1959. The series was presented by actor Bernard Braden and actress Barbara Kelly, both Canadians, who examined a single theme of contemporary Britain in each of the 28-minute issues. Youth culture, the role of women in British society, Britain's scientists and London were all explored through a series of interviews, mostly shot on location.
Producer: Central Office of Information
Sponsor: Commonwealth Relations Office
Production company: Independent Television News
Original distribution: Canada
Archive: BFI Archive Footage Sales
Source: COI catalogue cards; *Films from Britain*; film copies; production files (INF 6) and COI monthly divisional reports (INF 8)

DO YOU KNOW?

Dates: 1950–1952
History: *Do You Know?,* sponsored by the Co-

operative Wholesale Society (CWS), describes how different products such as cigarettes (issue no. 4) and jam (issue no. 1) were made at various CWS works across the country.

Sponsor: Co-operative Wholesale Society

Production company: Co-operative Wholesale Society Film Unit

Archive: BFI National Archive

Source: *Film User* no. 63 p. 28 (January 1952); BFI Film & TV Database

EARTH MOVER

Dates: 1970

History: *Film User* describes the second issue of *Earth Mover* as a colour 'excavator cine-magazine' featuring stories on a motorway project, a tribute to those who built the railways, and a comic piece set in Carnaby Street. This issue lasted nineteen minutes.

Sponsor: J. C. Bamford (Excavators)

Production company: Warners (Commercial Film Division)

Source: *Film User* no. 282 p. 10 (April 1970)

THE EMPIRE PICTORIAL

Dates: 1927

History: The first issue of the *Empire Pictorial*, produced by William Jeapes, was released in 1927.

Producer: William Jeapes

Production company: British Pictorial (European)

Source: *British Film Catalogue* vol. 2 ID no. 06336 p. 242

ENTERPRISE

Dates: 1967

History: *Enterprise* was a colour cinemagazine reporting on various construction projects of its sponsor, John Laing & Son. The first issue was twenty-three minutes long and featured work on a reservoir at Wraysbury, a 35-storey building in the City of London, reconstruction work at Avonmouth and the building of a new jetty at West Thurrock oil terminal.

Sponsor: John Laing & Son

Production company: John Laing & Son

Source: *Film User* no. 251 p. 34 (September 1967)

THE ENTHUSIASTS

Dates: 1967

History: *The Enthusiasts* was a series of six black-and-white films produced by the Central Office of Information (COI). Each issue focused on a personality of the day – Stuart Turner, David Attenborough, Caroline Loizos, Anthony Wedgwood Benn, Sandy Dunbar and Peter Parker. The format was similar in each case, with the subject introduced through background material and then interviewed in the studio, often by Michael Smee, the regular presenter of *London Line (Colour Series 2)*. The series was distributed to the USA, Canada and Australia but in slightly different forms – in Canada and the USA it was seen as *The Enthusiasts*; in Australia it made up every other issue of another COI series, *London Line (Colour Series 2)*. A contract with Gauntlet Productions for special coverage of material for *The Enthusiasts* issue no. 8 indicates that the series was originally conceived as a longer one.

ANTHONY WEDGWOOD BENN, *The Enthusiasts* issue no. 4, 1967

Producer: Central Office of Information

Sponsor: Commonwealth Affairs Office and Foreign Office

Production company: United Motion Pictures (London) Ltd

Original distribution: Australia, Canada and the USA

Archive: BFI Archive Footage Sales

Source: COI catalogue cards; film copies; production files (INF 6)

ESSO FARM REVIEW *see* FARM REVIEW

ESSO GAZETTE

Dates: 1951–1953

History: Three issues of *Esso Gazette* were released on an annual basis to keep employees abreast of the activities of Esso both at home and abroad. Subjects included an Esso exhibition in London, a poster competition and work at a refinery at Fawley.

Sponsor: Esso

Production company: Esso Film Unit

Source: BFI Film & TV Database

EVENTS

Dates: 1935–1939 and 1947

History: *Events* was an annual cinemagazine designed to review the achievements of the London Midland and Scottish Railway company. The first issue, EVENTS OF 1935, lasted twenty minutes and covered a new diesel rail car, the construction of new stations, the naming of locomotives and the Sliver Jubilee of Transport at Euston. The series continued in the same vein until the outbreak of the Second World War when EVENTS OF 1939 was abandoned. EVENTS OF 1947 signalled a short return before railway nationalisation brought the series to an end in 1948.

Sponsor: London Midland and Scottish Railway

Production company: London Midland and Scottish Railway Film Unit

Archive: The Railway Film Archive

Source: S. Foxon Collection

EVE'S FILM REVIEW

Dates: 1921–1933

History: *Eve and Everybody's Film Review* was launched in June 1921 as Pathe's cinemagazine aimed at the female audience, a compliment to its already successful *Pathe Pictorial*. The series began with a title competition, asking members of the public to suggest a better name for the magazine. It seems as though none was forthcoming, as the title remained, often shortened to *Eve's Film Review*, throughout the cinemagazine's 12-year run. *Eve's Film Review* was produced by Pathe's Periodicals Department under the direction of Fred Watts, who described the series in a promotional essay, 'Just "Pic and Eve"' in 1928, as 'a most comprehensive and attractive "light" periodical'. It was assembled mostly from library footage, the occasional specially shot story (using manpower from the *Pathe Gazette* camera team) and bought-in series, for example, *Living Masterpieces* (March 1922–March 1924) and *Sportlights* (April 1925–May 1926).

Eve's Film Review's main content, in keeping with its 'fashion, fun and fancy' slogan was film of women doing interesting novel jobs and hobbies, fashion displays and novelty items ranging from excerpts of musicals and plays to slow-motion camera studies of nature. The mixture was lively and varied, reflecting art, home, fashion, stage, recreation and cartoons. Cartoons featured prominently in the series. *Eve's Film Review* was the first context in which British audiences saw Felix the Cat cartoons, which were shown in *Eve* from June 1922 until January 1926 (when Ideal began to distribute 'whole' Felix cartoons as a separate entity), and they became extremely popular. Many promotional Felix the Cat souvenir items remain from this association, from wool winders to china figurines, all bearing the legend 'Pathe's Eve's Film Review'. After Felix, *Eve's Film Review* continued to finish each reel with a cartoon, running Krazy Kat (January 1926–May 1927), and Sammy and Sausage (May 1928–April 1929). Combined with the other content of the reel, *Eve's Film Review* provided everything a 1920s' woman could desire for cinematic entertainment.

Indeed, the longevity of this cinemagazine does suggest that it was a popular exhibition choice. *The Bioscope* celebrated *Eve's Film Review*'s tenth year in 1931, saying that the series 'has been one of the most appreciated of all the screen topicals, and during the ten years it has thrived, it has been noteworthy for the bright and interesting nature of its contents' (20 May 1931, p. 32). Evidence from the surviving correspondence between Pathe and the public suggests that alongside the critics and the women for whom the series was intended, *Eve's Film Review* also had an appreciative male audience, perhaps because of the frequent shots of women wearing very little, but also because of the variety of subjects covered, and the amusing, often ironic, intertitles composed by Watts.

Eve's Film Review was one of the longest-running cinemagazines of the 1920s, ending in December 1933. Its demise can be attributed mainly to Pathe's business strategy rather than any failure of the series itself. *Eve* did not make the transition to sound and the content was incorporated into *Pathe Pictorial*.

Production company: Pathe

Original distribution: National cinema distribution

Archive: ITN Source and BFI National Archive

Source: *Kinematograph Weekly*; *The Bioscope*; BUFVC Pathe Collection

FARM REVIEW

Dates: 1950–1954

History: *Farm Review* or *Esso Farm Review* (both names are used) utilised the cinemagazine format to describe new tractor and farming innovations, whilst by association showing the advantages of Esso fuel. The first issue was produced in Kodachrome and covered four stories including the RASE forage harvester trials at Shillingford and spraying of sugar beet with vaporising oils. This was first shown at the 1950 Smithfield Show, receiving favourable comment from the farming press, especially with regard to the colour. It seems to have been produced annually with each issue lasting around twenty-eight minutes.

Sponsor: Esso

Production company: Esso Film Unit

Source*: Imagery* vol. 3 no. 2 (June 1951); *Film User* no. 92 p. 274 (June 1954)

FARMING REVIEW

Dates: 1950–1952

History: Two issues of *Farming Review* were released each year and featured 'various ingenious ways in which farms, big and small, use their tractors'. These included stories on hop picking, ploughing, the wine harvest and reclamation of marginal land in Wales.

Producer: Film Producers Guild

Sponsor: Harry Ferguson

Production company: Greenpark Film Productions

Original distribution: Shown by Manchester Oil Refinery's mobile exhibition unit

Source: *Imagery* vol. 3 no. 2 (June 1951); *Film User* no. 52 p. 84 (February 1951); BFI Film & TV Database

FEDERAL SPOTLIGHT *see* RHODESIAN SPOTLIGHT

FILMAGAZINE

Dates: 1946–1947

History: *Filmagazine* was produced by Andrew Buchanan, directed by Henry Cooper and filmed by Charles Francis. It seems only two issues were ever produced, released annually and lasting around fifteen minutes each. These included stories on the praxinoscope, the sculpture work of Princess Biancha Loewenstein, rare books owned by the British and Foreign Bible Society, and a man who collected antique music boxes and automatons.

Producer: Central Office of Information

Production company: Films of Great Britain

Archive: BFI National Archive

Source: *Monthly Film Bulletin* no. 163 p. 103 (July 1947); *British Film Yearbook* 1949–50 p. 371; BFI Film & TV Database

FORDSON NEWSREEL

Dates: 1953–1960

History: *Fordson Newsreel* was intended as a public relations tool for Fordson tractors. Although called a newsreel by Ford, in terms of content the series was more like a cinemagazine. Most of the 16mm colour issues contained footage of Fordson tractors, often as incidental parts of stories about land drainage or construction, in order to encourage viewing by social and educational 16mm users.

The series ran for fifty issues, from 1953 until 1960.

Sponsor: Ford Motor Company

Production company: Ford Motor Company

Original distribution: Distributed by Ford Film Library, free of charge.

Source: *British National Film and Video Catalogue* Retrospective File; *Film User*; BFI Film & TV Database

FRONTIER

Dates: 1964–1965, 1969

History: *Frontier* was a series of fourteen black-and-white films on science and technology produced by the Central Office of Information (COI) on behalf of the Commonwealth Relations Office. The films were made by various companies, including United Motion Pictures (London) Ltd, British Films and Eyeline Films, and directed by documentary filmmakers such as Michael Orrom and Margaret Thomson. Each 13-minute film dealt with an aspect of current British research such as radio astronomy, the development of computers, the invention of the hovercraft and the progress of nuclear power. The series was intended primarily for English-speaking countries but three language versions were available – Arabic, Persian and Asian English. Early in 1969 the series was resurrected in colour as *Frontier (Colour Series)* but was limited to five films after it was decided to produce a new science magazine series called *Living Tomorrow*. The films were again contracted out to companies such as United Motion Pictures (London) Ltd, New Decade Films and Viewpoint Productions. Each 13-minute film examined topics such as radio astronomy, research into car safety and the uses of radio isotopes. The colour series was produced in seven foreign-language editions including Arabic, French, German, Thai and Latin American Spanish, reflecting the extending scope of the COI's international distribution.

Producer: Central Office of Information

Sponsor: Foreign and Commonwealth Office

Production company: Ipsolon Films Ltd/ United Motion Pictures (London) Ltd/Derek Stewart Productions/Marcus Cooper Ltd/Eyeline Films Ltd/British Films Ltd/Philomel Productions Ltd/ Overseas Film & Television Centre Ltd/ New Decade Films Ltd/Viewpoint Productions Ltd

Original distribution: Worldwide

Archive: BFI Archive Footage Sales

Source: COI catalogue cards; *Films from Britain* 1968–1969; film copies; production documents (INF 6) and COI monthly divisional reports (INF 8); COI production files at BUFVC; *British National Film Catalogue*

GAUMONT MIRROR

Dates: 1927–1932

History: *Gaumont Mirror* began in January 1927 as a partner to the well-established newsreel *Gaumont Graphic*, although it had a weekly rather than bi-weekly release. It was described by Gaumont as a screen periodical and advertised with the slogan, 'Reflects Everything New and Novel'. Novelty, however, was not the *Gaumont Mirror*'s sole preoccupation. Women were the prime target audience and many of the subjects covered were intended to be of 'special interest to women': for example, women in sport, fashions and hints for the home. Gaumont seems to have intended the *Gaumont Mirror* as direct competition for both of Pathe's popular cinemagazines – *Pathe Pictorial* and *Eve's Film Review*. Not only was the series aimed at women, but it was also advertised as a 'pictorial review' (*The Bioscope*, 29 December 1927), suggesting similar appeal to *Pathe Pictorial*.

R. S. Howard, *Gaumont Mirror*'s editor, had moved from *Gaumont Graphic* to become editor of all Gaumont periodicals in November 1930. Although the cinemagazine and newsreel were frequently advertised together, they were different products and there is no indication that cinema exhibitors were obliged to take both. Indeed, one advert in *The Bioscope* (31 December 1930) suggests the contrary.

Very early in the series, *Gaumont Mirror* launched its animated star Dismal Desmond. He was already an established character 'seen in every toy shop and ... extensively advertised in the press' (*Kinematograph Weekly*, 4 November 1926) and thus a tried-and-tested investment. Dismal Desmond cartoons were shown at the end of the reel, and intended to please both children and adults. In addition, they provided Gaumont with plenty of opportunity for merchandising, with toys and novelty items available from the cinemas as well as toy shops. In 1928, the *Mirror* ran a competition to establish the relative popularity of the various items of interest included in the reel each week but unfortunately the results have not survived.

Gaumont Sound Mirror, the British Acoustic sound version of *Gaumont Mirror,* was released on 29 September 1930 at the Capitol, Haymarket. This 'De Luxe Sound Magazine' was run alongside its silent original to cater for cinemas reluctant to adopt the new technology. It is unclear whether these issues, released simultaneously, were made up of the same stories and footage. As an incentive to patrons to take the risk of adopting sound, Gaumont Sound Periodicals offered free insurance policies to subscribers against loss of takings due to technological faults in the sound equipment. In April 1932, this was extended to cover all equipment in the cinemas. Due to the interest in the *Gaumont Sound Mirror,* its silent sibling lost much coverage after the beginning of 1931. However, it does seem likely that the silent *Gaumont Mirror* continued to be produced into the middle of 1931. *Gaumont Sound Mirror* continued to grow in popularity as more cinemas became wired for sound, and the final issue that we have recorded was issue no. 78, released in late March 1932.

Production company: Gaumont

Original distribution: National cinema distribution

Archive: BFI National Archive

Source: *Kinematograph Weekly; The Bioscope*

GAUMONT SOUND MIRROR *see* GAUMONT MIRROR

GOOD COMPANY

Dates: 1958

History: *Good Company* was a cinemagazine for Dexion employees.

Sponsor: Dexion

Source: *Film User* cover (June 1958)

HELICOPTER MAGAZINE

Dates: 1952 and 1956

History: *Helicopter Magazine* was designed to show developments within the helicopter department of the Bristol Aeroplane Company as an aid to the sales department both in Britain and abroad. The first 20-minute issue previewed the first twin-engined helicopter in the world, the company's Type 173 twin-rotor helicopter. It was shot with a Paillard camera and edited by the company's own staff. Although silent, the intention was to add a sound commentary later. It took four years for the next issue to appear, which was half the length and produced with Verity.

Sponsor: Bristol Aeroplane Company

Production company: Bristol Aeroplane Company/Verity

Original distribution: Worldwide

Source: *Film User* no. 71 pp. 469–470 (September 1952); *Film User* no. 122 p. 580 (December 1956)

HOLIDAY OMNIBUS

Dates: 1956–1961

History: *Holiday Omnibus* was a series of colour films produced by Butlin's, featuring various aspects of holidays at the camps. There were six issues produced between 1956 and 1961.

Sponsor: Butlin's Ltd

Production company: Butlin's Ltd

Source: *Film User* no. 123 p. 6 (January 1957); *Film User* no. 183 p. 39 (January 1962)

HOME AND AWAY

Dates: 1954–1961

History: *Home and Away* was a series of black-and-white cinemagazines made for employees and the communities surrounding Babcock & Wilcox plants in Paisley and Renfrew, Scotland. Initially devised as a quarterly magazine, it described itself as 'a film review of Babcock achievements, sport, social and local events for members of the Babcock & Wilcox family'. The first issue covered the Cowal Games, the Scottish Industries Exhibition, Calder Hall atomic power station and the Babcock boilers at Castle Donington power station. A Scottish commentator was used but a 'broad accent' was avoided because, although primarily shown within Scotland, it also had some international distribution. The company claimed in 1956 that each issue, of around fifteen minutes, was seen by 60,000 people in eleven cinemas over three weeks. It was then shown for another three weeks throughout the Babcock works at Renfrew and Dumbarton using a mobile van seating 150. It was estimated that 2,000 employees viewed the film this way. Twenty issues of the series were produced, with many of the stories repackaged as *Babcock Review*.

Producer: Film Producers Guild

Sponsor: Babcock & Wilcox (Steam)

Production company: Technical and Scientific Films

Original distribution: Primarily Scotland with some international distribution

Archive: BFI National Archive

Source: *Imagery* vol. 8 no. 2 pp. 18–21 (October 1956); Babcock & Wilcox publicity material

HOW, WHAT AND WHY

Dates: 1948–1949

History: *How, What and Why* was a science cinemagazine, made for the children's cinema clubs under the Children's Entertainment Films (CEF) banner. Each issue was compiled by Basic Films from another children's series, *Our Club Magazine*. Although Mary Field suggested that the series ran to three series, this may have been a mistake, as only three issues remain on record.

Producer: Children's Entertainment Films

Source: *Good Company: The Story of the Children's Entertainment Film Movement in Great Britain 1943–1950* by Mary Field

IDEAL CINEMAGAZINE

Dates: 1926–1932

History: *Ideal Cinemagazine* was first trade-shown on 15 January 1926 at the New Gallery Kinema, Regent Street, London. Thirteen issues were advertised at first and the series was originally limited to twenty-six single reels, to be released fortnightly. The series was launched as part of Ideal's Laughter Festival and immediately

established a motto, 'Learn a Little, Laugh a Lot'. Ideal was the only company to publicly define 'cinemagazine,' stating, 'It's an arresting series of one-reel pictures devoted to everyday things, viewed from strange and unconventional angles.' This wide variety of subjects was arranged around a title, frequently a pun, such as NEW VAMPS FOR OLD (issue no. 2), which often surprised the critics by its unusual nature. Despite this unconventional beginning, by January 1927 the content of *Ideal Cinemagazine* was much more recognizable as cinemagazine fare. The programme then provided sport, through bought-in Grantland Rice *Sportlights* footage; music, in the guise of Ideal's own *Singsong* series from issue no. 14 onwards (*Kinematograph Weekly*, 6 January 1927, p. 76); travel from the *Hodge Podge* series; and, of course, a cartoon.

In common with *Eve's Film Review* and *Gaumont Mirror*, *Ideal Cinemagazine* also attempted to attract a female audience, in this case, through the inclusion of an illustrated household hint. It was at this point, 1927, that *Ideal Cinemagazine* began to be advertised as 'The Champagne of Shorts', though Ideal was careful to maintain that it contained 'something to attract, amuse and enchant every class of patron' (*Kinematograph Weekly*, 24 February 1927). By May 1927, *Ideal Cinemagazine* was released twice a week, though still only one reel in length.

Ideal embraced sound production in August 1931, producing the weekly *Ideal Sound Cinemagazine* with sound-on-film technology provided by Peerless Pictures Ltd. In July of that year, Ideal boasted that it was already booked in 550 theatres (*The Bioscope*, 15 July 1931, pp. 6–7). It was also around this time that Ideal began to advertise that Andrew Buchanan edited the series (although he had, in fact, been editor from the beginning). In 1932, Buchanan moved production to Gainsborough Studios, presumably to facilitate sound recording to a greater degree. At this point the slogan was changed to 'Cinemagazine – the "Punch" of the Screen' – like other cinemagazines, drawing a direct comparison with print media. The last issue on record is BATH OF A NATION (issue no. 297), released on 9 May 1932.

Production company: Ideal

Original distribution: National cinema distribution

Archive: BFI National Archive

Source: *Kinematograph Weekly*; *The Bioscope*

INDUSTRIAL NOTEBOOK

Dates: 1959–1961

History: *Industrial Notebook* was first issued in 1959 and seems to have been produced annually. Each issue related to a general theme such as electricity generation and distribution (1960) or iron and steel (1961).

Sponsor: Shell-Mex BP

Production company: Random Film Productions

Source: *Film User* no. 167 p. 518 (September 1960); BFI Film & TV Database

INFORMATION PLEASE

Dates: 1948

History: *Film User* provides the only reference to *Information Please*, which was thirty-eight minutes long and distributed by Ron Harris.

Production company: Ron Harris

Source: *Film User* no. 20 p. 398 (July 1948)

INGOT PICTORIAL

Dates: 1949–1959

History: *Ingot Pictorial* was produced by Technical and Scientific Films, and later Verity Films, for the sponsors, Richard Thomas and Baldwins Group (RTB). It was distributed by Sound Services, a mobile cinema service, on 16mm to leisure groups and schools. Four quarterly editions were produced each year. The purpose of the series, according to Howard Marshall, director of RTB personnel and public relations and a frequent commentator for the series, was to instil a 'sense of pride' in the company. Issues were shown at the company's works, during 20-minute lunch-time shows from a mobile van and at local cinemas to which employees could take their wives and families. In this way, RTB claimed that each issue was seen by 25,000 workers in thirty works scattered from Lancashire to South Wales (*Film User* no. 66 p.

176, April 1952). The series ran for thirty-five issues, although records only exist for issues nos. 2 through 34. There is evidence of some international distribution in a reference to *Ingot Overseas* issue no. 3.

Sponsor: Richard Thomas and Baldwins

Production company: Technical and Scientific Films/Verity Films

Original distribution: 16mm through Sound Services and some international

Archive: BFI National Archive

Source: *Film User; Imagery;* BFI Film & TV Database

JUST BILLINGHAM

Dates: 1947–1960

History: *Just Billingham* was a colour cinemagazine made by the Billingham Film Unit of ICI to explain the work of the Billingham division to its employees. Each issue lasted around eighteen minutes and stories ranged from profiles of apprentices on their first day to award ceremonies where employees were presented with long-service medals. By 1960 twenty-seven issues had been released and distributed internally.

Sponsor: ICI Billingham

Production company: Billingham Film Unit (sound by United Motion Pictures)

Original distribution: For internal use only within ICI Billingham.

Archive: Northern Region Film and Television Archive

Source: *Film User* no. 160 p. 84 (February 1960)

KINEMACOLOR FASHION GAZETTE

Dates: 1913

History: *Kinemacolor Fashion Gazette* was a short-lived magazine that employed the early colour process Kinemacolor. It only ran from September to December 1913,

Producer: Abby Meehan

Production company: Natural Color Kinematograph Company

Source: Charles Urban papers, URB 3/1 pp. 18, 24 & 25

LAING NEWS REVIEW

Dates: 1954–1955

History: *Laing News Review* was intended to inform social groups and educational audiences about the work and culture of John Laing & Co. Ltd. The films told a 'story of work in progress or recently completed, both in this country and overseas'. Each issue was in Kodachrome and lasted around twenty-eight minutes. The first issue featured nine items including stories describing the action taken to deal with the 1953 flood, which devastated parts of the east coast of Britain, and the construction of the Lusaka–Chirundu road in Northern Rhodesia. Later issues tended to treat fewer subjects with more depth. Just six issues were made, released between January 1954 and December 1955.

Sponsor: John Laing & Co. Ltd

Production company: Public Relations Department of John Laing

Original distribution: Distributed to interested audiences on 16mm

Archive: BFI National Archive

Source: BFI Film & TV Database

LETTER FROM LONDON *see* MIDDLE EAST NEWSPOTS

LIVING TOMORROW

Dates: 1969–1983

History: *Living Tomorrow* was a long-running colour science magazine series produced by the Central Office of Information (COI) for broadcast on overseas television, initially to Japan, French Canada, Brazil and Portugal. It effectively replaced two existing series, the science series *Frontier (Colour Series)* and the lighter magazine *London Line (Colour Series 2)* by amalgamating the content of the former with the style of the latter. Each issue lasted around twelve minutes and consisted of between three and five items. *Living Tomorrow* was produced by the same team as *London Line* and although initially presenter-led, generally relied on a commentary to link the stories together, facilitating the production of different language versions. Although the series

Title frame from *Living Tomorrow* 1969

BFI/COI

shared much of its content with its 'sister' series *Tomorrow Today* and *Haçia El Manana*, the style and distribution were very different. In 1974 production of *Tomorrow Today* ceased and the distribution of *Living Tomorrow* was extended to Canada, Australia, New Zealand and the Caribbean. The series was designed not only to project a progressive Britain but also to support the country's export drive, and it certainly provoked interest among viewers about some of the products featured. Indeed, by the late 1970s three people were employed by the COI to answer viewers' letters about some of the topics. Although *Living Tomorrow* finished in 1983, the production of science series by the COI continued with *Perspective*.

Producer: Central Office of Information

Sponsor: Foreign and Commonwealth Office

Original distribution: Worldwide

Archive: BFI Archive Footage Sales and BFI National Archive

Source: COI catalogue cards; film copies; production files (INF 6); COI production files held at BUFVC

LOGBOOK

Dates: 1950 and 1953

History: *Logbook* was compilation of motor-racing highlights filmed for Shell-Mex BP and released on a regular basis.

Sponsor: Shell-Mex BP

Production company: Shell-Mex BP/Random Film Productions

Source: *Film User* no. 96 p. 469 (October 1954); BFI Film & TV Database

LONDON LINE

Dates: 1964–1979

History: *London Line* was the Central Office of Information's (COI) first studio-based magazine programme produced at the Granville Studios in Fulham, London. It was jointly sponsored by two government departments, the Foreign Office and the Commonwealth Relations Office, and made in four versions for weekly distribution: one version for the 'Old Commonwealth' – Australia and Canada; one for the 'New Commonwealth', primarily the newly independent states of Africa and the Caribbean; for Latin America as *Aqui Londres*; and an Arabic edition *Adwa Wa Aswat*. Generally an issue would contain primarily cultural stories, many featuring live music and scientific breakthroughs mixed in with interviews.

BFI NATIONAL ARCHIVE/COI

Title sequence from *London Line (Colour Series 2)* c. 1968

Although there was some crossover of content, many stories were specifically designed for the target audience of each edition. For example, one of the earliest issues of *London Line (New Commonwealth Version)* featured an interview with the Reverend Ogundura, a parish priest from Nigeria working in Britain, together with a music item from Mike Falana and the African Mes-

sengers. Above all the style of *London Line* was completely contemporary, reflected in the studio, the presenters and most evocatively in its title sequence, which was specifically foregrounded. These sequences were particularly important since they were repeated on a regular basis and effectively functioned in a way similar to an advertisement, distilling Britain into a single package lasting around twenty seconds. Designed by Eddie Newstead, the *London Line* titles utilised the latest techniques of graphic design to present a rapidly cut collage of black-and-white illustrations including a London street map, Nelson reflected in a woman's sunglasses, television sets, tower blocks, and the Beatles, culminating in the words 'London Line African Correspondents Reporting From London'. Indeed many of its 'correspondents', for example Lionel Ngakane and John Bankole-Jones, became well-known personalities in countries such as Uganda and Kenya.

In 1966 production started on a weekly series of thirteen colour magazine programmes, *London Line (Colour Series 1)*. This was designed as an experiment in colour production and distribution to meet existing demand from the USA and potentially from Canada, which was experimenting with colour transmissions in September 1966. Although there is no record of release or broadcast dates for this series, some of the existing production documents indicate when the programmes were made. The first issue was filmed in November 1966 so it is likely that it was broadcast the following month. The series was essentially a colour successor to the 'Old Commonwealth' version of *London Line*. The format virtually remained unchanged with presenter Mike Smee joined by Howard Williams, Carol Binstead and occasionally Molly Parkin, founder and fashion editor of the magazine *Nova*. The content was mainly cultural with regular stories on fashion and 'live' studio performances by bands such as Gerry and the Pacemakers.

This experiment in colour was deemed a success and a second series was commissioned for distribution in the USA, replacing *Calendar*, and Canada. The first issue of *London Line (Colour Series 2)* was filmed in September 1967 and was broadcast in the USA the same month. Although the opening titles and studio design changed, the format was similar to *London Line (Colour Series 1)* with Mike Smee now anchored behind a London Line desk regularly supported by presenters Ian Morrison, Marion Foster and Howard Williams. The content for this series was more oriented towards science and technology, although there was still a good proportion of fashion, live music and the arts. Although this programme was distributed primarily to the USA, Canada, Australia and New Zealand, there was a subsidiary distribution in monochrome for the West Indies, Gibraltar, Malta and Hong Kong. Within five months, however, British Information Services (BIS) in New York had decided that the programme did not satisfy its information goals and wanted to end it. This precipitated an internal enquiry, the Samples Review into the role and nature of television production within the information services, which eventually agreed with the wishes of BIS New York, and the series stopped transmission in the USA in September 1968. It continued production for around another six months while its impact was assessed in Canada and Australia but without the financial contribution from BIS New York the series proved too expensive. In 1969 the colour series of *London Line* was replaced by two series, *Living Tomorrow* and *The Pacemakers*. The Samples Review also signalled the end for two other versions of London Line, *Aqui Londres* and *Adwa Wa Aswat,* as the format changed from general magazine programmes to single-themed issues. However the continuing popularity of the African version ensured that the series remained in production for another decade.

Producer: Central Office of Information

Original Sponsor: Foreign Office and Commonwealth Relations Office

Production company: Central Office of Information

Original distribution: Latin America, Africa, Middle East, Commonwealth, USA

Archive: BFI Archive Footage Sales and BFI National Archive

Source: Production files (INF 6) and correspondence (INF 12); COI catalogue cards; film copies; COI production files held at BUFVC

LOOK AT LIFE

Dates: 1959–1969

History: *Look at Life* emerged in vibrant Eastman colour from the ashes of two newsreels, *Gaumont British News* and *Universal News*, which had been rationalised out of existence by the Rank Organisation in November 1958. The combination of falling cinema audience figures and the new dynamic force of television news had compelled Rank to rethink its presentation of the news within the cinema programme. The result was a ten-minute news magazine that became the weekly pre-feature staple for millions of Odeon cinema-goers for a decade until its demise in 1969. Taking its cue from the successful relaunch of *Pathe Pictorial* as a colour series in 1955, Rank melded a topical magazine format with a more in-depth 'documentary' approach of a single story using 'direct speech and natural sound'. When the first issue of *Look at Life*, MARRAKESH, was released in March 1959, it was hailed in the trade journals as an 'exciting venture in film journalism' and Rank announced that this new innovation would have 'a more lasting impact than the present ephemeral newsreel content'. It was a popular formula but one that remained frozen in time while television led audiences into a documentary world that had more grit and less glamour. By 1969 Rank could no longer ensure the survival of the series which had, by this time, simply become part of the furniture.

Producer: Rank Organisation

Production company: Special Features Division, Rank Organisation

Original distribution: United Kingdom and overseas via the Central Office of Information

Archive: BFI National Archive

Source: *Daily Cinema*; BFI Film & TV Database

LOOKING AROUND

Dates: 1952

History: *Looking Around* was produced by Burroughs Wellcome and featured different aspects of its work. Made by the company's own film unit under the direction of Douglas Fisher, each colour issue lasted around ten minutes. The first issue was released in 1952 and included the use of synthetic resin in museum preservation, and a profile of the East African naked mole rat, and TABALLET, a 'Tabloid' production as light entertainment, with mock-heroic verse commentary and musical accompaniment, with stop-frame animation in Technicolor.

Sponsor: Burroughs Wellcome & Co.

Production company: Burroughs Wellcome Film Unit

Archive: Wellcome Trust Medical Film and Video Library

Source: *British National Film and Video Catalogue* Retrospective File; Wellcome Trust Medical Film and Video Library online catalogue

LOOKING AT BRITAIN

Dates: 1959–1962

History: *Looking At Britain* was a series of black-and-white films produced by the Central Office of Information (COI) on behalf of the Colonial Office. The films were made by Kinocrat Films Ltd, Max Munden Productions and Impact Telefilms. Each 13-minute film dealt with a single aspect of life in Britain, including a comprehensive school, Royal Windsor and the world of a New Town housewife. Although the films were primarily designed for distribution in Africa, there is evidence from the music licenses that they were also destined for countries such as Australia.

Producer: Central Office of Information

Sponsor: Colonial Office

BFI/COI

Title frame from *Looking At Britain* 1961

Production company: Kinocrat Films/ Max Munden Productions/Impact Telefilms

Original distribution: British colonies, particularly Africa and the Commonwealth

Archive: BFI Archive Footage Sales and BFI National Archive

Source: Production files (INF 6); COI catalogue cards; *Films From Britain* 1964–65; *Central Film Library* catalogue 1971–72

THE MAGAZINE OF GENERAL KNOWLEDGE

Dates: 1929

History: *The Magazine of General Knowledge* was a light educational series produced by Visual Education. It was produced and directed by Leslie Howard Gordon and Christopher A. Radley. Issue no. 8 featured stories on training polo ponies, the Cheddar caves, catching turtles and winter sports.

Producer: Leslie Howard Gordon and Christopher A. Radley

Production company: Visual Education

Source: *British Film Catalogue* vol. 2 ID no. 06413 p. 246; BFI Film & TV Database

THE MARCH OF TIME

Dates: 1935–1951

History: *The March of Time* was an American news magazine that was released in Britain and had an associated British film unit. It was founded in 1935 by Louis de Rochemont as an adjunct to *Time* magazine, though *The March of Time* had existed as a CBS radio series since 1931. The radio programme specialised in using actors to give voice to statements made by leading figures of the day, and this combination of dramatisation and documentary was incorporated in the film version. Critics praised its dynamic nature and its engagement with controversies of the day, frequently contrasting its approach with that of the conventional newsreels. *The March of Time* was first released in Britain in 1935, with a slightly different numbering sequence (British releases were given as Year/ Number whereas American releases were Volume/Number). Some stories were shown only in Britain, such as SCOTLAND: HIGHLAND

PROBLEMS (British Series Third Year Number 2), whilst others were controversially considered inappropriate for British audiences, such as LEAGUE OF NATIONS UNION (American Series Volume 2 Number 5, May 1936). Those working on the British edition included Harry Watt, Arthur Elton and Len Lye, while John Grierson was hired as a consultant. Originally each 20-minute issue consisted of three or four stories, but by the end 1938 it had changed to a single story for each monthly release, starting with the renowned INSIDE NAZI GERMANY. The series continued in this form until its demise in 1951 (Sixteenth Year).

Producer: Time Inc.

Production company: March of Time Inc.

Original distribution: Worldwide

Archive: BFI National Archive

Source: *The March of Time* press information; *Documentary News Letter*; *Monthly Film Bulletin*; *The March of Time 1935–1951,* by Raymond Fielding

MAY WE INTRODUCE

Dates: 1948

History: *May We Introduce* was a 'magazine of other people's lives' made by Leslie Laurence Productions. Each of the three issues lasted around seventeen minutes and included stories on the Hungerford Club for the Deserving Poor, pilchard canning, and the Royal Society for the Prevention of Cruelty to Animals.

Producer: Leslie Laurence

Production company: Leslie Laurence Productions

Distribution: MGM

Source: *Monthly Film Bulletin* no. 171 p. 34 (31 March 1948); BFI Film & TV Database

MEAT VIDEO MAGAZINE

Dates: 2000–2005

History: *Meat Video Magazine* was a series of video magazine programmes for Key Stage 4, GNVQ and AS-Level students on aspects of meat – uses of meat in cooking, health and safety issues and catering considerations. Produced on a term-by-term basis, issues were freely available from the British Meat Education Service. Other topics included production methods, standards in McDonald's burger production and the components of a balanced diet.

Sponsor: British Meat Education Service

Original distribution: Videos distributed to schools through the British Meat Education Service

Archive: British Meat Education Service

Source: BFI Film & TV Database

MIDDLE EAST NEWSPOTS

Dates: 1960–1969

History: *Middle East Newspots* was a black-and-white series of topical stories produced in Arabic, Persian and French language versions by the Central Office of Information (COI) for the Foreign Office. The films, each lasting around four minutes, were made and distributed weekly. The first issue was shot in January 1960 and seems to have replaced *People and Places*, also known as *Arab Televiews* (1959–1960) and *Report from London*, also known as *Persian Televiews* (1959–1960). Although only records of the lead stories survive, it does seem likely that a few issues were taken from another COI series *Portrait* (1959–1965), such as LABORATORY ASSISTANT (issue no. 50) and FARMER (issue no. 51). From issue no. 87 in 1961 the title changed to *Letter from London,* although the format seems to have remained the same. There is some evidence that *Letter from London* may also have been 're-versioned' for Australia under the same title.

Producer: Central Office of Information

Sponsor: Foreign Office

Original distribution: Middle East and possibly the Commonwealth

Source: COI catalogue cards; *Films from Britain 1968–1969*; COI monthly divisional reports (INF 8)

MINING REVIEW

Dates: 1947–1983

History: The original idea for *Mining Review* came from a proposal by the Labour government for *Factory Newsreel*. The aim of the series was to increase morale and keep workers informed of new manufacturing and industrial developments, (as *Worker and Warfront* had done during the Second World War). It would have a cinema distribution with a particular focus on industrial areas. Although *Factory Newsreel* never materialised, the National Coal Board (NCB) was persuaded by the idea, and, when it took control of the coal industry in 1947, sponsored a series on similar lines: *Mining Review*. The first six issues (1947) were made by Crown and had a national monthly release. Following this, the next 162 issues (1948–1961) were made by the production company DATA and numbered in years, (i.e. 1st Year Number 5) in the manner of the British version of *The March of Time*. From 15th Year Number 1 (September 1961), the NCB's own film unit produced the series until its demise in 1983.

All issues of *Mining Review* were distributed to cinemas on 35mm, by National Screen Services until 1955, and then by DATA Distribution. The films were also available from the NCB Film Library on 16mm for public and private showings, as were composite editions made up of several stories on the same theme, such as mechanisation. Normal issues were made up of several topical items covering production techniques, staff news and general interest, but these issues were also interspersed with single-item issues, such as one the making of the series itself (17th Year Number 8, 1964).

In 1972, with declining cinema audiences and general retrenchment in the mining industry, the NCB decided to limit its sponsorship of the cinemagazine to six issues per year rather than twelve. To ease this change, issues were remodelled to a single story, and the cinemagazine was renamed *Review*. *Review* began with 26th Year Number 1 in September 1972, with alternate issues offered to outside sponsors who had a public service message to present. These sponsors included the Spastics Society, the Metropolitan Police and the Dairy Council. *Review* continued to be made available on 16mm and distributed on 35mm to cinemas all over the UK, including London West End venues. The final issue of *Review*, 36th Year Number 5, was released in April 1983, just a year before the NCB Film Unit itself closed.

Sponsor: National Coal Board

Production company: Crown Film Unit/ DATA/NCB Film Unit

Original distribution: National cinema distribution through National Screen Services and then DATA Distribution. Worldwide through the Foreign Office and Central Office of Information

Archive: BFI National Archive

Source: National Coal Board collection; *Film User*, *Kinematograph Weekly*; North West Film Archive online catalogue; *The British Documentary Movement and the 1945–1951 Labour Government*, by A. P. Hogenkamp

MISSIONARY MAGAZINE

Dates: 1949

History: *Film User* announced the preparation of *Missionary Magazine*, noting that it was designed to stimulate British interest in missionary work. The material was shot in Africa during the course of a 25,000-mile round trip by a 20-year-old cameraman, Donald J. Nicholson.

Sponsor: Christian Film Council

Source: *Film User* no. 38 p. 681 (December 1949)

MR THERM'S REVIEW

Dates: 1956

History: *Mr Therm's Review* was a colour promotional cinemagazine made by Film Workshop for the Gas Council. The 'Mr Therm' of the title was a cartoon figure, reminiscent of a flame, that had been used in Gas Council advertising since the 1930s. Each ten-minute issue contained four or five general interest stories on subjects such as the Chelsea Flower Show or dog breeding, at least one of which had a connection with the gas industry. Each issue was generally introduced by the entertainer Richard Murdoch and featured at least one celebrity. Issue no. 5 showed the film star Zena Marshall receiving advice on orchids in her Mayfair flat. The series ran for ten issues with 16mm copies available from the Gas Council Film Library.

Sponsor: Gas Council

Production company: Film Workshop

Original distribution: 16mm distribution through the Gas Council Film Library

Source: *Film User* no. 109 p. 585 (November 1955); BFI Film & TV Database

MOBILVIEW

Dates: 1961–1962

History: *Mobilview* was intended as a public relations tool for Mobil. It appears that only two black-and-white issues of the 16mm magazine were made, in 1961 and 1962, each lasting around fifteen minutes. These included stories on petrol stations, the maiden voyage of the *Empress of Canada* and atomic power stations.

Sponsor: Mobil Oil Company

Production company: Technical and Scientific Films

Source: *British National Film and Video Catalogue* Retrospective File; *Film User*; BFI Film & TV Database

MONTAGE

Dates: 1960–1963

History: *Montage* was a colour series that ran for eight issues between 1960 and 1963. It featured Dunlop products and their uses, making this series more of an advertising tool than many of its predecessors. Dunlop itself described the films as 'eighteen minutes of colourful entertainment with an instructive background' in *Film User* advertisements. The series was frequently advertised for hire to 16mm users.

Sponsor: Dunlop Rubber Co.

Production company: Dunlop Rubber Co.

Original distribution: Non-theatrical use, primarily educational and social groups, through the Dunlop Film Library

Archive: BFI National Archive

Source: *British National Film and Video Catalogue* Retrospective File; *Film User*

MORRIS GAZETTE

Dates: 1947

History: *Morris Gazette* was a series of 20-minute cinemagazines describing the company's activities outside the factory. The single reference in *Film User* mentions several issues.

Producer: Morris Motors

Sponsor: Morris Motors Ltd

Source: *Film User* no. 8 p. 287 (June 1947)

MOSLEMS IN BRITAIN

Dates: 1961; 1964

History: *Moslems in Britain* was a short-lived black-and-white series made by United Motion Pictures (London) Ltd for the Central Office of Information (COI) and sponsored by the Foreign Office. The first two films, MANCHESTER and CARDIFF, were presented in Arabic by Gamal Kinay and featured interviews with both Muslim women and men about their lives in Britain. Shooting scripts for a further two films on Liverpool and Sheffield were commissioned in October 1961 but neither went any further. A more thematic approach was adopted with PLACES and PEOPLE, the final two films in the series, released in 1964.

Producer: Central Office of Information

Sponsor: Foreign Office

Production company: United Motion Pictures (London) Ltd

Original distribution: Middle East

Archive: BFI National Archive

Source: Production files (INF 6) and COI monthly divisional reports (INF 8)

MOTORING SCENE

Dates: 1968–1969

History: *Motoring Scene* was conceived by the Ford Film Unit as a reply to requests from overseas for racing and rallying reports. It was essentially a public relations series, released on a quarterly basis, which provided 'a kaleidoscope of subjects to reflect the fast world of Ford'. Each colour issue lasted between twelve and fifteen minutes; a total of five issues seem to have been produced. *Motoring Scene No. 3* included stories on Roger Clark's saloon car success at Nurburgring, a cricket match featuring a team of Grand Prix drivers and the FordSport Day at Mallory Park. The series was distributed through the Ford Film Library, both nationally and to twenty European and Commonwealth countries.

Sponsor: Ford Motor Company
Production company: Ford Film Unit
Original distribution: 16mm distribution through the Ford Film Library
Source: *Ford Film Library* catalogues; *Film User* no. 266 p. 10 (December 1968)

THE NEW SCREEN MAGAZINE

Dates: 1921
History: The first edition of this weekly magazine seems to have been released in June 1921.
Production company: Herald
Source: *British Film Catalogue* vol. 2 ID no. 06057 p. 225

NORTH EASTERN GOES FORWARD *see* REPORT ON MODERNISATION

OIL REVIEW

Dates: 1950–1953
History: *Oil Review* was produced by Greenpark Productions for the Anglo-Iranian Oil Company Ltd, under its trading name BP. BP described it as 'a screen magazine about oil – how we get and use it and how essential it is to every one of us'. Issues described modernisation work being carried out by the Anglo-Iranian Oil Company at its bases in the Middle East and processing works in Europe, and the uses of oil at home in Britain. Eighteen issues were produced between 1950 and 1953, released bimonthly on 16mm, through the Petroleum Films Bureau. They were also used for internal relations purposes within the company.
Sponsor: Anglo-Iranian Oil Company/BP
Production company: Greenpark Productions
Original distribution: 16mm from the Petroleum Films Bureau
Archive: BFI National Archive and BP Library
Source: *Film User, Imagery;* BP Archive

THE ORKNEY MAGAZINE

Dates: 1957
History: THE DRIFT BACK was the first issue of *The Orkney Magazine*, made by the Edinburgh company Ancona Films and directed by Margaret

Tait. This ten-minute black-and-white film described the return of farmer Neil Flaws and his family to the island of Wyre. Ronald Aim, leader of the Orkney Strathspey and Reel Society, composed the signature tune for the series, and the commentary was spoken by 'a well-known Orcadian, Harald Leslie'. The series was produced for the Rural Cinema Scheme in the Orkneys, a programme of special films designed to encourage large audiences to attend the local cinema evenings in the Scottish Highlands and Islands. In addition to circulation on the islands themselves, 16mm copies were screened as part of the normal programme at the Phoenix Cinema in Kirkwall and in a programme of Orkney films at the Aberdeen branch of the Caithness, Orkney and Shetland Association on 23 October 1964. There is no evidence that any further films in this series were made.
Sponsor: County Council of Orkney Education Committee
Production company: Ancona Films
Original distribution: 16mm local distribution
Archive: Scottish Screen Archive
Source: Scottish Screen Archive online catalogue; *Film User* no. 126 p. 166 (April 1957)

OUR CLUB MAGAZINE

Dates: 1945–1950
History: *Our Club Magazine* was made by Wallace Film Productions for the Children's Educational Film Department (CEF), a division of Gaumont British Instructional Films and the Rank Corporation. The unusual situation of an outside company producing material for a Rank department is explained by the date of the beginning of the series. With studio time limited because of the Second World War, CEF productions were squeezed in by any company able to spare the time. After the war, Wallace continued to produce the series. Issues of this black-and-white cinemagazine were about eleven minutes long, regularly containing four stories that featured children from the Odeon and Gaumont cinema clubs. The first issue included scenes of children taught 'safety first' on the roads. Rank alone had 400 clubs in the United Kingdom with an estimated

audience of 400,000 per week. *Our Club Magazine* was meant to be entertaining as well as educational and it seems to have been very popular with young audiences, partly because it featured children their own age. Fifty-eight issues had been produced by the time the series ended in 1950 with the demise of the CEF.

Sponsor: Rank Corporation/G. B. Instructional

Production company: Wallace Film Productions

Original distribution: 35mm distribution to Odeon and Gaumont cinemas.

Archive: BFI National Archive

Source: *The Cinema*; BFI Film & TV Database; Children's Film Foundation publications

OUR CLUB SCRAPBOOK

Dates: 1951

History: Issues 1 to 5 of *Our Club Scrapbook* are mentioned in the *Monthly Film Bulletin* and the format indicates a possible continuation of *Our Club Magazine*.

Production company: G. B. Instructional

Source: *Monthly Film Bulletin* no. 209 p. 286 (June 1951); *Monthly Film Bulletin* no. 210 p. 303 (July 1951)

OUR MAGAZINE

Dates: 1952–1956

History: *Our Magazine* was produced by Wallace Film Productions for the Children's Film Foundation (CFF) as a successor to *Our Club Magazine*. Each of the sixteen issues was eleven minutes long, containing four stories that featured young children who were normally engaged in educational or sporting activities. The magazines were shown at children's cinema clubs, or Saturday matinees, around Britain. Issuc no. 2 of the series, along with the CFF feature film STOLEN PLANS (1952), was awarded 'Best Complete Programme for Children 11–14' at the Venice Film Festival 1952. Issue no. 6 was entered for the festival in 1954, and issue no. 7 in 1955.

Producer: A. V. Curtice

Sponsor: Children's Film Foundation

Production company: Wallace Film Productions

Original distribution: National cinema distribution

Archive: BFI National Archive

Source: *The Cinema*; BFI Film & TV Database; Children's Film Foundation publications.

OUR NATIONAL HERITAGE

Dates: 1964

History: At least four issues *Our National Heritage*, a travel magazine series sponsored by National Benzole, were produced, with Leon Bijou directing issue no. 4.

Sponsor: National Benzole

Production company: Cecil Musk

Source: *Film User* no. 209 p. 151 (March 1964)

OUR WORLD MAGAZINE

Dates: 1950

History: *Our World Magazine* was produced as a more international version of the popular *Our Club Magazine* series by Wallace Film Productions but only ran for three issues.

Sponsor: Rank Organisation/G. B. Instructional

Production company: Wallace Film Productions

Original distribution: 35mm distribution to Odeon and Gaumont cinemas

Source: *Good Company: The Story of the Children's Entertainment Film Movement in Great Britain 1943–1950,* by Mary Field; *Monthly Film Bulletin* no. 195 p. 53 (March 1950)

THE PACEMAKERS

Dates: 1969–1971

History: *The Pacemakers* was a series of twenty-six colour magazine programmes produced by the Central Office of Information (COI) for the Foreign and Commonwealth Office. Each programme focused on an individual who in some way was challenging the status quo in their chosen profession or area of interest and creating something new. This could be an object itself, in the case of Sam McGredy's roses, or its application, as was Eric Laithwaite's vision for the linear motor. New ideas in education and play were

BFI/COI

Title frame from *The Pacemakers* 1969

discussed by those who were implementing them, such as Henry Pluckrose, headmaster of a primary school in central London. Each programme was around thirteen minutes long and often presented by the subjects themselves, for example the actress Glenda Jackson and the pioneering conservationist Bob Boote. The series was distributed to Canada and Australia and replaced *London Line (Colour Series 2)*. It was also slightly re-edited and packaged as *No Two the Same,* with language tracks in Arabic, French and Latin American Spanish for worldwide distribution.

Producer: Central Office of Information

Sponsor: Foreign and Commonwealth Office

Original distribution: USA, Canada, Australia and New Zealand

Archive: BFI Archive Footage Sales

Source: COI catalogue cards; film copies; production files (INF 6)

PANORAMA

Dates: 1951–1956

History: *Panorama* was intended to promote the activities of various ICI branches to the company's workers, and in doing so bring the divisions together. Each issue lasted around eighteen minutes and usually featured around four stories ranging from the manufacture of cardboard packets for washing soda to the use of explosives in quarrying. The series was the internal side of the extensive ICI film production programme and was shown to employees in after-hours mobile shows in works' canteens, theatres and local halls. It was also available on free loan to the public from the ICI Film Library. Twelve issues of *Panorama* were made between 1951 and 1956.

Sponsor: ICI

Production company: ICI

Original distribution: Internal and 16mm library distribution from the ICI Film Library

Archive: ICI Film Collection

Source: *Film User, Lens* (November 1951); BFI Film & TV Database

PARADE

Dates: 1963–1973

History: *Parade* was a cinemagazine series produced by the Central Office of Information (COI) for the Foreign and Commonwealth Office. Following the successful launch of the Technicolor cinemagazine *Roundabout* in South and South-East Asia in May 1962, it was decided to pilot a similar magazine for distribution in English-speaking Commonwealth territories in Africa, the Caribbean, the South Pacific and the Mediterranean in January 1963. The first issue was launched in March 1963 and was distributed to cinemas and non-theatrical outlets on a bimonthly basis until June 1964 and then monthly until July 1973. Each issue carried topical stories about developments in Britain and the Commonwealth, as well as items focused on the territories in which it circulated. Initially *Parade* was made by Associated British Pathe but in 1970 the contract passed to British Movietonews, which produced the series from issue no. 83, released in October 1970.

Producer: Central Office of Information

Sponsor: Foreign and Commonwealth Office

Production company: Associated British Pathe/British Movietonews

Original distribution: Africa, the Caribbean, the South Pacific and the Mediterranean

Archive: BFI Archive Footage Sales and BFI National Archive

Source: Production files (INF 6) and the COI monthly divisional reports (INF 8); COI production files at BUFVC; COI catalogue cards; *Films from Britain* 1968–1969

PATHE MONTHLY

Dates: 1925

History: It appears that *Pathe Monthly* was only in production for eleven months, from February to December 1925. It was first released on the third Monday of every month, and later, the fourth. This suggests that the series may have had some problems with completion in time for release, which may also explain its untimely demise. *Kinematograph Weekly* described *Pathe Monthly* as an 'untheatrical ... new Scientific, Travel and Interest film periodical'. It was made up of three regular stories, 'The Secrets of Life', a microscopic study of insects and natural subjects; 'Romances of Science', a series of studies of scientific processes through diagrams and cartoons, made by Bray Studios; and 'The Trials of Judge Rummy', a comic cartoon series, also made by Bray.

Production company: Pathe

Original distribution: National cinema distribution

Source: *Kinematograph Weekly*; *The Bioscope*

PATHE PICTORIAL

Dates: 1918–1969

History: First released in March 1918, *Pathe Pictorial* was the longest-running series in the history of the British cinemagazine, in continuous production for over fifty years. It established the general format of the genre, focusing on stories of general interest, acting as a supplement to the company's newsreel *Pathe Gazette*. Its longevity can partly be explained by its willingness to adapt and rebrand itself, although to the audience it was always *Pathe Pictorial*. In October 1931 (issue no. 704) it finally absorbed sound and transformed into *Pathe Sound Pictorial,* after Pathe had experimented with the sound cinemagazine format with *Pathe Sound Magazine* from August 1930.

In 1936 it became *New Series Pictorial*, shortened to *New Pictorial* in 1944. As competition from television became more heated in the mid-1950s, colour was introduced in January 1955 to mark its topical stories out from its rivals'. Another

Pathe Pictorial lobby card c. 1969

competitor, the Rank cinemagazine *Look at Life,* was produced in 1959 but with the introduction of colour television in the mid-1960s the days of both cinemagazines were numbered, with *Pathe Pictorial* finally ceasing production in March 1969.

The early editorial arrangements for *Pathe Pictorial* are unknown, but by 1928 it was being edited by Fred Watts. He continued in this role until 1944, when Howard Thomas seems to have taken editorial control as 'production manager.' Watts resigned the following year, and seems to have been replaced by Terry Ashwood. By 1962 Ashwood was being credited as 'executive producer' of *Pathe Pictorial*, and the 'editor' was Douglas Warth, who continued in this post until the end of the cinemagazine in 1969.

Production company: Pathe

Original distribution: National cinema distribution

Archive: ITN Source and BFI National Archive

Source: British Pathe Paper Archive

PATHE SOUND MAGAZINE

Dates: 1930–1931

History: Pathe had announced a trade show of the first four issues *Pathe Sound Magazine* on 18 June 1929, hard on the heels of the launch of the first regular British sound newsreel, *British Movietone News*, released on 9 June 1929. It stated in the trade paper *Kinematograph Weekly* that there was 'an item for every patron – that's what this different departure in audible entertainment offers … the *Pathe Sound Magazine* Covers the whole Entertainment Field!' By August it was an established part of Pathe's regular topicals using the strap line, 'the Eyes and Ears of the Screen'. The stories mainly featured items that exhibited sound to its best advantage, with interviews and musical numbers shot in a specially adapted studio. It was effectively absorbed into *Pathe Pictorial* when the cinemagazine adopted sound in October 1931.

Production company: Pathe

Original distribution: National cinema distribution

Archive: ITN Source

Source: *Kinematograph Weekly*

PATHETONE WEEKLY

Dates: 1930–1941

History: *Pathetone Weekly* was first released weekly in March 1930 with a view to incorporating all the semi-news events that passed into the Pathe organisation around the world. The series was created by Fred Watts, who ran all of Pathe's cinemagazines. He seems to have remained in editorial control throughout its history. In 1935 *Kinematograph Weekly* noted that, like *Pathe Pictorial*, *Pathetone Weekly* incorporated 'the novel, the amusing and the strange'. *Pathetone Weekly* continued in production until February 1941.

Production company: Pathe

Original distribution: National cinema distribution

Archive: ITN Source and BFI National Archive

Source: British Pathe Paper Archive; *Kinematograph Weekly*

PEOPLE AND PLACES

Dates: 1959–1960

History: *People and Places*, also known as *Arab Televiews*, was made by Kinocrat Films on behalf of the Central Office of Information (COI) for the Foreign Office. This series consisted of 13-minute black-and-white films, each covering a different aspect of British life such as HOME NURSE (issue no. 6), BRITISH POLICEMAN (issue no. 8) and

LEARNING IN BRITAIN (issue no. 11). Ali Nour usually presented these films in Arabic but occasionally Hannah Jamil or Hassan Massudi would introduce them.

Producer: Central Office of Information

Sponsor: Foreign Office

Production company: Kinocrat Films

Original distribution: The Middle East

Source: COI catalogue cards; production files (INF 6) and COI monthly divisional reports (INF 8); *British National Film Catalogue* 1963

PIPELINE

Dates: 1979–1990s

History: The first issue of *Pipeline*, a quarterly videocassette magazine programme for employees of BP, was released in April 1979. It included stories on company profits for 1978, the effect of the oil crisis on BP, and the company's activities in the North Sea. Attendance at screenings was voluntary for staff but BP reported that the first issue was seen by 35 per cent of its employees. Records at the BP Video Library suggest that the series ran well in to the 1990s.

Sponsor: British Petroleum

Original distribution: Internal video distribution

Production company: World Wide Pictures

Archive: BP Video Library

Source: *Screen Digest* p. 117 (June 1979); BP Video Library

POINT OF VIEW

Dates: 1939–1941

History: *Point of View* was a monthly series which aimed to counter what its producers perceived as being the 'propaganda' bias of the documentary film by presenting pro and cons of social and political issues of the day. Each issue focused on questions such as SHOULD NON-VOTERS LOSE THE VOTE? (issue no. 3, 1939) or IS IDLENESS A VICE? (issue no. 7, 1940), and different points of view were put forward in each case. For example, in SHOULD WE GROW MORE FOOD? (issue no. 5, 1939) a farmer and housewife discussed whether Britain should grow more food, or import more produce. There were nine issues in all, covering eleven topics. A special edition, GUNS AND BUTTER, was released in October 1939.

Production company: Spectator Short Films
Original distribution: United Kingdom
Source: *Monthly Film Bulletin*; *Today's Cinema*; *Documentary Newsletter*

PORTRAIT

Dates: 1959–1965

History: *Portrait* was a black-and-white series of 13-minute films, each describing a different occupation followed in Britain. Forty-six jobs were described throughout the course of the series, including BRICKLAYER (issue no. 1), SCHOOL-TEACHER (issue no. 10) and NURSE (issue no. 23). *Portrait* was produced by the Central Office of Information (COI) for the Foreign Office and Commonwealth Relations Office, with each issue contracted out to one of two production companies, New Decade Film Ltd and United Motion Pictures (London) Ltd.

Title frame from RACING CYCLIST, *Portrait* issue no. 4, c. 1963

Although originally intended solely for distribution in the Middle East, with the working title *Arab Televiews*, it was soon 're-versioned' and dubbed for different territories. By 1964 it was produced in Arabic, French African, Brazilian Portuguese, Persian, Latin American Spanish, Malay English and Hindi. Initially the release was quite sporadic but by 1962 the intention was to release it on a monthly basis, primarily for television audiences. The production did become more regular but never reached these levels by the time the series ended in 1965.

Producer: Central Office of Information
Sponsor: Commonwealth Relations Office and Foreign Office
Production company: New Decade Film Ltd and United Motion Pictures (London) Ltd
Original distribution: Originally the Middle East and then worldwide
Source: COI catalogue cards; production files (INF 6) and COI monthly divisional reports (INF 8); *Films from Britain* 1968–1969

PRISONS VIDEO MAGAZINE

Dates: 1991–

History: *Prisons Video Magazine* began in September 1991 as an experimental video project sent to every prison governor in England. It has become a monthly magazine programme made by former prisoners and sent throughout the British Isles. Each issue runs for thirty to forty minutes, and contains five or six stories filmed in prisons in England, Scotland and Ireland. Subjects covered include new facilities in individual prisons, the RAPt drug rehabilitation programme, poetry in prisons and resettlement. Five copies of *Prisons Video Magazine* are sent to every prison in Great Britain, as well as to the minister responsible for prisons, the Prisons Inspectorate, the Prisons and Probation Ombudsman and prisons' staff organisations.

Production company: Prisons Video Trust
Distribution: Limited video distribution
Archive: Prisons Video Trust
Source: Prisons Video Magazine website

PULSE PICTORIAL

Dates: 1961

History: *Pulse Pictorial* was sponsored by Bayer Products and designed to advertise the use of Bayer products to those in the medical profession. The first issue lasted twenty-five minutes and featured stories ranging from the growth of Bayer Products' weekly newspaper *Pulse* to the dangers of ill-fitting shoes.

Sponsor: Bayer Products
Production company: Bayer Products
Source: *Film User* no. 179 p. 488 (September 1961)

RACING OUTLOOK

Dates: 1924

History: *Racing Outlook* was a horse-racing cinemagazine produced by Stoll Film Studios and directed by John Betts. It seems to have been released on a monthly basis with twelve issues produced in all.

Production company: Stoll Film Studios
Archive: BFI National Archive
Source: BFI Film & TV Database

RACING PERSONALITIES

Dates: 1952

History: *Racing Personalities* featured interviews with stars of the motor-racing world. This issue, and only reference to the series, included the drivers Les Graham talking about the MV Agusta and Stirling Moss demonstrating his racing skills.

Sponsor: Shell and BP
Source: *Film User* no. 65 p. 131 (March 1952); BFI Film & TV Database

RAIL REPORT *see* REPORT ON MODERNISATION

REPORT FROM LONDON

Dates: 1959–1960

History: *Report from London*, also known as *Persian Televiews*, was a series of 13-minute black-and-white films each covering a different aspect of British life such as THE SCHOOLMASTER (issue no. 3), BRITISH POLICEMAN (issue no. 10) and LEARNING IN BRITAIN (issue no. 8). Many of these shared the same content as *People and Places* and were regularly presented in Persian by Hussein Darabaghi.

Producer: Central Office of Information
Sponsor: Foreign Office
Production company: Kinocrat Films
Original distribution: The Middle East

Source: COI catalogue cards; production files (INF 6) and COI monthly divisional reports (INF 8); *British National Film Catalogue* 1963.

REPORT ON MODERNISATION

Dates: 1959–1972; 1980

History: *Report on Modernisation* was a colour series describing different aspects of railway modernisation, ranging from track improvements to the latest coaches and railway training schools. It was designed to keep British Rail employees up to date with the latest developments and was generally released annually. Although there seems to be a break in production in 1962 it is possible that this was filled by *North Eastern Goes Forward*.

The genesis of this production goes back to 1959 when John Grierson was asked by Edgar Anstey, head of British Transport Films, to look at the possibilities of making a film on railway modernisation in the north of England. He reported that one was not enough, and although these ideas were then shelved for financial reasons, they eventually informed *North Eastern Goes Forward*, produced at the request of the North Eastern Region of British Railways. Although only one issue was produced in 1962, it informed the later style of *Report on Modernisation*. These ran for twenty minutes and showed the building of

BTF Film Unit filming RAILWAYS CONSERVE THE ENVIRONMENT *Rail Report*, issue no. 11 1970

new marshalling yards, improvements to passenger and freight facilities and the design of modern aids for speed and safety on the track. Using many of Grierson's original ideas, it helped staff of the division keep pace with the rapidly developing social and industrial needs of the area.

In 1965 the name was changed from SIXTH REPORT ON MODERNISATION to RAIL REPORT 6: THE GOOD WAY TO TRAVEL, although the format remained the same until the series was cut in 1972. It was briefly resurrected in 1980 with RAIL REPORT 13: ON TRACK FOR THE 80s, but despite proposals for another issue it did not survive the demise of British Transport Films in 1984.

Production company: British Transport Films

Original distribution: Internal

Archive: BFI National Archive

Source: S. Foxon Collection; BFI Film & Television Database

REVIEW *see* MINING REVIEW

RHODESIAN SPOTLIGHT

Dates: 1955–1963

History: *Rhodesian Spotlight* was a black-and-white cinemagazine produced by the Central African Film Unit (CAFU) and distributed within the Federation of Rhodesia and Nyasaland. A typical ten-minute issue would comprise around six stories ranging from the construction of a new court at Blantyre to an exhibition at the Rhodes National Gallery (issue no. 66, 1958). The name was changed twice, to *Federal Spotlight* in 1959 and *Spotlight* in April 1963. The *Spotlight* series was basically designed to promote the Federation both at home and abroad through a topical mix of stories and from the mid-1950s was generally regarded as CAFU's most important activity. With the collapse of the Federation in 1963 CAFU was wound up and *Spotlight* ceased production at the end of year.

Producer: Central African Film Unit

Production company: Central African Film Unit

Original distribution: Federation of Rhodesia and Nyasaland

Archive: BFI National Archive

Source: BFI Film & TV Database; *Rhodesian Spotlight* production documents

---

ROUNDABOUT

Dates: 1962–1974

History: In late 1960 Charles Beauclerk of the Central Office of Information (COI) conducted a

Title frame from *Roundabout* c. 1965

two-month trip to South-East Asia to report on the film operation in the region. One of his recommendations was that 'a monthly film magazine in colour' should be produced for cinema and non-theatrical distribution in the region. In May 1962 the first issue of a new monthly Technicolor cinemagazine, *Roundabout*, was released, sponsored by all three overseas departments of the British government. Each issue carried topical stories about developments in Britain and the Commonwealth, as well as items with a particular focus on South and South-East Asia. By the late 1960s it was issued in eight languages – English, Burmese, Mandarin Chinese (sub-titled), French, South Vietnamese, Indonesian, Thai and Malay. Initially *Roundabout* was made by Associated British Pathe but with the closure of its cinemagazine unit in 1969, the contract passed to British Movietonews, with *Roundabout* issue no. 99 released in August 1970.

Producer: Central Office of Information

Original Sponsors: Colonial Office, Commonwealth Relations Office and Foreign Office

Production company: Associated British Pathe/British Movietonews

Original distribution: South and South-East Asia

Archive: BFI Archive Footage Sales and BFI National Archive

Source: Production files (INF 6) and COI monthly divisional reports (INF 8); COI catalogue cards; *Films From Britain* 1968–1969; COI production files at BUFVC

RSPB MAGAZINE

Dates: 1968

History: This single reference to *RSPB Magazine* describes the following stories featured in issue no. 1: the production of RSPB print magazine *Birds*, an RSPB exhibition, birds feeding from a garden table and the creation of a woodland pond.

Sponsor: Royal Society for the Protection of Birds

Source: BFI Film & TV Database

RSPCA FILM MAGAZINE

Dates: 1960–1964

History: *RSPCA Film Magazine* described the activities of the charity and possibly had an annual release. Issue no. 5, released in 1964 with commentary by Michael Aspel, included stories about orphaned animals and the annual open-air service for animals held at Hexham Abbey.

Producer: A. W. Kornell

Sponsor: Royal Society for the Prevention of Cruelty to Animals

Production company: RSPCA Film Unit

Source: BFI Film & TV Database

SCRAPBOOK

Dates: 1949–1960

History: The Shell catalogue described *Scrapbook* as 'a cinemagazine for farmers'. Issues were generally around eighteen minutes long and focused on improvements to farming technology using Shell and BP products. The films were shown on request, using mobile film units, to rural social groups and farming organisations as part of an audio-visual programme specially tailored to a farming audience. During 1949–1950 the Shell-BP Farm Service organised 400 film shows. The most popular item on the programme was *Scrapbook*, which was requested 325 times.

Sponsor: Shell-BP Farm Service

Production company: Random Film Productions

Original distribution: National non-theatrical distribution through the Shell-BP Farm Service.

Source: *Imagery* vol. 2 no. 2 (June 1950); *Film User*, *Monthly Film Bulletin*; Shell-Mex and BP catalogues; BFI Film & TV Database

SHELL CINEMAGAZINE

Dates: 1938–1952

History: *Shell Cinemagazine* was one of the first sponsored industrial cinemagazines, with each ten-minute issue looking at the activities of the company and the benefits of oil to the community. It was produced by the Shell Film Unit, which had been established by Jack Beddington in 1936 and run by Arthur Elton (Realist Film Producers and later Film Centre), on a consultancy basis. The series maintained high production values and was well received critically, acclaimed as 'technically unsurpassed in any field'. The magazine was intended for non-theatrical distribution both at home and abroad, acting both as a public relations exercise and also a counterbalance to the large volume of technical films produced by Shell. In 1940 foreign-language versions were produced in French, Spanish, Portuguese and Dutch. Twenty issues were made over fourteen years.

Sponsor: Shell International Petroleum Company

Production company: Film Centre/Shell Film Unit

Original distribution: 35mm and 16mm non-theatrical distribution from the Petroleum Films Bureau

Archive: Shell Film and Video Unit and BFI National Archive

Source: *Documentary News Letter*, *Film User*, BFI Film & TV Database

SPOTLIGHT *see* RHODESIAN SPOTLIGHT

SPOTLIGHT ON AGRICULTURE

Dates: 1974

History: *Spotlight on Agriculture* was intended to

provide better communication and information services between the National Farmers' Union (NFU) and its members. It was financed by a variety of companies that supplied the farming goods featured in the films. INTO EUROPE (issue no. 1), for example, was sponsored by Fisons, Alfa-Laval and the Wellcome Foundation. The series was released through the six regional offices of the NFU on 16mm for use at county and local branch meetings and similar events.

Producer: National Farmers' Union

Sponsor: Various

Production company: Gerard Holdsworth Productions

Original distribution: Non-theatrical 16mm distribution

Source: *Screen Digest* p. 190 (December 1974)

SUMMING UP

Dates: 1947–1951

History: *Summing Up* was an educational news magazine designed for teachers of current affairs. Ten-minute issues were released quarterly and covered the main items of home and foreign news of the preceding three months. Great care was taken to maintain a factual balance, with A. L. Rowse, historian at All Souls College, Oxford, on hand to ensure it. James McKechnie provided the commentary. At least eighteen issues were produced between 1947 and 1951.

Production company: Pathe Pictures/British Instructional Films

Archive: ITN Source

Source: *Newsreels across the World*, edited by Peter Baechlin and Maurice Muller-Strauss, p. 69; *Film User* no. 7 p. 247 (May 1947); *Monthly Film Bulletin*

TEXACO VIDEO NEWS

Dates: 1980–1981

History: *Texaco Video News* was a bimonthly in-house video magazine. At the time of production, there were just sixteen videocassette recorders located in Texaco offices around the UK.

Producer: Peter Fairley

Sponsor: Texaco

Production company: Company Management Communications

Original distribution: Internal video

Source: *Screen Digest* p. 138 (July 1981)

THINGS THAT HAPPEN

Dates: 1936–1937

History: *Things That Happen* was a black-and-white monthly cinemagazine lasting around ten minutes per issue and originally shot on 16mm. Focusing on Scottish topical items, it also included dramatised stories such as the reconstruction of a bank robbery in Glasgow (issue no. 3, 1937) and the 'first sighting' of the Loch Ness monster (issue no. 1, 1936). There are no references to indicate that the series lasted beyond issue no. 3.

Production company: Scottish Film Productions

Archive: Scottish Screen Archive and BFI National Archive

Source: Scottish Screen Archive online catalogue

THIS IS BRITAIN

Dates: 1946–1951

History: *This Is Britain* was a black-and-white cinemagazine initially produced by the Ministry of Information for the Board of Trade, and then from 1 April 1946 by its successor the Central Office of Information (COI). Fifty-one issues were produced over six years. The first thirty-six were produced by Merlin Films and the remainder by the Crown Film Unit until the series was cut in 1951. Each issue lasted around twelve minutes and consisted of around three stories ranging from kitchen bath units to sorting London's mail. Primarily designed to promote Britain's exports overseas, each issue generally focused on developments broadly within industry and manufacture, with the odd story dedicated to leisure-oriented topics. The last nine issues adopted a completely different format, initially focusing on a single theme with separate associated stories, such as HEALTH (issue no. 43, 1950), and then developing the more fluid approach of SENSE OF TASTE (issue no. 48, 1950).

Producer: Ministry of Information/Central Office of Information

BFI/COI

RESTOCKING THE THAMES WITH ELVERS, *This is Britain* issue no. 7, 1946

Sponsor: Board of Trade

Production company: Merlin Films/Crown Film Unit

Original distribution: Worldwide

Archive: BFI National Archive and BFI Archive Footage Sales

Source: Production files (INF 6) and COI monthly divisional reports (INF 8); COI catalogue cards; *Central Film Library* catalogue 1949

THIS MODERN AGE

Dates: 1946–1951

History: *This Modern Age* was a monthly news cinemagazine produced by the Rank Organisation. It was similar in style to *The March of Time*, to which it was often compared, usually unfavourably. There were forty-one issues in all, released between October 1946 and January 1951. Each issue was devoted to a single story, lasting around twenty minutes. Initially it covered only domestic issues and then gradually branched out to cover more international themes. Among its notable productions were PALESTINE (issue no. 6, 1947), COAL CRISIS (issue no. 7, 1947), THE BRITISH – ARE THEY ARTISTIC? (issue no. 16, 1948) and WOMEN IN OUR TIME (issue no. 22, 1948). The executive producer was Sergei Nolbandov, Eric Cross the chief cinematographer, and the commentators were Bruce Belfrage, Leo Genn, Robert Harris and Bernard Miles. It was commercially distributed to around 200 cinemas in the United Kingdom and to more than thirty other countries.

Producer: Rank Organisation

Production company: This Modern Age Ltd

Original distribution: Worldwide

Archive: BFI National Archive

Source: *Documentary News Letter*; *Monthly Film Bulletin*; *The Non-Fiction Film in Britain 1945–51*, by Leo Enticknap

THIS WEEK IN BRITAIN

Dates: 1959–1980

History: *This Week in Britain* was the longest-running magazine series produced by the Central Office of Information (COI) for overseas distribution. It was a weekly five-minute film on a single topic introduced by a presenter from the country or territory it was destined for. Some of these 'reporters', such as Noelene Pritchard, became well-known figures, particularly in Australia where the programme occupied a regular slot just before the evening news for many years. Initially it was distributed in Canada, Australia and Latin America but the formula proved so popular and inexpensive that the distribution was extended in the early 1960s to include the Middle East, Africa and parts of South-East Asia. With the restructuring of television production within the COI in 1969 all editions of *This Week in Britain* were cut except for two, one destined for Australia and the other for Mexico and re-titled *24 Horas*. However, both editions developed a subsidiary distribution in the 1970s, to Latin America and the Caribbean among other countries. In 1980 the series was cut when its regular slot on Australian television was lost, by which time over 1,100 stories had been produced over twenty-one years.

Producer: Central Office of Information

Original Sponsors: Commonwealth Relations Office and Foreign Office

Production company: British Movietone News and later Central Office of Information

Original distribution: Commonwealth, Latin America, Middle East and Africa

Archive: BFI National Archive and BFI Archive Footage Sales

Source: Production files (INF 6) and COI monthly divisional reports (INF 8); COI production files at BUFVC; COI catalogue cards

TICKET TO LONDON

Dates: 1963

History: *Ticket to London* was a fifteen-minute series produced by the Central Office of Information (COI) for broadcast on Canadian and Australian television. Each issue covered a variety of topical stories presented by an Australian or Canadian reporter. Although the details for only three issues have been found, there were certainly more produced, but little to indicate the survival of the series beyond 1963.

Producer: Central Office of Information

Sponsor: Commonwealth Relations Office

Original distribution: Canada and Australia

Source: COI catalogue cards; *British National Film Catalogue* 1963.

TOMORROW TODAY

Dates: 1969–1974

History: *Tomorrow Today* was a colour science magazine series produced by the Central Office of Information (COI) for broadcast on overseas television. It effectively replaced two existing series, the science series *Frontier (Colour Series)* and the lighter magazine-style *London Line (Colour Series 2)* by amalgamating the content of the former with the style of the latter. *Tomorrow Today* was produced by the same team as *London Line (Colour Series 2)* and initially used many of the same presenters such as Ian Morrison and Howard Williams. Although it shared much of its content with its 'sister' series *Living Tomorrow,* it differed in its use of presenters, a characteristic it shared with the Spanish version *Haçia El Manana.* It was distributed primarily to Australia, Canada, New Zealand and the Caribbean, with occasional placement in countries such as India and Singapore. In 1974 financial pressure forced a restructuring of programme content that brought this strand to an end, although *Living Tomorrow* was still distributed to these countries until 1983.

Producer: Central Office of Information

Sponsor: Foreign and Commonwealth Office

Production company: Central Office of Information

Original distribution: Primarily to Australia, New Zealand, Canada and the Caribbean

Archive: BFI National Archive and BFI Archive Footage Sales

Source: COI catalogue cards; production files (INF 6); COI production files at BUFVC

TOPIC

Dates: 1958–1959

History: *Topic* was a magazine series of thirteen black-and-white films produced by the Central Office of Information (COI) on behalf of the Foreign Office, primarily for broadcast on television in the USA. It was produced more or less on a monthly basis and sent to British Information Services in New York which would then distribute the 16mm films throughout the USA. *Topic* was designed to 'introduce' Americans to various aspects of British life, hence its alternative title *Meet the British.* An American couple, Joan and Julius Evans, presented most of the issues, exploring a variety of subjects, ranging from the 'typical housewife' to a Member of Parliament, and also looked at Oxford, Coventry and Northern Ireland. The series was contracted to two production companies, Anvil Films which made most of the films, and Independent Television News.

Producer: Central Office of Information

Sponsor: Foreign Office

Production company: Anvil Films and Independent Television News

Original distribution: USA

Archive: BFI Archive Footage Sales

Source: Production files (INF 6) and COI monthly divisional reports (INF 8); COI catalogue cards; *Films From Britain* c. 1960

TRANSATLANTIC TELEVIEW

Dates: 1954–1958

History: *Transatlantic Teleview* was the brainchild of Charles Dand, Director of the Films Division of British Information Services in New York in 1954. In a memo to the Foreign Office he outlined the need for and format of magazine film series for television that would introduce British political figures to an American audience through a series of studio interviews. By December 1954 the first issue of *Transatlantic Teleview*, an interview with the Secretary of State for the Colonies

Title frame from *Transatlantic Teleview* 1955

Lennox Boyd, was on its way to New York. Most of these interviews were conducted by Robert McKenzie, then Foreign Editor of *Picture Post*, who explored a wide variety of topics from labour relations with Vic Feather of the Trades Union Congress (issue no. 4, 1955) to the future of Jamaica with Norman Manley (issue no. 10, 1955). An issue was produced roughly each month, usually by World Wide Pictures and normally lasted around fourteen minutes. The format was successful enough to continue for three years and persuade the Commonwealth Relations Office to produce its own version, *Commonwealth Teleview*, for Canada and Australia.

Producer: Central Office of Information
Sponsor: Foreign Office
Production company: World Wide Pictures
Original distribution: USA
Archive: BFI Archive Footage Sales
Source: COI catalogue cards; *Overseas Film Library* catalogue c. 1958; production files (INF 6) and COI monthly divisional reports (INF 8)

ULSTER MAGAZINE

Dates: 1953

History: *Ulster Magazine* was a twenty-minute magazine looking at contemporary Ulster, including its constitutional position, agriculture, new light industries and its relations with Great Britain and the USA.
Sponsor: Government of Northern Ireland
Production company: Random Film Productions
Source: *Film User* no. 80 p. 319 (June 1953)

UNILEVER MAGAZINE

Dates: 1950–1956

History: *Unilever Magazine* was a public relations tool designed to show the 'different parts of a uniquely varied industrial group'. These 'closely packed' reviews of the company's activities included stories ranging from canning fruit to trick photography, the construction of a new soap tower at Bristol and an underwater farm. Initially each issue lasted around twelve minutes but this was soon extended to twenty minutes. Increasing demand led the company in 1957 to advertise compilations of single magazine stories along particular themes, particularly for educational purposes. Nine issues were made periodically between 1950 and 1956, although the original intention was to produce it on a quarterly basis.
Sponsor: Unilever/Lever Brothers
Production company: Editorial Film Productions
Original distribution: Distributed, free of charge, by Unilever Film Library on 16mm
Archive: BFI National Archive
Source: *Film User; British National Film and Video Catalogue* Retrospective File; BFI Film & TV Database; North West Film Archive online catalogue

VANITY FAIR

Dates: 1922

History: The first issue of the weekly cinemagazine *Vanity Fair* was released at the beginning of January 1922. It was advertised prior to the launch of the first issue as 'the Big All-British Weekly Attraction depicting art-science-industries-sport-fashion-travel-slow movement-& natural colour photography'. It was produced by Jack Andrews and Norman Whitten and shot by Pat Tobin. Although it had a good critical reception, records indicate that this short-lived imitation of *Around The Town* only survived for thirty-one issues with the last released on 31 July 1922.

Producers: Jack Andrews and Norman Whitten
Production company: Walturdaw Co. Ltd
Source: *Kinematograph Weekly*

VARIETY FARE

Dates: 1949

History: This single reference to *Variety Fare* issue no. 1 describes it as a single black-and-white silent reel including stories on a mannequin parade, the Royal Tournament and all-in wrestling.

Producer: J. S. Frieze
Production company: Peak Film Productions
Source: *Film User* no. 26 p. 678 (December 1948)

VIDEO EDUCATION MAGAZINE

Dates: 1985–1986

History: *Video Education Magazine* was an hour-long video magazine on educational issues. Topics included community education, multi-ethnic curriculum and computers in the classroom. Three were issued each year, initially by subscription.

Production company: Reference Tapes
Original distribution: For hire or purchase from Pergamon Educational Productions
Source: *British National Film and Video Catalogue* 1986

VIEWPOINT

Dates: 1957–1960

History: *Viewpoint* was a series of twenty-one five-minute black-and-white films produced by the Central Office of Information (COI) on behalf of the Commonwealth Relations Office. These were primarily designed for broadcast on Canadian television in the Canadian Broadcasting Corporation's own series of the same name. In each of these slots a prominent personality would be interviewed about his views on a topical subject, usually by Robert McKenzie, who by this time was already presenting two other COI series, *Transatlantic*

Teleview and *Commonwealth Teleview*. For example in *Viewpoint* issue no. 4, Sir John Cockcroft, head of Britain's Atomic Research Establishment, talked about the latest developments and future application of nuclear power.

Producer: Central Office of Information
Sponsor: Commonwealth Relations Office
Production company: World Wide Pictures and Independent Television News
Original distribution: Canada
Archive: BFI Archive Footage Sales
Source: COI catalogue cards; production documents (INF 6) and COI monthly divisional reports (INF 8)

THE WAY AHEAD (NATIONAL)

Dates: 1963

History: *The Way Ahead (National)* was made by British Transport Films as an expansion of the popular news-based *The Way Ahead (Wyvern)*. The series had a rather complicated structure, pairing national stories with individual stories made for each region of British Rail. Thus, Southern Area would view the same national stories as Northern, but each would also view its own local stories as part of the same issue.

Sponsor: British Rail
Production company: British Transport Films
Archive: BFI National Archive
Source: Film copies (S. Foxon viewing notes)

THE WAY AHEAD (WYVERN)

Dates: 1962

History: *The Way Ahead (Wyvern)* was made by British Transport Films as a local cinemagazine dealing with new developments in the Midlands.

Sponsor: British Rail
Production company: British Transport Films
Archive: BFI National Archive
Source: Film copies (S. Foxon viewing notes)

THE WEALTH OF THE WORLD

Dates: 1950–1951

History: *The Wealth of the World* was a two-reeler made by Pathe's Documentary Unit for cinema distribution. Reflecting an international dimension, the theme of this series was the development of natural resources in the service of mankind. Each issue was sponsored by an industrial concern; the Petroleum Films Bureau for example, sponsored the first issue, OIL.

Sponsor: Various industrial companies, both private and nationalised

Production company: Pathe Documentary Unit

Archive ITN Source

Source: *Monthly Film Bulletin* no. 197 p. 93 (June 1948); *Newsreels across the World*, edited by Peter Baechlin and Maurice Muller-Strauss

WEST COUNTRY GAZETTE

Dates: 1948

History: The first ten-minute issue of *West Country Gazette* included stories on the North Somerset Agricultural Show at Ashton Court, Gloucestershire cricket team and a glider being loaded into a BAC freighter at Filton for a sales trip to Portugal. Although another issue was released, it is not clear whether the series survived into the following year.

Production company: Bristol Cine Services

Archive: BFI National Archive

Source: *Film User* no. 21 p. 445 (July 1948); BFI Film & TV Database

THE WHIRLPOOL OF WAR

Dates: 1914–1915

History: *The Whirlpool of War* was a First World War weekly news cinemagazine produced by Cherry Kearton and the Warwick Trading Company in tandem with the newsreel *Warwick Bioscope Chronicle*. The first issue was released in August 1914, and from October each film had an individual title such as WAR WITH TURKEY (issue no. 20, 1914). When the series ended in February 1915, thirty-three issues had been released, each lasting between four and six minutes.

Producer: Cherry Kearton

Production company: Warwick Trading Company

Archive: BFI National Archive

Source: *The Bioscope*

WORKER AND WARFRONT

Dates: 1942–1945

History: *Worker and Warfront* was an official news magazine produced by Paul Rotha Productions for the Ministry of Information between May 1942 and January 1945. Each issue lasted between ten and twelve minutes and usually comprised around four stories covering topics such as wartime recipes, camouflage netting, a children's clothing exchange, and reshaping the landscape around concrete works. After issue no. 18 the series was renamed *Britain Can Make It*.

Producer: Ministry of Information

Production company: Paul Rotha Productions

Archive: Imperial War Museum

Source: *Catalogue of Films of General Scientific Interest Available in Great Britain* (1946)

THE YORKSHIRE PROJECTOR

Dates: 1976–1977

History: *The Yorkshire Projector* was a compilation of topical items made by local independent filmmakers. It was shown in village halls and community centres by mobile units throughout the county by the Yorkshire Arts Association and in the area's regional film theatres. The first issue ran for seventeen minutes and comprised three items.

Production company: Yorkshire Arts Association

Source: *Screen Digest* p. 25 (February 1977); BFI Film & TV Database

ZOO MAGAZINE

Dates: 1964

History: The only reference to *Zoo Magazine* mentions the 1964 issue, indicating that it had an annual release.

Sponsor: Dudley Zoological Society

Production company: Birmingham Community Films

Source: *Film User* no. 217 p. 637 (November 1964)

Peter Greenaway directing a model at Liverpool Street station for ZANDRA RHODES, *Insight* issue no. 1, 1981.

BFI/COI

RESEARCHING OFFICIAL CINEMAGAZINES AT THE NATIONAL ARCHIVES

Linda Kaye

A researcher stepping into the world of 'official' cinemagazine and television magazine series produced by the Central Office of Information (COI) will enter virtually uncharted territory, perhaps occasionally stumbling across faint traces of footprints only to see them rapidly disappear. For bibliographical sources a few have reached the border, providing signposts in the form of good contextual introduction to British government information policy and film production in the early years of the COI, generally from 1946 to 1951. From the demise of the Crown Film Unit in 1952, the trail virtually peters out, leaving mainly contemporary accounts of the COI and the Overseas Information Service. So with very little on COI films from 1952 and nothing on television production except the odd public information film, how do you start mapping out the territory?

As far as primary source material for productions is concerned, the main source of information for cinemagazines is held at The National Archives (TNA), the official archive of the UK government. It has a comprehensive website, with an online catalogue and downloadable research guides (http://www.nationalarchives. gov.uk/catalogue/researchguides index.asp) providing an overview to areas of the collection. *The Arts, Broadcasting and Film: An Overview*, *British Propaganda in the 20th century* and *Coal Mining Records within The National Archives* all provide a good starting point. It is worth noting at this point that the term cinemagazine is rarely used so series do have to be identified as such in advance.

All records created or inherited by the COI from 1915–1998 are held in the INF series. All film production documents related to the COI and its predecessors, including the Ministry of Information and the GPO Film Unit, are held in INF 6. Each film is then given an individual number within the series. Production files for issues of *Britain Can Make It*, for example, can be found in INF 6/592–595. The files here, however, will not provide a comprehensive record of what was produced. Only production documents for films that have been selected as public record and preserved at the BFI National Archive are retained by TNA. So only a *selection* of production documents can be found in INF 6. Thirty-five films were produced for the series *Looking at Britain* but only thirteen files are retained at TNA.

BFI/COI

Films from Britain catalogue 1968-69

There are over 2,500 records in INF 6 and the numbers within it do not relate to an alphabetical or chronological sequence. For example, the files that relate to *Looking at Britain* in the order of production the references run like this: INF 6/2015–2016; 840–842; 844; 1478; 845; 1362; 846; 1053; 2018; 2017. It is worth noting that films may not always be catalogued under the series name and title, sometimes they can appear as a single item under individual titles within the series, such as 'Roundabout Series No 58 Doctor in Vietnam 1966' or just on their own, 'Round about Farnborough '70'. Also many titles listed under a series, for example *London Line*, may not actually be part of it. One way of double-checking that you have all the material related to a series is to see whether all the components share the same MI number. The MI number was the production code given to films and series produced by the Ministry of Information and then the COI. Thus, *Looking at Britain* is MI 920 and issues are sequentially numbered, so the first issue is MI 920/1 and the last MI 920/35. In the TNA online catalogue this can be found in the Former reference (Department) field. The MI numbers were allocated retrospectively so once again they do not necessarily correlate with a chronological sequence.

The production history of a series can be gleaned from references made in the monthly divisional reports of the COI, which are held in INF 8, and general correspondence and reports held in INF 12. The divisional reports only run from 1946 to 1963, when they were replaced with more general 'progress' reports: these do not appear to have been retained. Audience reception of these series, which were primarily distributed overseas, is particularly difficult to trace. There was little systematic evaluation with feedback from the main overseas posts, both informally through correspondence and formally through annual service reports, forming the main channel. Very few of these reports have survived, the vestiges covering the period 1969 to 1976, with the odd one from the early 1980s, can be found in INF 18. These noted what film and television material was shown and with what degree of success, together with recommendations and requests. INF 12 provides information in the form of unpublished reviews, reports and correspondence on the policy behind COI productions, but this can often be like hearing one side of a conversation. Shifts in overseas information policy and the place of film and television within it were informed by a variety of factors emerging from different departments, and are often scattered across TNA in the files of the Foreign Office – in FO or Foreign and Commonwealth Office, FCO, for example. Command Papers covering different aspects of the Overseas Information Service are currently held at TNA on microfiche although there are plans to digitise them.

Once this basic production infrastructure has been provided through The National Archives, it can then be extended to other sources. BFI Archive Footage Sales, the commercial agent for the COI, retains a file of catalogue cards that effectively provide an index to COI series. Unfortunately it is only the lead story that is generally listed if the issue contains more than one item. A selection of COI production material has been digitised and is available on CD-ROM. An additional set of these CD-ROMs is held at the BUFVC together with hard copy relating to series described in this volume. These production files generally relate to films that have *not* been selected for the public record but still in most cases exist. However, even when taken with those held at TNA they rarely constitute a full set of production material for an entire series.

What proves invaluable at this stage are documents that have rarely been retained in any systematic and comprehensive way: catalogues. Of the following catalogues only odd examples have survived and are scattered across the BUFVC, BFI Archive Footage Sales and the BFI National Archive. Catalogues produced by the Central Film Library provide details of individual stories for series made during the Second World War and into the late 1940s that were distributed nationally, such as *Britain Can Make It* and *This Is Britain*. From the mid 1950s the COI started producing its own catalogues for distribution overseas. Initially these incorporated both film and television material but from the mid-1960s these were separated. The fragmented existence of these catalogues renders the *British National Film Catalogue* (later the *British National Film & Video Catalogue*) an essential safety net, catching productions that might otherwise have remained invisible.

Data on over 7,000 official magazine stories can now be found on the British Universities Newsreel Database together with their provenance, but this still only represents a fraction of COI production. The map is still a rudimentary one but it is hoped that its existence will encourage researchers from all disciplines to extend and develop it.

BFI ARCHIVE FOOTAGE SALES

21 Stephen Street, London W1T 1LN

Tel: 020 7957 8932 Fax: 020 7580 7503

Web: http://www.bfi.org.uk/afs

Holdings: *Architectural Newsreel; British Sporting Personalities; Calendar, Carrousel Britanico; Commonwealth Review; Commonwealth Teleview; Dateline Britain; The Enthusiasts; Frontier, Living Tomorrow; London Line; Looking at Britain; The Pacemakers; Parade; Portrait; Roundabout; This is Britain; This Week in Britain; Tomorrow Today; Topic; Transatlantic Teleview; Viewpoint*

BFI NATIONAL ARCHIVE

21 Stephen Street, London W1T 1LN

Tel: 020 7255 1444 (switchboard) Fax: 020 7580 7503

Web: http://www.bfi.org.uk/archive

Holdings: *Around the Town; Behind The Scenes; Beladuna; Britain Can Make It; British Screen Tatler; British Sporting Personalities; Calendar, Carrousel Britanico; Cinegazette; Colonial Cinemagazine; Commonwealth Review; Commonwealth Teleview; Do You Know?; Eve's Film Review; Filmagazine; Frontier, Gaumont Mirror, Home and Away; Ideal Cinemagazine; Ingot Pictorial; Laing News Review; Living Tomorrow; London Line; Look at Life; Looking at Britain; March of Time; Mining Review; Montage; Moslems in Britain; Oil Review; Our Club Magazine; Our Magazine; Parade; Pathe Pictorial; Pathetone Weekly; Racing Outlook; Report on Modernisation; Rhodesian Spotlight; Roundabout; Shell Cinemagazine; Things That Happen; This is Britain; This Modern Age; This Week in Britain; Tomorrow Today; Unilever Magazine; The Way Ahead (National); The Way Ahead (Wyvern); West Country Gazette; The Whirlpool of War*

BP VIDEO LIBARY

52/54 Southwark Street, London SE1 1UN

Tel: 020 7357 7521 Fax: 020 7357 9953

E-mail: bpvl@bp.com

Web: http://www.bpvideolibrary.com

Holdings: *Oil Review; Pipeline*

IMPERIAL WAR MUSEUM FILM AND VIDEO ARCHIVE

Lambeth Road, London SE1 6HZ

Tel: 020 7416 5291 Fax: 020 7416 5379

E-mail: film@iwm.org.uk

Web: http://collections.iwm.org.uk

Holdings: *ABCA Magazine; Worker and Warfront*

ITN SOURCE

200 Gray's Inn Road, London WC1X 8XZ

Tel: 020 7430 4480 Fax: 020 7430 4453

E-mail: uksales@itnsource.com

Web: http://www.itnsource.com

Holdings: *Eve's Film Review; Pathe Pictorial; Pathe Sound Pictorial; Pathetone Weekly; Summing Up; The Wealth of the World*

LONDON TRANSPORT MUSEUM

Covent Garden Piazza, London WC2E 7BB

Tel: 020 7379 6344 Fax: 020 7565 7254

E-mail: research enquiries form via the website

Web: http://www.ltmuseum.co.uk

Holdings: *Cinegazette*

NORTHERN REGION FILM AND TELEVISION ARCHIVE

c/o Tyne and Wear Archives Service, Blandford House, Blandford Square, Newcastle upon Tyne NE1 4JA

Tel: 0191 277 2250 Fax: 0191 230 2614
E-mail: contact page via the website
Web: http://www.nrfta.org.uk
Holdings: *Just Billingham*

NORTH WEST FILM ARCHIVE

Manchester Metropolitan University, Minshull House, 47-49 Chorlton Street, Manchester M1 3EU
Tel: 0161 247 3097 Fax: 0161 247 3098
E-mail: contact page via the website
Web: http://www.nwfa.mmu.ac.uk
Holdings: *Unilever Magazine*

THE RAILWAY FILM ARCHIVE

17 Kingsway, Leicester LE3 2JL
Tel: 0116 289 0531
Holdings: *Events*

SCOTTISH SCREEN ARCHIVE

National Library of Scotland, 39-41 Montrose Avenue, Hillington Park, Glasgow G52 4LA

Tel: 0845 366 4600 Fax: 0845 366 4601
E-mail: ssaenquiries@nls.uk
Web: http://ssa.nls.uk
Holdings: *City Sidelights; Home and Away; The Orkney Magazine; Things That Happen*

SHELL FILM AND VIDEO UNIT

Video Media Services, Shell Centre, London SE1 7NA
Tel: 020 7934 3318 Fax: 020 7934 4918
E-mail: jane.paynor@shell.com
Web: http://www.shell.com
Holdings: *Shell Cinemagazine*

WELLCOME LIBRARY, MOVING IMAGE AND SOUND COLLECTIONS

183 Euston Road, London NW1 2BE
Tel: 020 7611 8766 Fax: 020 7611 8765
E-mail: misc@wellcome.ac.uk
Web: http://library.wellcome.ac.uk
Holdings: *Looking Around*

BFI ARCHIVE FOOTAGE SALES

21 Stephen Street, London W1T 1LN

Tel: 020 7957 8932 Fax: 020 7580 7503

Web: http://www.bfi.org.uk/afs

Holdings: BFI Archive Footage Sales is a commercial agent for the Central Office of Information (COI) and holds documents related to its film and television productions. These include: digitised copies of COI production files (those not held by The National Archives) on CD-ROM; catalogue cards indexing COI series by lead story; COI catalogues including *Central Film Library, Films from Britain,* the *Overseas Film Library* and *Catalogue of Films Available Overseas.*

BFI NATIONAL ARCHIVE

21 Stephen Street, London W1T 1LN

Tel: 020 7255 1444 (switchboard) Fax: 020 7580 7503

Web: http://www.bfi.org.uk/archive

Holdings: The BFI National Archive holds documents that relate to its moving image collections, some of which are associated with cinemagazines. These include: Babcock & Wilcox publicity material for *Home and Away; The March of Time* press information; *Mining Review* material within the National Coal Board collection; *Rhodesian Spotlight* production documents; COI catalogues including *Central Film Library* and *Films from Britain.*

BP ARCHIVE

Modern Records Centre, University of Warwick, Coventry CV4 7AL

Tel: 024 7652 4521 Fax: 024 7652 4523

E-mail: BPArchive@bp.com

Web: http://www2.warwick.ac.uk/services/library/mrc

Holdings: The BP Archive dates back to 1921 and holds material, such as publicity brochures, relating to BP plc (incorporated as Anglo-Persian Oil Co. Ltd in 1909). It is also holds the archives of several major jointly owned subsidiaries: Kuwait Oil Co. Ltd, Iraq Petroleum Co. Ltd, and Shell-Mex and BP Ltd. Visits need to be pre-booked and materials ordered in advance.

BRITISH UNIVERSITIES FILM & VIDEO COUNCIL

77 Wells Street, London W1T 3QJ

Tel: 020 7393 1518 Fax: 020 7393 1555

E-mail: newsreels@bufvc.ac.uk

Web: http://www.bufvc.ac.uk

Holdings: The BUFVC holds the British Pathe Paper Archive, including production documents and other papers for *Pathe Pictorial* and *Eve's Film Review;* digitised copies of COI production files (those not held at The National Archives) are held as hard copies (for series included in this volume) and on CD-ROM together with written accounts by ex-COI staff; *Rhodesian Spotlight* production documents included in BUFVC's British Movietone Paper Collection; various catalogues including *Catalogue of Films of General Scientific Interest Available in Great Britain* (1946), *Central Film Library, Ford Film Library Catalogue* (c.1972), *Shell-Mex and BP Film Library Catalogue.*

THE NATIONAL ARCHIVES

Kew, Richmond, Surrey TW9 4DU

Tel: 020 8876 3444

E-mail: via contact form on website

Web: http://www.nationalarchives.gov.uk

Holdings: The National Archives holds a variety of material including production documents and correspondence relating to selected government film and television production. Material associated with the Central Office of Information and its predecessor the Ministry of Information can be found in the INF series while *Mining Review* production files can be found in COAL 30 and 32. For more details regarding this collection see 'Researching official cinemagazines at The National Archives' in this volume.

NATIONAL MEDIA MUSEUM

Bradford, West Yorkshire BD1 1NQ

Tel: 0870 7010 200 (for Insight) Fax: 020 7393 1555

E-mail: enquiries@nationalmediamuseum.org.uk

Web: http://www.nationalmediamuseum.org.uk/Collections

Holdings: Papers relating to the early film pioneer and cinemagazine producer Charles Urban held in Insight, the Museum's extensive Collections & Research Centre.

BFI NATIONAL LIBRARY

21 Stephen Street, London W1T 1LN

Tel: 020 7255 1444 (switchboard) Fax: 020 7436 2338

E-mail: Via contact form on website

Web: http://www.bfi.org.uk/filmtvinfo/library

Holdings: The BECTU History Project, an oral history initiative, includes over 500 interviews with members of the British film and television industries, a number of whom worked on cine-magazines.

BRITISH UNIVERSITIES FILM & VIDEO COUNCIL

77 Wells Street, London W1T 3QJ

Tel: 020 7393 1518 Fax: 020 7393 1555

E-mail: newsreels@bufvc.ac.uk

Web: http://www.bufvc.ac.uk

Holdings: A number of interviews were conducted during the course of the BUFVC's 'Cinemagazines and the Projection of Britain' project with people involved in the production of cinemagazines. They broadly fall into two groups: those who produced official cinemagazines at the Central Office of Information (COI) and those making sponsored cinemagazines. The following audio interviews are held on CD-ROM: John Chittock (sponsored); Cyril Frankel (COI); John Hall and Adam Leys (COI); Deh-Ta Hsiung (sponsored); Janice Kay (COI); Robert Kruger (sponsored); Peter Pickering (sponsored); Peter Steel (COI); Brian Taylor (COI and sponsored).

ARCHIVES, LIBRARIES AND SPECIAL COLLECTIONS: ONLINE

BBC NATION ON FILM

http://www.bbc.co.uk/nationonfilm
This archive of historical film clips, hosted by the BBC with the Open University, includes extracts from the ICI cinemagazine *Just Billingham* in its Chemical Industry section.

BRITISH PATHE

http://www.britishpathe.com
Up to 3,500 hours of material are available for free as a low-resolution download, covering the whole of the Pathe newsreel and cinemagazine film library. Series available include *Pathe Pictorial* and *Eve's Film Review*. The collection is managed by ITN Source.

BRITISH UNIVERSITIES FILM & VIDEO COUNCIL

http://www.bufvc.ac.uk/cinemagazines
The British Universities Newsreel Database's online Video Showcase currently features editions of *Around the Town* and will include a wider range of cinemagazines in the future.

THE MARCH TOWARD WAR

http://xroads.virginia.edu/~MA04/wood/mot/html/home_flash.htm
A website produced by the American Studies Program at the University of Virginia which contains items from the *March of Time,* available in the Timeline section.

THE NATIONAL ARCHIVES

http://www.nationalarchives.gov.uk/films
The National Archives (formerly the Public Record Office) has cinemagazine content in its online exhibition of public information films.

SCOTTISH SCREEN ARCHIVE

http://ssa.nls.uk
Clips of cinemagazines such as *Home and Away* and *City Sidelights* can be viewed on the website along with over a thousand clips from the Scottish Screen Archive collection.

SCREENONLINE

http://www.screenonline.org.uk
This guide to British film and television history contains several hundred hours of streamed video but is only accessible only to UK schools, colleges and libraries. Cinemagazine material available includes *Cinegazette* and *Mining Review.*

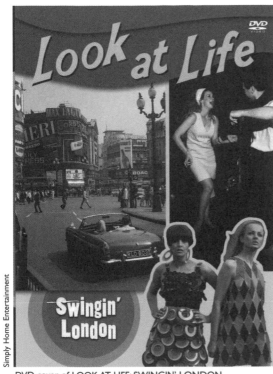

Simply Home Entertainment

DVD cover of LOOK AT LIFE: SWINGIN' LONDON

ROUNDABOUT VOLUME 1

Examples from the Central Office of Information's 1960s' cinemagazine *Roundabout*, designed for exhibition overseas to promote the British way of life.
DVD (region 2), 56 mins.
Available from http://www.moviemail-online.co.uk

LOOK AT LIFE: BRITISH COLD WAR JETS

A compilation of nine editions of the Rank cinemagazine *Look at Life* featuring military aviation footage from Lightnings, Vulcans and Victors, Scimitars, Sea Vixens, Gannets and Buccaneers.
DVD (region 2), 84 mins.
Available from http://www.moviemail-online.co.uk

LOOK AT LIFE: SWINGIN' LONDON

Sixteen *Look at Life* stories focusing on London in the 1960s including: REPORT ON THE RIVER, SHOPPING BY THE TON, RISING TO HIGH OFFICE, COFFEE BARS, IN GEAR, CHANGE AT THE TOWER, FIRE OVER LONDON, GOOD-BYE, PICCADILLY, MARKET PLACE, MEMBERS ONLY, TOP PEOPLE, ON THE METER, EATING HIGH, DOWN LONDON RIVER
DVD (region 2), 124 mins.
Available from http://www.amazon.co.uk

LAND OF PROMISE: THE BRITISH DOCUMENTARY MOVEMENT 1930–1950

This major retrospective of documentary film-making from the BFI, featuring 40 films over four DVDs, includes two cinemagazines: *Britain Can Make It* and *Mining Review*.
DVD (region 2), 720 mins.
Available from http://www.moviemail-online.co.uk

BIBLIOGRAPHY

BOOKS AND ARTICLES

Aitken, Ian (ed.), *Encyclopedia of the Documentary Film* (London: Routledge, 2005)
Three-volume encyclopedia of documentary films worldwide, with an entry on cinemagazines by Luke McKernan.

Baechlin, Peter, and Maurice Muller-Strauss (eds.), *Newsreels across the World* (Paris: Unesco, 1952)
A comprehensive analysis of worldwide newsreel production and distribution which includes a section on 'screen magazines' including The Wealth of the World, Summing Up, This Is Britain *and* Shell Cinemagazine. *Available online at http://unesdoc.unesco.org/images/0003/000301 /030104eo.pdf (8.5MB).*

Berry, Dave, 'Jerry the Tyke – Felix's Canine Cousin', in Alan Burton and Laraine Porter (eds.), *Crossing the Pond: Anglo-American Film Relations Before 1930* (Trowbridge: Flicks Books, 2002)
An essay on the cartoon character Jerry the Tyke, who appeared in Gaumont Mirror *in the 1920s.*

Broughton, Mark, 'In and Out of the Whirlpool of War', *Viewfinder* no. 45, December 2001
A short article on Cherry Kearton's First World War news magazine The Whirlpool of War.

Enticknap, Leo, *The Non-Fiction Film in Britain, 1945–51* (Ph.D. thesis, University of Exeter, 1999)
Doctoral thesis on British non-fiction film, which includes a chapter on the magazine films, focusing on This Modern Age. *Available online at http://www.enticknap.net/leo/index.htm.*

Erhardt, Erwin F., *War Aims for the Workforce: British Workers Newsreels during the Second World War* (Ph.D. thesis, University of Cincinnati, 1996)
Doctoral thesis on workers' newsreels and magazine films during the Second World War, including the Ministry of Information's Worker and Warfront.

Field, Mary, *Good Company: The Story of the Children's Entertainment Film Movement in Great Britain, 1943–1950* (London: Longmans, 1952)
Mary Field was head of the Children's Entertainment Department at Gaumont-British Instructional, and later Executive Officer of the Children's Film Foundation. Her book lists the organisation's cinemagazine output and goes into some detail about the motivation behind it.

Fielding, Raymond, *The March of Time, 1935–1951* (New York: Oxford University Press, 1978)
The standard history of the American news cinemagazine The March of Time, *with an account of its British unit.*

Gifford, Denis, *British Animated Films, 1895–1985: A Filmography* (Jefferson, NC, London: McFarland, 1987)
Comprehensive filmography of British animation, which includes the cartoon characters which appeared in British cinemagazines: 'Pongo the Pup' (Pathe Pictorial*), 'Dismal Desmond'* (Gaumont Mirror*), 'Jerry the Troublesome Tyke'* (Gaumont Mirror) *and 'Sammy and Sausage'* (Eve's Film Review*).*

Gifford, Denis, *The British Film Catalogue Vol. 2: Non-fiction Film, 1888–1994* (London: Fitzroy Dearborn, 2001)
Catalogue of British non-fiction film production, which includes details of many (though not all) British cinemagazines.

Gifford, Denis, *Entertainers in British Film: A Century of Showbiz in the Cinema* (Westport, CT: Greenwood Press; London: Flicks Books, 1998)

Exhaustive guide to entertainers in British films (fiction and non-fiction), including the many variety performers to be found in cinemagazines such as Around the Town, Eve's Film Review, Pathetone Weekly *and others.*

Gölzhäuser-Newman, Nicola, *Eve's Film Review. Genre und Gender im britischen screen magazine der 1920er Jahre* (Passau: Karl Stutz, 2004)
Published dissertation on Eve's Film Review.

Hammerton, Jenny, *For Ladies Only? Eve's Film Review: Pathe Cinemagazine 1921–33* (Hastings: The Projection Box, 2001)
A lively history and analysis of Pathe's cine-magazine for women.

Hammerton, Jenny, 'The Spice of the Perfect Programme: The Weekly Magazine Film during the Silent Period', in Andrew Higson (ed.), *Young and Innocent? The Cinema in Britain 1896–1930* (Exeter: University of Exeter Press, 2002).
British cinemagazines in the context of 1920s British cinema.

Hogenkamp, Albert, *The British Documentary Movement and the 1945–51 Labour Governments* (Ph.D. thesis, Westminster College, Oxford, 1991)
Doctoral thesis on the postwar relationship between the government and the British Documentary Movement includes many official cinemagazines, such as Mining Review, *together with a useful, if incomplete, filmography of official film production in this period.*

Kaye, Linda, 'Reel Britannia', *History Today* vol. 56 no. 4, April 2006
Article on the hidden history of the use of the cinemagazine format by the Central Office of Information.

Kaye, Linda, 'Cinemagazines and the Projection of Britain', *Viewfinder* no. 60, October 2005
Overview of the BUFVC's 'Cinemagazines and the Projection of Britain' project.

Knight, Derrick and Vincent Porter, *A Long Look at Short Films: An A.C.T.T. Report on the Short Entertainment and Factual Film* (London: Pergamon Press, 1967)
An assessment of British short film production, arguing that magazine series such as Look at Life, *produced by Rank for distribution on its own circuit, have effectively hindered the successful development of a short film industry in Britain.*

McKernan, Luke (ed.), *Yesterday's News: The British Cinema Newsreel Reader* (London: British Universities Film & Video Council, 2002) *Collection of historical and commissioned essays on British newsreels, including an essay by Jenny Hammerton on Pathe cinemagazines and another by Sarah Easen on women in British newsreels and cinemagazines.*

Noble, Peter (ed.), *British Film Yearbook* 1949–50 (London: Skelton Robinson, 1950)
Lists cinemagazine productions including ABCA Magazine *and* Filmagazine.

Robinson, David, and Ian Wright, 'Shorts and Cinemas', *Sight and Sound* vol. 36 no. 2, (Spring 1967)
This article assesses whether the 'monopolistic' practices pursued by the Rank Organisation and others, which included the production of series such as Look at Life *for distribution on its own circuit, were the sole cause for the poor state of the British short film industry.*

JOURNALS, TRADE PRESS AND MAGAZINES

Any research into cinemagazines from the 1920s will rely heavily on trade journals such as *The Bioscope* (1908–1932) and *Kinematograph Weekly* (1907–1959). *Daily Cinema* (1957–1968) and *Today's Cinema* (1969–1971) are useful for tracing the development of later series such as *Look at Life* and smaller sponsored series. *Screen Digest* and *Film User,* published by Current Affairs from 1946, are valuable for tracing sponsored series. *Imagery*, published by the Film Producers Guild, an association of producers and distributors of industrial (amongst other) films, describes the productions of companies such as Verity Films, Greenpark Productions, and Technical and Scientific Films as well as other cinemagazine producers. Both *Lens*, the newsletter of the ICI Film Unit in the 1950s and *Coal*, a magazine produced by the National Coal Board and considered by it to be the print equivalent of *Mining Review*, provide valuable context as well as data. The *Monthly Film Bulletin* and *Documentary News Letter* are particularly helpful for the news magazines and sponsored material during the Second World War and immediate postwar period.

CATALOGUES

The Central Office of Information published a number of catalogues for film and television productions distributed nationally, the *Central Film Library* catalogue (1940s–1990s), and internationally: the *Catalogue of Films Available Overseas* (1949 and 1951), *Films from Britain* (1950s and 1960s) and *Overseas Film Library* (1950s). *Films on Coal*, published by the National Coal Board covers *Mining Review* from the 1960s until 1983. Both Shell and Ford published their own catalogues: *Shell Mex and BP Film Library Catalogue* (later *Shell Film Library Catalogue*) and *Ford Film Library* respectively. The *British National Film and Video Catalogue* (1963–2001) and the *British National Film and Video Catalogue* Retrospective File (data relating to productions prior to 1963 and held at the BUFVC) provide details for many series that would otherwise be lost. The *Catalogue of Films of General Scientific Interest Available in Great Britain* (1946), compiled by the Scientific Film Association, and the *Marketing Video Library Catalogue* are also useful.

ONLINE CATALOGUES

BFI Film & TV Database
http://www.bfi.org.uk/filmtvinfo/ftvdb
British Universities Newsreel Databases
http://www.bufvc.ac.uk/newsreels
Imperial War Museum
http://www.iwmcollections.org.uk
The National Archives
http://www.nationalarchives.gov.uk/catalogue
North West Film Archive
http://www.nwfa.mmu.ac.uk
Scottish Screen Archive
http://ssa.nls.uk
Wellcome Trust Medical Film and Video Library
http://library.wellcome.ac.uk/catalogues.html

INDEX